ANCESTORS ON THE MOVE

ANCESTORS ON THE MOVE

A HISTORY OF OVERSEAS TRAVEL

KAREN FOY

Images on p. 72 and p. 78 courtesy of Kath Jones; all other images are from the author's collection.

First published 2014

The History Press
The Mill, Brimscombe Port
Stroud, Gloucestershire, GL5 2QG
www.thehistorypress.co.uk

British Library Cataloguing in Publication Data.
A catalogue record for this book is available from the British Library.

ISBN 978 0 7524 9938 3

Typesetting and origination by The History Press
Printed in Great Britain

CONTENTS

ACKNOWLEDGEMENTS

Ancestors on the Move: A History of Overseas Travel is a huge topic to tackle in just one volume and I have deliberated long and hard over what subjects to include and what to leave out. Everyone's story will take them down a different path, so naturally it is impossible to cover every eventuality. That said, I have thoroughly enjoyed writing and researching the various aspects of this book and hope I have provided a starting point and inspiration to encourage you to follow the trail of your forebears that threw caution to the wind and travelled, or emigrated, abroad.

I would like to thank The History Press for commissioning me to write this (my third title for them) and fellow family historian, Kath Jones, for providing information and images relating to her genealogical experiences. Most of all, I would like to thank my husband, Jeff, for encouraging me through the fun times and frustrations of book writing!

Happy history hunting to all!

INTRODUCTION

From the early reed vessels of the Ancient Egyptians and the oar-powered longboats of the Vikings, to the tall-masted nineteenth-century clipper ships and iron-clad ocean liners, ships and boats are our oldest form of transportation. Even today, three-quarters of the world's goods must travel from country to country across the oceans and seas.

Early foreign trade brought the need for increased passenger travel and gradually ships were built to meet the demand of accommodating their precious 'human cargo' on crossings to all four corners of the globe. Conditions varied depending upon the historical period (era) in which the journey was undertaken and the social status of the passenger; the traveller's personal circumstances and reason for the voyage could greatly affect their experiences onboard.

Throughout the centuries, the seas around Britain have become a bustling highway and a means of entering, or escaping, our island nation. It is these migrational patterns that have had a huge impact on our genealogical roots. Perhaps you've been researching your family history only to discover that individuals, or even whole family groups, have disappeared from certain decades of the census? Maybe you've found anomalies in surname spellings, or that stated birthplaces are far beyond British shores? Is there talk of a budding explorer within the branches of your tree, of a great aunt with exotic features, or of a criminal cousin who fled his homeland to escape punishment?

As family historians, migration from one's country of origin is likely to have affected the majority of us in one form or another. Just like today, money was at the forefront of everyone's minds when planning any trip, move or venture, but prior to the First World War there were far fewer 'legal' restrictions upon our ancestor's movements. No thought had to be given to getting a photo ID prepared, visas did not have to be requested, and passports were not compulsory. We rarely think of our British ancestors as nomads, but in many cases, and depending upon the circumstances, this is exactly what they were.

Some left permanently to set up home in another country, while others travelled to distant lands temporarily in search of work, fame, fortune, or simply for the good of their health. The hand of fate was not always kind, with some never really recovering from the enforced trauma and upheaval. Others, especially the younger generations, made a success of the opportunities – however small – that came their way, and the branches of our trees took a new direction as they flourished overseas. By comparison, those of foreign origin may have arrived from far-flung destinations to start a new life in Britain, giving us a whole new nationality to add to our 'genealogical mix'.

There are a myriad of reasons that may have prompted individuals to seek a life beyond their place of birth. In this book I have chosen to focus on those which have had the greatest effect on the largest number of people, and to examine why their actions have become deeply etched in our personal histories. Questions may have arisen which have prompted you to want to investigate further. If so, the following chapters could help you to increase your knowledge of your ancestor's travels. Starting points to consider include:

- Did your forebear commit a crime and were they transported for their punishment? Can you build a back story as to what their voyage was like and the conditions experienced onboard ship? Did they return home once they had served their sentence?
- Did they take advantage of one of the many government incentive schemes? Maybe they were given free passage to an expanding British colony and the opportunity to acquire cheap land once they arrived? Did they make a success of their new venture?
- What level of society did they originate from? Did they come from an already wealthy family and were taking up a business opportunity abroad? Were they plantation owners with interests in the West Indies, or were they high-ranking officials with the East India Company overseeing business interests in Asia? Or perhaps they were merchants seeking out products to transport to the British Isles?
- You may come from a military background. Was your forebear stationed at some far-flung outpost, or did he join a colonial unit? Perhaps he fought for a cause and enlisted as a soldier in a foreign campaign?
- Or was your ancestor simply an avid traveller, eager to see the world either under his own steam or by working his passage to pay for his fare?

All journeys before the invention of air travel would have been made by sea and then over land. By discovering more about why and how our ancestors travelled we can begin to dig deeper. I have tried to provide details of the essential sources, websites, libraries and societies that can point you to the records most likely to reveal more about your forebears' activities. In order to expand upon what you can learn about their lives from 'official resources' I also discuss some of the collectables and memorabilia you may have been lucky enough to inherit, or can acquire, to illustrate your family story.

Understandably, for the majority affected by forced migration – prompted by war, conflict, religious persecution, poverty and famine – items later handed down as evidence of their previous lives and experiences are going to be scarce. Any possessions that may have survived are likely to be small – something that could have been carried upon their person or taken within their belongings at a moment's notice. It is also worth considering that anything of value may have been sold to enable them to pay for their passage. But not everyone travelled or emigrated under such dire circumstances and any memorabilia that you discover relating to past adventures will be priceless to you and future generations. Whatever the circumstances, it is essential to think 'outside of the box' if you wish visually to portray your family tale. There is a whole array of paper-based ephemera that can really add interest – and new information – to your research.

Each chapter of this book provides suggestions of what to look out for, or case studies explaining the information you can glean from each example. Many of you will discover intriguing items that are unique and personal to your own ancestry, so simply use these ideas as a starting point to track down and expand upon the physical objects within your genealogical archive.

With a little thought and creativity you can preserve and chronicle your forebear's lives in a very appealing way. For example, don't fall into the trap of thinking that once you have *one* newspaper report of an event that you shouldn't try to seek out another. Each will vary, perhaps written from a different perspective, and may include contrasting versions of facts and information. One may focus on an eyewitness account, whereas another could be written from a political point of view.

Postcards may show scenes from different angles or include a variety of shots of a similar landscape, giving you greater detail of an area where an ancestor lived, travelled to, or settled in.

Prints, engravings, journals, personal letters and diaries can all provide new clues to follow, raising questions you had, perhaps, previously not thought of. Published books written about specific events in history, in which your ancestor may have been involved, are fantastic for enabling us to understand the bigger picture, but primary sources often shed new light on how individuals were affected.

Ticket stubs and printed passenger lists give us an exact date of travel; advertisements tell us the route along which a voyage was taken, while logbooks describe the weather conditions faced on the journey.

From my own experiences I have found that handwritten notes can show us what was important to, or what fascinated our forebears; these are often concerns and issues that today we would simply take for granted. A letter to relatives back home in Britain from a family member who had settled in the United States during the early 1900s, describes how there are oranges and lemons growing on the trees – sights they had never seen before. Another note mentions a train journey across America, the distance covered, and how long the trip would take during that era, while a selection of postcards – again sent to loved ones back home – provides views of the nearest US city to where the family made their new life, each one with a simple message on the back describing the shops and department stores they now frequented. It is often the minutia that adds 'flesh to the bones' of a good story and these morsels of information – experienced by the 'ordinary man or woman' – can easily be related to your own ancestor's encounters in similar situations.

By combining these details with what we know was actually happening in the world at a particular time, we can begin to understand the decisions our ancestors made and why they chose to uproot. This then becomes a captivating journey – not only experienced by your forebears – but also by you as a family historian as you piece together the important incidents and adventures in their lives.

1

LIFE ON THE OCEAN WAVE

'The world is a book and those who
do not travel read only one page.'
Augustine of Hippo

Events in history have dictated why many of our ancestors have been prompted to 'up sticks and move', completely changing the path our family stories have taken. Before we focus on how they were drawn to, and away from, specific countries, we take a look at those ancestors who chose to travel for pleasure, discovering that for some, the saying 'it's not about the destination, it's the journey that counts' really was true!

We are all familiar with the term 'holiday' – a chance to take a break from our busy lives and enjoy a well earned rest or a period of change. This often involves travel and the chance to experience a new destination. For our ancestors, travelling abroad was an exciting – and ultimately rewarding – prospect. Yet, with no television to visually relay what countries looked like, they relied on books, atlases, personal memoirs and recollections to form a picture of what to expect when visiting a foreign land.

Although these trips could be for extended periods, travellers always intended to return home once they had completed their itinerary. This form of 'pleasure seeking' was seen as a 'rite of passage' for the wealthy; a pastime unaffordable to the lower classes that could only dream about the prospect of short-term travel taken purely for recreation and enjoyment.

Today, in our twenty-first-century world, we take foreign travel for granted. We have a choice of transport to get us off our island, and once we set foot in another country we have the option of planes, trains and automobiles to take us further on our journeys.

By comparison, our ancestors had much fewer options and travel abroad would mean a completely life-changing experience. To enable us to follow their trail around the globe we must investigate their methods of transport and the conditions encountered by the varying classes. We will begin with those who were eager to see the world from a different perspective, soak up the atmosphere and culture of their new destination, and enjoy life on the ocean wave in comfort.

TAKING THE TOUR

From the late 1600s, it was customary for upper-class men, and later, women, to undertake what became known as a Grand Tour of Europe, enabling them to advance their cultural education and mix with those of a similar social status on the Continent. By the nineteenth century, their contemporaries in the United States had also joined in on these European jaunts, along with the wealthy middle classes who were seeking to mingle with the fashionable elite, making beneficial contacts for when they returned to home.

Eventually, the development of the railways made overland travel much more enjoyable compared to the stagecoach journeys of the past, while maritime advancements ensured greater comfort and speed as vessels changed from sail-driven barques and clipper ships to steam-powered liners. Naturally, conditions onboard varied depending upon the class of cabin a passenger could afford. Those travelling for pleasure and education would enjoy the luxury of comfortable accommodation, while adventurers hoping to seek their fortune were prepared to endure the basics of third class or even steerage, with its limited facilities and privacy.

Adverts, ship plans and personal sketches of cabin layouts help us learn more about the vessels on which our ancestors travelled.

For many, the Grand Tour could take anything from a few weeks to several months to complete as the 'tourists' soaked up the arts, antiquities and customs of the countries they visited. Along the way they would purchase items unlike those found in Britain: sculptures, books, furniture and other works of art became a permanent reminder of their trip to Europe, displayed on walls and in cabinets, and passed down within a family as an early form of memorabilia.

Each tour naturally had a 'tour guide' to explain the intricacies of etiquette and tradition within each country visited, as well as providing a commentary on the sights, offering advice on local behaviour, and providing a translation of foreign language should it be required.

But it was not only the wealthy who wished to have a 'window on the world', and when Thomas Cook saw the opportunity to extend his popular British excursions overseas, the scheme was met with enthusiasm. After a series of 'grand circular tours' of Europe, he extended his routes to include Italy, Switzerland, Egypt, and later, the United States. By charging for travel arrangements, food and accommodation over a fixed period along a specified route, Thomas Cook's company established 'inclusive independent travel' and the pre-booked holiday. His series of guide books (known as 'Cook's Travellers Handbooks') were aimed at educating a wide, middle-class audience and preparing them for the sights, sounds and experiences that lay ahead.

CASE STUDY: MEMORIES IN THE MAKING

Seasoned travellers often chose to share their own encounters with others through publication, either relaying their adventures to newspapers back home or writing books on their experiences upon their return. During the 1890s, W. Lawrence Liston wrote a fascinating personal account – later published in *The Girl's Own Paper* to educate young ladies – of a voyage that he undertook for health reasons, enabling us to visualise what a traveller could expect to see and experience on the journey between Port Said and Suez. Initially, he comments that:

> Port Said is not a beautiful town and this is rarely worthwhile for any lady passengers to land, a motley crowd of men on shore, in long robes and turbans, come to row passengers ashore in boats. Many land here for the purpose of telegraphing home the news of their safe arrival and one is frequently pestered by self constituted guides, who offer, for the sum of two pence, to show the way to the post office or Telegraph Depot.

Comically, he explains about an Egyptian juggler who comes on board to provide entertainment for the passengers and 'performs marvellous tricks ... his ample robes enable him to secrete endless chickens and rabbits, which he utilises for his tricks: the marvel is that he does not sit on them'. Liston also gives us an insight into how the ships were refuelled at this time:

> At night [...] it is a striking sight to see the coal barges come up to the side of the ship. At the end of each barge is hung out a kind of large beacon fire, and all the barges swarm with dark bodied Arabs and Egyptians, who, as they come alongside, sing a kind of wild dirge-like melody, which they keep up during the whole coaling. To watch these men coaling the ships and walking up to the bunkers is like seeing the links of a great revolving human chain. They leave the ship in a shocking state of dirt and dust, and it is a great relief when the engine room bell sounds and we are once more moving.

When the steamer enters the Suez Canal, Liston explains that it can only travel at a rate of 4 or 5 miles an hour due to the shallowness of the water. Any ship that navigated this channel at night was required to have a searchlight that illuminated 1,000yd in front, lighting up the sandbanks and making them look like ridges of snow. He adds, 'On the return voyage one will hear our Australian cousins, who have never seen snow, asking if this is what it is really like.' It turns out the author had a good knowledge of how the Suez Canal operated, after travelling this route on several occasions in the past:

> By far the greatest numbers of trading vessels passing through are bound for, or have come from, England. At each station – known as a 'gare' – there is a set of signals which indicate to an approaching ship whether she is to enter the canal or put into a siding [...] Other ships take second place to the mail packet steamers. On the entrance of the ship into the canal this fact is noted at the chief office at Tewfik, where there is a model of the canal and a set of model ships. The clerk receiving notice of the entrance of the ship places a model with corresponding flag in the little trough, and telegraphs directions concerning it to the next 'gare', so that at any particular time the position of any ship in any part of the canal is accurately known.

Today, in our computerised world, this operation seems quaint and antiquated, but it obviously worked sufficiently well to get the majority of ships through the passage with little or no trouble. It is fascinating for the family historian to come across personal accounts or published articles that explain these mammoth projects from the viewpoint of the passenger and how it affected their journey. Your own ancestor may well have travelled along this route and these snippets of information can really 'add weight' to your own family story.

Liston mentions a whole host of sightings passed by on this particular voyage, including the town of Suez, Moses Wells marked by a group of palm trees, the famous Mount Sinai, and one particular port of call – Aden. This was the first addition to British territory in the reign of Queen Victoria and was secured in 1839 by the East India Company and Royal Marines to help prevent attacks by pirates on British shipping to India. It was an extremely valuable acquisition as a centre for Asiatic and European trade, as well as being an important military and coaling station. But it is not only the *places* that Liston describes but also the *people*, and to many passengers, everything they witnessed would be new and exciting:

> A wonderful collection of human beings assembles to greet each ship, most noticeable of who are the divers. Their heads are all clean shaven and they generally come out to the ships in threes in little boats, one rowing and the others diving about. For the most part, they disdain all copper coins, affecting to be unable to see them, and crying out, 'Throw silvah, sah!' The impunity with which they swim about among the sharks is miraculous: they will, for a shilling, dive under the ship and, come up on the other side: or, having clambered up the rigging, will dive from it into the sea. Having secured the coin for which they have dived, they cram it, along with all the others that they may have gained, into their mouths, being apparently, like monkeys, endowed with pouches there.

This last comical observation shows just what people believed when they came into contact with new nationalities and cultures. He continues:

> Another interesting set of people are the natives who come on board with all sorts of fabrics, embroidery, jewellery, boxes, bottles of Attar Roses, and ostrich feathers also form a large part of their stock in trade. They invariably ask more than double the sum that they expect to receive. These gentlemen bring a certain quantity of material on board, and hope to take a certain amount of money back, so that towards the end, when they have made that sum, they will sell what remains of their stock at very much reduced prices, and then is the time to buy. All these natives are controlled and kept in order by the native police, who, with their little round caps bordered with yellow, look quite imposing. Their methods of dealing with their brethren generally take the form of fearful blows delivered anywhere and anyhow with a thick stick.

WHERE TO WINTER?

In the late nineteenth century there was nothing that affluent Brits hated more than to spend a cold wet winter in Britain. Turn to the back pages of any *Illustrated London News* and there would be adverts to entice prospective globetrotters, often under the heading of 'Where to Winter'.

The Grand Hotel at Biarritz was just one of the fashionable places to be seen and 'frequented by the elite and a rendezvous of the English colony'. In 1895, it boasted 'views to satisfy all the comforts which travellers may desire [...] charmingly situated facing the ocean with a climate as mild and delightful as that of Nice and Italy'. During the winter season the rates were from 10 francs per day, depending upon the floors occupied, and visitors could expect the luxury that all private rooms were carpeted!

But perhaps Europe did not fit the bill and there were those Victorians who preferred a destination a little further afield. Thirty Guinea Tours to Palestine, Egypt and Constantinople could be enjoyed by those prepared to travel by steamship on a thirty-day cruise. The Peninsular and Oriental Company advertised the 'excellent opportunity of reaching Egypt or Bombay' on their steam-navigation vessels, while the Royal Mail Steam Packet Company offered sixty-five days for £65 on their 'magnificent vessels' touring the West Indies. The promise of 'a string band, electric lights, electric bells, hot and cold baths, and high-class cuisine' tempted many travellers from their draughty mansions or London flats. Newspaper coverage of the P&O liner SS *Cathay* reported that:

> The magnificent oil burning steamship described by Lord Inchcape, two or three years ago when she was launched as the last word in comfort in ocean travel, left Tilbury Docks on a severely cold winter's day, bound for Australia. The atmosphere was Arctic, and all the passengers long for the warmer air and genial sunshine anticipated during the next day or two.

On this particular vessel it seems most of the travellers were bound for Australia (Adelaide, Melbourne, Sydney or Brisbane), some for New Zealand, some for Colombo or Rangoon, and others for Khartoum and further destinations in the desert. A passenger on board confirmed the luxurious conditions they were experiencing on the voyage:

> Truly, she is all we could desire. Cabins for one and two passengers, each with something like a real bedstead, large and airy, electric lights, wardrobes, chests of drawers, paper racks above your bed, and a small folding table attached to the wall on which your early cup of tea is placed at 6.30 in the morning. There are hot and cold saltwater bathrooms in plenty; a charming music room with easy chairs, smoking room, and a library of books free to passengers.

Along with all these 'mod cons' was the regular dining: 'You are amply fed, and the cuisine is excellent. Breakfast is at 8.30, lunch at one, afternoon tea at four, and dinner at 6.30. Then later in the evening are dainty sandwiches and during the forenoon a Steward takes round biscuits.'

Although security upon entering a foreign country was not what it is today, for some, the encounter was still memorable and worth noting in their diaries: 'The experience with customs officers at Marseilles is really most curious,' explained one traveller writing in 1925:

> After your bags are opened and examined in the usual way, and you innocently try to march out of the Customs House following your porter, you are stopped by other officials asking further questions; then a third attack is made upon you by a man who might be anybody or nobody, but who is in reality a plainclothes detective, who insisted on feeling my pockets for tobacco, but apparently was satisfied, and then allowed us all to pass on. (I had heard about these plainclothes men before.)

Period photographs, like this example taken on the SS *Spartan Prince* in 1899, help us visualise what life was like on-board ship for late-nineteenth and early-twentieth-century passengers.

Even the requirements surrounding travel with a passport had still not reached the strict regulations enforced during the latter part of the twentieth century. On a journey from Algiers to Marseilles on board a steamer of the Compagnie Générale Transatlantique, one traveller recalled:

> Whilst on the ship having dinner, the gentleman sitting opposite overheard us talking about passports (which we had never yet shown since leaving home) and afterwards told me our conversation had reminded him that he had forgotten his own passport in Algiers (where he lived) and that he had immediately wirelessed home for this to be posted to Paris, as he was proceeding to England, and would be held up in Paris until it came.

When the same diarist proceeded to Cannes, it is interesting to note his amazement about the developments in travel times and transport: 'Cannes is a resort most charming, refined and sweet. It is difficult to imagine that in this May-like weather we are only about twenty-seven hours' journey from wintry England. In six weeks time this journey will be done in eight hours by seaplane!'

Diaries and journals capture the thoughts, feelings and observations of emigrants and adventurers during their voyage, and in the foreign lands they visited.

PASSENGER TRAVEL – A GROWING INDUSTRY

As Britain strove to find a faster way to reach the furthest outposts of its colonial empire, ship building and sea travel was enjoying a continued period of success. P&O vessels took passengers and cargo to Sydney, Singapore and Hong Kong, the Royal Mail Steam Packets went to the exotic ports of Rio, Buenos Aires and the West Indies, while the Union Castle lines headed for the Cape Colonies.

Founded in 1837, P&O was originally known as the 'Peninsular Steam Navigation Company' and built its reputation carrying mail from the UK to Spain and Portugal. When the contract was altered to include the carrying of Egyptian mail, the term 'Oriental' was added to the company moniker. Gradually the routes expanded, encompassing East Ceylon, Singapore and Hong Kong. The steam vessels were developed and improved to meet the requirements of a mail service to Australia, and by 1859, P&O became the first steamer to carry a cargo of tea from China to the UK. Although the company had always carried cargo, the focus was on mail transportation; this changed in 1896 when its first purpose-built cargo ship was launched.

But sea travel was a constantly evolving business and with the turn of the new century, P&O entered the market of passenger travel, offering a programme of pleasure cruises, later purchasing a string of shipping liners to fulfil the demand for this area of their business.

In 1866 P&O employed 12,000 people across ten different companies and this number only increased as the years went by. Your ancestor may well have travelled on one of their vessels but also consider that they could have chosen a 'working life' on the ocean wave. Visit www.poheritage.com to search their online database of ships and their family history research guides to tracking down passengers and crew. Their gallery of vintage posters, photo and art highlights bring their vessels and services offered to life.

WORKING YOUR WAY AROUND THE WORLD

Not everyone had the finances to be able to afford a holiday overseas, and for those with a passion to experience the countries they had previously only read about, there was always the option of working their passage. There were plenty of situations for men who were prepared to take on any role on both cargo and passenger ships, but for the women it was not quite so easy. From the 1870s, competition grew between steamship companies to provide the finest accommodation and facilities with their passengers in mind. Vacancies for stewardesses and other female roles gave women an opportunity to experience onboard travel to a foreign destination without the need to find their fare. But competition for these positions was tough.

Newspapers, journals and printed ephemera provide numerous examples of those who were prepared to meet the challenge head on, yet required a little guidance to get their adventure underway. In 1890, a young adventurer named Fanny wrote to a magazine column for advice as she hoped to work her passage to Australia as a stewardess. Sadly, she received quite a curt reply from the journal correspondent and one wonders if she ever had the nerve to follow her dream after such a negative – and public – response: 'You must apply to some of the great firms for passenger steamships. We fancy that a situation as a stewardess is somewhat difficult to obtain by one who has had no practical experience.'

Three years later another young woman was about to set sail for America to take up a position as a housekeeper. Before her trip she had decided to write in to the miscellaneous column of the popular *Girl's Own Paper* to seek their opinion on what clothing she should take for the journey. The detailed answer was published and no doubt proved extremely helpful. It is examples of paper-ephemera such as these periodicals (which can be picked up at garage and car boot sales, collectable fairs or online) that provide us with a personal view of the lives of individuals at a particular time:

> It will be a great mistake to make such a voyage without such warm clothing as is necessary for our own country and European travel. You should start in serge (tailor-made), having a good deep pocket on each side of the skirt in the front seams, and a warm Ulster with a roomy hood to match. Until you arrive at Port Said you will not find it too warm. A lighter material might then be worn both in gown and jacket. A wide brimmed hat, at least enough so to shade the eyes, and a couple of dark washing dresses would be suitable for ship use and travelling on arrival. Of course, on ship-board, it will be well to have a black silk, or silk and cashmere dress for dinner wear. As a young housekeeper in prospect you had better take out a good supply of house and table linen.

An *Illustrated London News* image from October 1857 depicting the method a ship would use to hoist a pilot on-board in order for him to sail the vessel safely into harbour.

From the published response you can visualise the poor girl getting anxious that she hasn't yet bought every item of apparel on the list, and that taking a 'good supply of house and table linen' with her on the journey, hadn't even crossed her mind!

With the invention of the Internet nearly 100 years in the future, it would be commonplace for people to seek advice on all manner of subjects by writing in to correspondence columns in weekly magazines and monthly publications. The editor of the column would then produce a published response, answering the question and offering guidance. During the latter part of the nineteenth century, a large proportion of these queries were immigration and travel based, giving us an insight into what were the most popular destinations for the migrant – or tourist – at this time, and revealing 'top tips' and recommendations for the novice traveller planning a trip overseas.

Another enquiry was in response to which countries were offering free or subsidised passages at a particular time. One published reply to a young woman named Susan informs us that in 1893:

> There are only two colonies that are now giving free passages, Queensland and Western Australia, and we are informed that this privilege is limited to selected female servants. Persons who have a small amount of capital are eligible for reduced passages to New Zealand. The passage to Dunedin, Christchurch, Wellington, and Auckland, takes about forty-five days. The price of a ticket, for men or women, by second class is from £36 15s to £42. And a steerage ticket, for either sex, from £16 16s to £21.

It is hard to contemplate a journey of forty-five days when we can now travel to the other side of the world within twenty-four hours (albeit by aeroplane and not ship). Did your ancestor travel to Australia or New Zealand at the end of the nineteenth century? Might they have paid these prices and spent over a month and a half at sea?

A SHARED EXPERIENCE

A cruise, expedition or unusual encounter in a different country often prompted travellers to record the experience in a letter sent back home, in a diary or journal, or on some occasions, in a talk to interested parties upon their return. A newspaper clipping from the early 1900s reports that:

> In the Fisher Street Wesleyan Schoolroom, Warrington [...] A most enjoyable and instructive lecture, descriptive of a tour on the banks of the Nile was delivered last Wednesday night. Mrs Garnett is a fluent and very entertaining speaker and her remarks were listened to with rapt attention. The peculiarities of several towns were graphically sketched; and other places such as the Pyramids and the great Sphinx were vividly brought before the audience, while half a dozen 'English Egyptians' were requisitioned to illustrate the manners and customs of the people. Messes Ladle, Hearsay and Gibson, together with two or three ladies, donned Egyptian costumes of various kinds and impersonated the dusky Arabs to perfection.

This tiny piece of ephemera is a gem of a find. Revealing the names of the people involved, the confirmation of foreign travel, and an 'address' of an area where the speaker may have lived.

Before the accessibility of television, people made their own entertainment and were eager to share their experiences with others. Church halls and meeting rooms provided the perfect place to stage these events and helped people to get a wider perspective on what was going on in the rest of the world. Lectures and talks were announced in local newspapers and parish newsletters. Look out for examples in the areas where your ancestors lived.

TAKING IT FURTHER

Unearthing christening notices, baptismal cards and even wedding invites in the belongings of an ancestor far from their native homeland can give us avenues of research to follow and reveal more about their childhood before their new life overseas. Equally, there were many travellers who eventually returned to their country of origin and it is not until we read an obituary that we discover more about their adventures. Track down published obituaries of your forebears (or re-read those you may already have) to look for fresh clues about destinations they may have visited; they may have had a life abroad that you had previously known nothing about!

When Mr Philip C. Garnett passed away in the early twentieth century his obituary revealed compulsory travel during the First World War, and a later voyage in an attempt to improve his health:

> He was one of the first to join the Sportsman's Battalion when it was formed in October 1914, and for many months underwent the rigorous training of a Private, which at his age was undoubtedly a great physical strain. In 1916 he received a commission in the Royal Field Artillery, and it was while serving in this force that he met with a serious accident. His leg was broken by a kick from his horse, and for more than a year he was under the treatment of various hospitals. On his recovery he transferred to the R.A.S.C. and in 1917 went out to France, where he acted as Captain in the Motor Transport. While on service there he contracted internal poisoning and has had indifferent health ever since his demobilisation in 1919. Last spring a sea voyage was advised and Mr Garnett went for a trip to the West Indies.

Just from this one paragraph the family historian has a number of leads to follow:

- What was the Sportsman's Battalion and to which areas of Europe were they sent?
- Can Mr Garnett's military records be traced?
- Do documents still exist which refer to his accident?
- Can his service in the R.A.S.C. be traced and where was he posted in France?
- How did he contract internal poisoning?
- Does he appear on the outbound passenger lists for his trip to the West Indies on the Ancestry or Findmypast websites?

Use this method of breaking down the information you have found to extend the avenues of research pertaining to your own ancestor's travels.

CASE STUDY: PRIMARY SOURCES AND POINTS OF VIEW

You don't always have to *own* a particular piece of ephemera to benefit from its existence. As you try to understand your ancestor's decision for moving overseas, or why they chose to travel to a particular destination, primary sources such as letters, diaries and memorabilia held in museums and private collections can shed light on those who have lived through similar circumstances.

To get an idea of what examples exist that are relevant to *your* ancestral story, type keywords into an Internet search engine and see what comes up. Use phrases such as French Revolution letters, famine diary, emigration diary, gold rush letters and ephemera to whittle down your search; the results may reside in public archives, or even be for sale on auction sites.

Once you embark on this quest you will soon discover that there are literally hundreds of questions you want to ask about your forebear's travels, not only about the destinations and the sights they witnessed, but perhaps starting with the conditions faced on board ship, or what food was likely to have been available during the journey.

Reading the diary of George Russell Rogers, a passenger onboard the SS *Rodney*, a clipper-ship bound for Australia in 1891, he vividly describes the system used for keeping 'fresh meat' available for the passengers' meals:

> The vessel carries a quantity of live beasts and birds for food. We have on-board 32 sheep, six pigs, 22 dozen fowls, eight dozen ducks and a dozen geese. These unfortunate creatures are stowed away in hutches or coops on the main deck and their lot indeed is a hard one. The sheep are packed very closely in hutches in which they can only just stand up whilst the birds are so crammed up in their coops that I doubt if some of them ever get at their food or water. Indeed it is no uncommon occurrence for the butcher to find on going about his rounds, two or more dead ducks or chickens. It seems absurd to bring these poor things to sea because in heavy weather they get very wet (although canvas is hanging in front of their coops) and they frequently go blind from the action of the salt water. The sheep bare their lot very well but look so hopeless, but the pigs have a very good time provided the hutch is not cleaned too often.

Personal ephemera can really give us a new outlook on the personalities of our ancestors, especially those observations written in their own hand. These statements, opinions and points of view are the thoughts and feelings of individuals who were actually there at the time, experiencing similar circumstances to those enjoyed or endured by your own forebears.

George obviously had a good sense of humour when he wrote the following description of how one of the pigs was prepared for dinner. Today, we might think these conditions and procedures barbaric, but back then, without the aid of pre-packed food and the prospect of weeks at sea, this was how our forebears survived:

> After lunch, 'Dennis' the second pig was killed and all hands nearly, and several male passengers turned up at the execution to pay their last respects. The butcher killed him off very well, although he (Dennis) made a great farce about having his throat cut. He was then popped into a tub filled with hot water and his bristles scrubbed off. He was then hung up to the rigging but as the vessel was rolling very much and the sea breaking over, he was shaken off his hook and was found rolling about the deck in the most ludicrous manner. He was captured and hung up again.

By contrast, Dr Abraham Pease, a journalist travelling on board the steamer SS *E.M.S.* in 1899, was one of many 'tourists' who chose to include keepsakes from their trips, pasted within their journals or scrapbooks. The menu from one of the evening meals shows that the choice of dishes was extensive for first-class passengers at this time.

It is not only the passengers of the ship that help us realise what was involved in eighteenth/nineteenth-century travel, but also the crew. If your ancestor worked their passage then any letters or diaries they may have left behind (or by others who were in a similar situation) can help you begin to understand what they were experiencing. The website 'The Diary Junction' at www.pikle.co.uk/diaryjunction.html is a fascinating Internet resource for those interested in historical diaries. With information and links to the works of over 500 diarists – many of them famous – you are guaranteed to find something to inspire, written from the perspective of those who were actually living during a particular period. Click on the links to be taken to extracts, transcriptions or digitalised versions of the original diary. From landowners and merchants to those who experienced life at sea, there are examples of various aspects of life from the early seventeenth century onwards.

2

UNITED KINGDOM

'There are no extraordinary men...
just extraordinary circumstances that ordinary men are forced to deal with.'
William Halsey

Every journey begins with a departure point, so it is fitting to start this 'global tour' by spotlighting the United Kingdom, concentrating on the arrival and 'official processing' of newcomers who chose to make Britain their home, before examining some of the contributing factors that prompted large numbers of our population to migrate.

ALIENS VERSUS IMMIGRANTS

Before you begin any research it is worth considering how your 'travelling' ancestor was perceived in Britain so that you can determine which records are likely to be the most beneficial to you. There is quite a difference between those individuals classed as 'immigrants' and those classed as 'aliens'.

An *immigrant* moves to a foreign country in order to settle and make a new life for themselves and their families, while an *alien* moves to a foreign country but *does not* intend to settle there. Over the centuries, a number of concerns have been raised by British people towards these 'newcomers', including the possibility of foreigners working for less money and taking jobs in times of economic crisis, and the chance they may be spies that pose a threat to the country. As a result, a number of records were introduced that have become worth their weight in gold for any genealogist trying to establish links with those ancestors who arrived in the UK from abroad.

From as early as the sixteenth century, regular surveys were produced that documented the number of strangers in the capital, while by the seventeenth century, Quarter and Borough Sessions recorded immigrants and those that employed them.

Enquire at your County Archives to see what examples they have in their collections. During the eighteenth and nineteenth centuries, foreign arrivals were obliged to register themselves at port and with the local Justice of the Peace, in order to notify them of their presence. Masters of ships were required to fill out certificates relating to any alien passengers they brought into the country, and although these certificates no longer survive before 1836, an index to them can be searched at The National Archives www.nationalarchives.gov.uk.

When trying to establish a person's nationality, certificates of arrival completed between 1826 and 1905 usually state the last port from which a person sailed, but as journeys were often taken in stages, this does not necessarily mean this was the country from which they originated.

If your ancestor arrived after the start of the First World War, then they would have been required to register at the local police station. Those documents that have survived should be held at the County Record Office for that area, while London records are likely to have been deposited at The National Archives. These Registers of Aliens can hold quite comprehensive information so expect to find the person's name, nationality and place of birth, their residential address with details of the type of tenancy, their occupation (even if they were not actually practising the trade at the time), their employer's address, as well as information about the individual's spouse and children.

Finding your Alien Ancestors

One of the best places to search for individuals arriving in the UK is in the Alien Arrivals Collection at www.ancestry.com. Documenting more than 610,000 non-British citizens (aliens) who set foot on British shores between the late eighteenth and early twentieth century, you will find the information available is split into three distinct groups.

First, Alien Entry Books can be searched online for the period between 1794 and 1921 and includes correspondence and documents created by the Home Office and the Aliens Office relating to aliens, naturalisations and applications for denization. The main focus of the second part of this collection covers Alien Arrivals in the period from 1810 to 1869, offering us:

- The name of the individual.
- Their age and profession.
- Their country of origin/nationality.
- Port and date of arrival.
- The name of the ship on which they arrived.
- The certificate number of the documentation on which this information is recorded.

The final era covered is from 1878 to 1960 and is a database known as the UK Incoming Passenger Lists. This index is most useful for researchers trying to understand more about those ancestors arriving in the United Kingdom from foreign ports outside of Europe and the Mediterranean, and the ships on which they travelled. Expect to find:

- The name of the passenger.
- Their age and date of birth.
- The vessel name.
- The port of departure.
- The port and date of arrival.

NEWCOMERS TO BRITAIN

From 1851 onwards – depending on the information provided – the census would indicate the origins of individuals born outside Britain. Naturalised British citizens were regularly recorded with the initials 'BS' meaning British Subject. It was not until the mid-nineteenth century that restrictions were put on immigrants arriving from the Commonwealth. Previously, those from the British Empire were automatically classed as citizens and did not have to apply for the right to live in Britain, but these new rules gave the individual two options and required them to apply for either:

- *A Patent of Denization*, which once granted by the sovereign, allowed the applicant some privileges of a British subject – such as the right to hold English land – and was known as a Denizen. They did not have any political rights and were unable to hold a civil, military or parliamentary post, or inherit property. The last known denization took place in 1848 and became obsolete when naturalisation was introduced.
- *For Naturalisation*, which gave foreign nationals the same rights as a native-born resident. The Naturalisation Act was enforced in 1844 and stated that anyone wishing to stay in Britain should declare their age, trade and residence as well as swearing an Oath of Allegiance to the country before they were granted permission – in the form of a certificate – and allowed to stay.

Before this date the acquisition of these documents was not obligatory so those from the poorer classes, who were desperate to flee their homelands, often didn't bother. Therefore, the discovery of a completed application can prove very useful, giving details about the hopeful candidate and their family. Surviving documents from 1800 onwards have been indexed at The National Archives. Successful naturalisation documents can reveal the name and address of the applicant, their country and place of birth, alongside their profession and marital status (note: women had one slight advantage and were able to become naturalised through marriage to a natural-born or naturalised British citizen – this ruling did not apply to men).

By 1870 these regulations had changed again with consideration only given to those applicants who had served the Crown or lived in Britain for at least five years. Many of the accepted immigrants decided to change their names by Deed Poll to an Anglicised version of their original, in the belief that this would give them a better chance of integrating into the community.

CASE STUDY: NATURALISATION CERTIFICATES

Before you begin your search to confirm whether an ancestor applied for British citizenship you should first try to obtain the following information: the person's full name, what country they came from, and the date you think that they may have applied for denization or naturalisation. For applications between 1801 and 1871 you can search online and download any copies you may find from The National Archives website at www.nationalarchives.gov.uk.

You would need to visit the archives at Kew to enquire about access to, and the survival of, applications after this date. Copies of Certificates of British Nationality issued between January 1949 and September 1986, or Certificates of Naturalisation issued between January 1981 and January 1986, can be ordered from The National Archives. For those issued after this date you would need to contact the UK Border Agency.

Our example shows a Certificate of Naturalisation granted on 9 December 1948 to a Mr Poldi Schlesinger. As you can see there is a treasure trove of information contained in this document under the 'Particulars Relating to Applicant' section. It provides:

- The individual's full name.
- His address in Putney, London.
- His trade as a stock keeper and machine scraper to a Hat Trimmer.
- His date and place of birth on 7 December 1877 in Maiersdorf, Austria.
- His nationality as Austrian.
- The name of his wife as Rosa.
- And the name and nationality of his parents as Ignaz and Betty Schlesinger, who were also of Austrian origin.

These details can help you to verify a marital relationship, confirm a previous generation in the form of parents' names, and reinforce specific facts that you may previously have found, such as their date and place of birth. Turn this particular certificate over

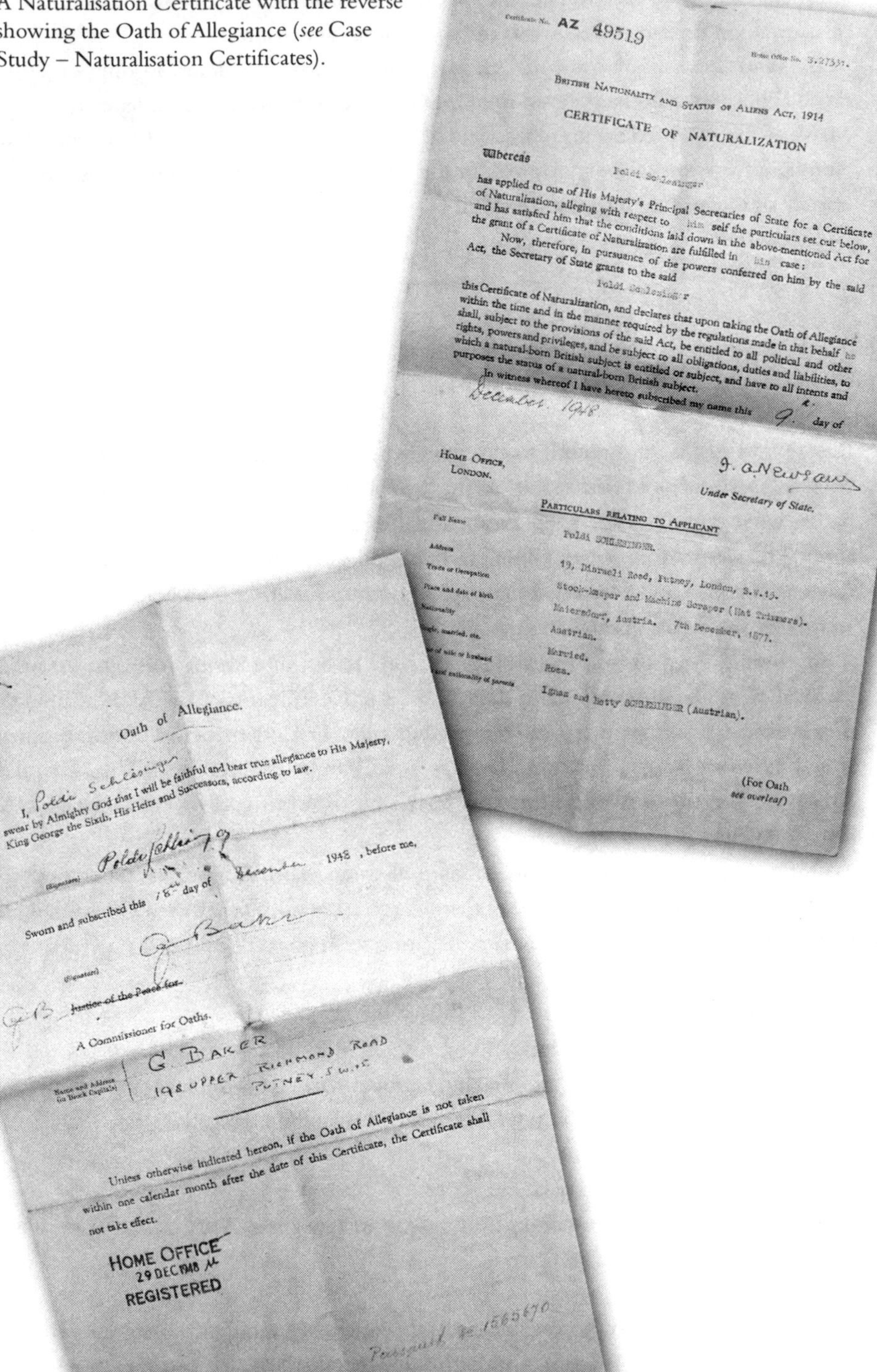

Certificate No. AZ 49519

Home Office No. S.27337.

British Nationality and Status of Aliens Act, 1914

CERTIFICATE OF NATURALIZATION

Whereas Poldi Schlesinger

has applied to one of His Majesty's Principal Secretaries of State for a Certificate of Naturalization, alleging with respect to him self the particulars set out below, and has satisfied him that the conditions laid down in the above-mentioned Act for the grant of a Certificate of Naturalization are fulfilled in his case:

Now, therefore, in pursuance of the powers conferred on him by the said Act, the Secretary of State grants to the said Poldi Schlesinger

this Certificate of Naturalization, and declares that upon taking the Oath of Allegiance within the time and in the manner required by the regulations made in that behalf he shall, subject to the provisions of the said Act, be entitled to all political and other rights, powers and privileges, and be subject to all obligations, duties and liabilities, to which a natural-born British subject is entitled or subject, and have to all intents and purposes the status of a natural-born British subject.

In witness whereof I have hereto subscribed my name this 9th day of December 1948.

Home Office, London.

J. A. Newsam

Under Secretary of State.

Particulars relating to Applicant

Full Name: Poldi SCHLESINGER.

Address: 19, Disraeli Road, Putney, London, S.W.15.

Trade or Occupation: Stock-keeper and Machine Scraper (Hat Trimmers).

Place and date of birth: Unterdorf, Austria. 7th December, 1877.

Nationality: Austrian.

Single, married, etc.: Married.

Name of wife or husband: Rosa.

Names and nationality of parents: Ignaz and Betty SCHLESINGER (Austrian).

(For Oath see overleaf)

Oath of Allegiance.

I, Poldi Schlesinger swear by Almighty God that I will be faithful and bear true allegiance to His Majesty, King George the Sixth, His Heirs and Successors, according to law.

(Signature) Poldi Schlesinger [illegible]

Sworn and subscribed this 18th day of December 1948, before me,

(Signature) G. Baker

G.B. ~~Justice of the Peace for~~

A Commissioner for Oaths.

Name and Address (in Block Capitals): G. BAKER 198 UPPER RICHMOND ROAD PUTNEY. S.W.15

Unless otherwise indicated hereon, if the Oath of Allegiance is not taken within one calendar month after the date of this Certificate, the Certificate shall not take effect.

HOME OFFICE 29 DEC 1948 REGISTERED

Passport No. 1565670

A Naturalisation Certificate with the reverse showing the Oath of Allegiance (*see* Case Study – Naturalisation Certificates).

and you can see an example of the Oath of Allegiance signed by the applicant. Here, Mr Schlesinger agreed to: 'swear by Almighty God that I will be faithful and bear true allegiance to His Majesty, King George the Sixth, His Heirs and Successors, according to law.' This oath was then signed by the applicant and countersigned by a Commissioner for Oaths, nine days after the Certificate of Naturalisation was produced. To confirm its authenticity and that the correct procedures had been carried out, the document was stamped by the Home Office.

PASSENGER LISTS

Introduced after a number of government acts, passenger lists were compiled to monitor the movement of people from country to country. Very early records required people to seek the permission of the Crown before they could leave their country of origin, while later record-keeping was a statistical exercise and designed to help control the numbers of immigrants arriving.

Each master of a vessel was required by law to provide a list of all his passengers to the officers at the port of departure. This information was then sent to the Board of Trade. When the vessel reached its destination a similar requirement was requested from the immigration authorities.

During the nineteenth century a formal layout of the passenger lists was introduced, which included columns for the name, age, occupation and home country of each individual. Later, details of where the passenger was travelling to were also added, along with the amount of money the individual possessed and whether they could read or write. There are a number of considerations to be taken into account when researching the information provided on a passenger list:

- You might be able to tie families together if they are recorded with consecutive ticket numbers.
- When the passenger applied for a ticket, their name will have been transcribed onto a master ticket list before being entered onto the Board of Trade list. Errors could easily have been made on either occasion so don't dismiss individuals as not your ancestors just because their surnames are not spelt correctly. Remember that it was not only languages that formed a barrier when providing personal details for the passenger lists. Strong regional accents could also impact on the way in which a name was spelt, especially if it was misheard by the listener.
- Those with less money or in large family groups would find it more economical to travel in third class. Third class passengers were required to pass a medical inspection prior to boarding; if they failed they would be refused passage. A line crossed

through the person's name could indicate that this was the case, or that they had simply cancelled their travel arrangements.

- When identifying an individual, it is best not to rely too much upon the age they have given just in case they were trying to appear younger, or older, than they actually were.
- The census is a fabulous tool for establishing the occupation of your ancestors at ten yearly intervals. If they happened to travel abroad during this decade you can confirm from the information they have provided whether they had continued in the same line of work or had changed vocation.
- On documents completed before departure, the passenger was required to state the country that they were intending to visit or reside in. You can find out more about their exact destination by checking the immigration records of that country.

Considering our history of record-keeping, the majority of passenger lists in Britain date from 1890, as previously they were only preserved for five years before being destroyed. You may have more luck if your ancestor travelled to the United States in the earlier part of the nineteenth century, as official records began here after 1820.

By the twentieth century thousands of passengers were travelling for pleasure and the passenger lists were designed to collect information to reflect this, distinguishing between tourists and immigrants.

Victorian travellers photographed on-board the ship *Spartan Prince*, taken in 1899.

BRITISH PORTS OF DEPARTURE

When trying to follow your ancestor's trail, it is important to try and establish the route they chose and the port from which they departed or arrived in Britain. You will then be able to widen your search and investigate the relevant documents in which your ancestor's details may appear:

- English Ports – Bristol, Cowes, Deal, Dover, Gravesend, Hull, Liverpool, London, Newcastle, Plymouth, Portsmouth, and Southampton
- Scottish Ports – Aberdeen, Edinburgh, Glasgow, Leith, and Stranraer
- Welsh Ports – Cardiff, Newport, and Swansea
- Irish Ports – Queenstown, Londonderry

ABSTRACT OF LOG.

R.M.S. "OCEANIC." COMMANDER: J. G. CAMERON, R.N.R.

LIVERPOOL TO NEW YORK, APRIL 16TH, 1902.

PASSED DAUNTS ROCK LIGHT VESSEL, APRIL 17TH, AT 9-55, A.M.

DATE.	MILES	LAT.	LONG.	REMARKS.
APRIL 17	52	51·24	9·32	
" 18	492	49·53	22·14	MOD. W'LY WINDS WITH FINE WEATHER
" 19	426	47·56	32·25	MOD. TO FRESH W.S.W. WINDS. MOD. W'LY SEA
" 20	464	44·15	42·27	FRESH GALE FROM W.S.W. TO N.W'LY
" 21	489	41·38	52·32	FRESH W.S.W. TO N.W'LY W'DS, H'VY HEAD SEAS
" 22	402	40·53	63·24	FRESH N'LY WINDS & HEAVY SEAS TO LIGHT VAR
" "	473	TO SANDY HOOK L.V.		LIGHT S.E'LY TO MOD. W'LY WINDS, FINE W'ER
TOTAL	2,891			ARRIVED APRIL 23RD AT

PASSAGE DAYS, HOURS, MINUTES.

AVERAGE SPEED KNOTS

An example of memorabilia produced especially for the passengers onboard the SS *Oceanic*, recording a log of the journey taken in 1902.

Outbound Passengers

One of the best places to search Britain's outbound passenger lists between 1890 and 1960 is on the fabulous research site www.findmypast.co.uk. These lists have varied in style and changed over time. Some include a myriad of detail, while others simply record the minimum amount of information. But whether typed or handwritten, if you can find an entry for your forebear, you will have yet another ancestral trail to follow.

The layout of the site makes searching the records very easy. Passenger lists for long-haul voyages to destinations outside Britain and Europe include countries such as the USA, Australia, Canada, New Zealand, India, and South Africa. Also covered are parts of Asia, the Caribbean, West Africa, and South America. En route there are even records for those passengers who disembarked at European destinations. British ports of departure are listed alphabetically, enabling you to try a variety of combinations if you are unsure of the location from which they left. (It should be noted that there are no digitalised records for incoming voyages to Britain. Any which exist are held at The National Archives in Kew.)

But it is not only emigrants that you can expect to find on the databases of this website. Civil servants and diplomats on government business, tourists on holiday trips, war brides en route to the United States after the Second World War, and 'Home Children' whose passage was paid for by charities in the hope of giving them a new start overseas – all feature within these documents. Even 'Ten Pound Poms' – the term used to describe those British nationals who took up the offer to emigrate to Australia on a £10 ticket sponsored by the Australian government – make an appearance, confirming that the records tell the stories of people from all walks of life. Once you've located an ancestor you can read the transcripts or choose to download and print scans of the original documents, making these images great additions to your collection of family history ephemera.

IRISH IMMIGRATION

In 1800 the population of Ireland was estimated at 4½ million residents; within forty years this had doubled to just over 8 million. When the economy began to feel the strain of such a rapid growth, the pressure was passed on to its inhabitants as land was divided into smaller plots, leaving many unable to grow enough food to support their families. The threat of destitution soon followed and the poorer/working classes became dependent on the potato as a staple food source to keep them from starvation.

In August 1845 – when it was thought the situation couldn't get any worse – the fungus *Phytophthora infestans* started to destroy the potato crops, causing a terrible stench as the green leaves began to blight and rot. A third of the country's crop was ruined, with the following year's crop deemed virtually unusable. Ireland was plunged into one of the bleakest periods in its history. Caught in the grip of famine and poverty, workhouses became full to overflowing and many died of starvation-related diseases.

The effects of the situation were further escalated when, unable to pay their rent, tenants were evicted by their landlords, who wished to clear their lands and modernise their estates. Some tried to 'fight' the situation, getting by as best they could, while others took the 'flight' option and joined the thousands leaving their homeland for good.

The lucky ones were given money by landholders, who contributed to the assisted emigration schemes, enabling those with very little to start a new life overseas. Others were simply turned out of their homes and left to fend for themselves without a roof over their heads and no means of support. Times were bleak and it is no wonder that the thought of escaping Ireland and a life of poverty, illness and death was all that

Irish Immigration First Day cover from 1999 commemorating early Irish settlers arriving in Boston. Find imaginative ways to illustrate specific incidents in your ancestor's history.

many had in mind. Between 1845 and 1854 over 1 million adult males and females are believed to have left Ireland as a direct result of the potato blight. Although huge numbers chose to take the long voyage to America, there were thousands of others who took the shorter journey across the Irish Sea to England.

Upon arrival in Liverpool, many attempted to make homes in the city – often escaping poverty in Ireland only to be confronted with it once again in the form of crowded housing and poor sanitary conditions. Liverpool became the migrant gateway for passage both in and out of the country, and its long history with Irish arrivals accounted for 17 per cent of the city's population being of Irish origin when the government census was taken in 1841. After the famine, this number rose to 22 per cent. It should also be noted that Liverpool was not solely influenced by the Irish. As the first port of entry to Britain for thousands of new arrivals, its diverse range of cultures included Indians, Chinese, Africans and migrants from many Europeans countries all living side by side.

Naturally, not all Irish immigrants decided to stay in Liverpool and instead travelled on to Manchester. Bustling with life and in the grip of the Industrial Revolution, the prospect of work seemed guaranteed. They set up their own communities (which became known as 'Little Ireland') in districts such as Ancoats and Chorlton-on-Medlock, but again, the lack of sanitation and poor housing meant these poverty-stricken areas were a breeding ground for disease.

Many Roman Catholics changed their religious persuasion as soon as they set foot on English soil, believing that a Church of England faith would give them a better chance of integrating into life on the mainland, so remember to check both sets of records when trying to track your ancestor down.

Sadly, there were those that didn't even reach England. Paupers who died at sea, and perhaps had no relatives willing or able to claim their bodies and pay for a funeral, would be buried at the expense of the parish. In 1806, the first Liverpool Parish Cemetery was opened and many of the victims of the Irish Potato Famine, who died during, or shortly after, the voyage from Ireland, were buried there. The burial of Catholic paupers continued in this cemetery up to 1890; after this date they were buried in the Catholic section of Anfield Cemetery.

By comparing documents with your growing knowledge of world history and events, it is possible to get a much clearer idea of what was happening during a specific period. For example, we can see how desperate Irish famine immigrants were to leave their homeland and travel much further afield simply because of the routes they took.

Before 1845, those wishing to emigrate to Canada would have left via Ireland's main ports or journeyed first to Liverpool and on from there. When conditions in Ireland worsened, such was the demand for vessels that emigrant ships were leaving from the much smaller ports of Kinsale, Westport and Killala in County Mayo. These were often packed to capacity, regularly carrying more than the legal limit, with little in the way of facilities onboard for the passengers, let alone berths to accommodate them. The only food they had for the six-week voyage was that which they had brought onboard themselves. The meagre ration of approximately two pints of water per day that they were given did little to keep them sustained – especially if they suffered seasickness. By the time they reached their destination there would be those that didn't have the strength to continue on, or had already died en route from starvation and disease. It is worth widening your search to see what passenger lists or information exists about the ships leaving from the smaller ports when you are trying to find emigrants who left Ireland at this time. You may discover just how desperate your ancestor's plight really was.

Even a person's choice of destination can tell us something about their situation. In many cases those that travelled to Canada and on to the United States had at least some money put by to pay for their passage, giving the impression they were slightly more 'prosperous' than their poorer kinfolk bound for Britain. Until assisted – and much sought after – passages became available, the poorest could not even afford the lowest fares to cross the Atlantic and instead paid the few pence required for deck passage across the Irish Sea.

Visit the website www.theshipslist.com, where you will find access to hundreds of passenger lists from Britain, Ireland, the US, Canada, Australia and South Africa. All the information is searchable for free and even includes immigration reports, shipwreck information, ship pictures and descriptions, shipping line fleet lists and newspaper records. There are 3,500 web pages with new databases added on a regular basis.

Sadly, there was no obligation to record departures from Ireland and it can be difficult establishing exactly which county your Irish ancestors originated from. Even if they are later recorded in the census, many chose simply to list 'Ireland' as their birthplace.

What may be helpful to consider is that famine immigrants tended to follow the patterns of their predecessors by heading to already established Irish communities when they arrived in Britain. Bradford, for example, attracted large numbers from Mayo, Sligo and Dublin, while Leeds saw an influx of immigrants from Mayo and Tipperary. A little 'local history' research in the area where your ancestor settled could help you whittle down a likely county of origin.

When the potato famine struck and prompted a mass exodus of Ireland's population, many of them left from Cobh (known as Queenstown between 1850 and 1920) – www.cobhheritage.com is the official website set up in conjunction with the Cobh Heritage Centre and is a 'must' for anyone researching this specific area of emigration. As Queenstown was a major Irish port, the website also deals with the history of larger vessels such as the *Titanic* and the *Lusitania*, which docked at Queenstown taking on passengers before continuing with their voyages between Liverpool and New York.

Thinking Outside of the Box

Items related to one of Ireland's worst periods in history – the potato famine – are likely to be few and far between and those that do exist can often fetch a large price at auction. One of the areas where you may find some references to the troubles of the time is in personal letters between individuals. These may take the form of brief notes, perhaps asking for assistance from other family members who might already be living overseas, but it must be remembered that not everyone in a dire situation at this time could read or write. As a result, much of the written material that survives would have been created by those with some education. Schoolteachers, who supported themselves before the famine by teaching the local children, would no longer have employment when the numbers dwindled. People in situations like this often wrote their grievances to the small press. Look out for examples such as these on eBay to piece together the thoughts and feelings of the public and the impact that the famine was having on all sections of society.

It is true that family memorabilia from this time is rare – especially when for so many, their only possessions were the clothes upon their backs – but there are ways in which you can depict this great change in their lives within your research; it just requires a little creative thinking.

Commemorative stamp issues, such as the example circulated in 1999 by the USA, portrays immigrant ships on the stamp with a postal cachet decorating the First Day Cover envelope showing the new arrivals disembarking in New York. Ireland has also released individual stamps to mark this period of its history using images of the ships as part of a postal release in 2000. Even scenes of families in the soup kitchens at the height of the famine were depicted on a stamp set issued in 1997. Wood-cut engraved printed illustrations, such as can be found in vintage newspapers like the *Illustrated*

London News (available on auction sites and at ephemera fairs), expose the poverty and hardship suffered, along with the hope of a fresh start in the 'New World'. Often you can find single images for sale, which have been removed from the newspaper, enabling you to purchase only the subject you are interested in. It should be noted that these particular examples of ephemera are increasing in value and can vary in price depending upon the 'newsworthiness' of the subject matter reported.

CASE STUDY: A CATASTROPHIC COLLISION

Although the famine had the greatest impact on Ireland's population and economy, over the years, people have chosen to emigrate for a variety of reasons. For some, the decision to leave their homes for a land many miles from their country of origin was a difficult one, while for others it was a time of excitement and anticipation for the adventure ahead. We have all heard stories of difficult voyages with dreadful conditions endured in order to fulfil ambitions, and sadly not everyone was destined to reach journey's end safely.

In November 1916, in the midst of a gale that raged in the Irish Sea, the passenger steamer *Connemara*, a vessel of 800 tons with ninety souls onboard, came into collision with a small boat named the *Retriever*, which was carrying Lancashire coal from Garston to Newry. Within fourteen minutes both vessels had sunk and despite being within sight of land only one man – James Boyle – survived. Those who perished came from all walks of life. The captain of the *Connemara* was a Carlisle man, although most of his crew were Welshmen. The stewardess, a Miss Williams, was going home to Wales to be married. There were three cattlemen aboard from Greenore, a luggage guard named John Hughes, and a number of soldiers returning from sick leave to rejoin their comrades at war. The majority of passengers were emigrants making for Holyhead on their way to America; sixteen of these were girls from the counties of Sligo, Monaghan, Cavan and Armagh, their dreams, and those of their respective families, shattered.

This incident was reported in the newspapers of the day and highlights how the collection of facts could provide the basis for further research. Have you discovered similar newspaper cuttings tucked within your forebear's belongings? Ask yourself why it was considered so important to be kept? Can you find out more about the incident reported and was one of your ancestors affected by it?

SCOTLAND'S GREAT MIGRATION

Since the defeat of the Jacobites at Culloden in 1746, and the effect of land enclosures during the Highland Clearances, Scotland has seen numerous instances in its history which have caused its citizens to migrate.

The decision to travel overseas would not have been an easy one, but with little to keep them on their native soil, some Scots were faced with few options. Those with farm animals sold their stock, while others – left with minimal possessions – used every last penny in their pockets to buy passage to America sailing from west-coast Scottish ports or their English equivalents.

By the 1780s another generation had faced the Scottish winters and unemployment hardships, and when the American War of Independence came to an end, a new wave of Scottish migrants headed to Canada. But it wasn't only the Americas that provided a big draw for the Scots.

Although the First Fleet had left for New South Wales loaded with convicts in 1787 (see Chapter 3), there were other opportunities in Australia – and later New Zealand – when the working man and his family was offered land at cheap rates to encourage new settlers. For many Scots – and other Brits alike – the prospect proved too much to resist as a future for their children beckoned without the threat of a dominant landlord and certain poverty.

In the early part of the nineteenth century Scottish farmers were having a pretty tough time of it. Land clearances were still being carried out to make way for more profitable sheep farms, and individual tenants were once again forced from their homes – left with little option but to try to make a living on unimproved land or move to coastal settlements and turn their hand to fishing.

Potatoes in the Highlands were often grown in raised beds and fertilised with seaweed, but when the potato blight swept through Ireland, it wasn't long before its effects were felt in Scotland, bringing yet more hardship and famine to the region, and the inevitable pressure to emigrate. A typical shipping agent's advert from the 1830s gave hope to those who no longer saw a future in their mother country, and it is no wonder that the wording seemed to provide an instant answer in what was for many, their darkest hour:

> The subscribers having established a regular succession of ships of the first-class to leave this port weekly from New York, beg leave to intimate to emigrants leaving Scotland, that they can rely on passages on the very lowest terms, and without the delay and alteration of days of sailing, which so often occurs to passengers in the seaports of Scotland. The quick and cheap communication from Glasgow and Greenock by steam packets daily, renders this the most desirable mode of passage from Great Britain to America.

> Emigration societies and families will be contacted with, and all letters (post paid) will receive immediate attention.
>
> Passages may be obtained at this office in superior ships, to Philadelphia, Boston, Baltimore, Québec...

For others though, this advert seemed like a distant, unachievable dream. With barely enough money to feed and clothe themselves, they could hardly raise the capital for the voyage no matter how cheap it promised to be.

As Scotland's poor sunk deeper into poverty it was realised that private landowners and public bodies had to step in to help. For five years, between 1852 and 1857, the Highlands and Islands Emigration Society assisted many to move to America, Canada, Australia and New Zealand.

When the Poor Law Amendment Act was introduced in 1850, another opportunity arose, as it allowed children under the age of 16 to be sent overseas to escape destitution, and although we've now discovered that many of the child emigration schemes set up were hugely flawed, this one piece of legislation lit the touch paper for the stream of child migrants who left Britain from this period right up to the 1950s.

En Route Research

Not every country has the same degree of organisation or availability of documents covering genealogical records as the next. We are extremely lucky when tracking British, US, Canadian, Australian and European routes, but try to research parts of Asia and Africa and you will undoubtedly encounter difficulties or dead-ends regarding the amount of information available.

But whatever country your forebears decided to emigrate to, or from, you can virtually guarantee that if you look hard enough there is a society or group of enthusiasts dedicated to covering the same areas of research as yourself. Like-minded genealogists are usually only too willing to share their findings, point others in the direction of relevant resources, and generally help to get you on the road to knocking down any 'brick walls' you may have been facing.

The Scottish people have always been known for their nomadic traits, but one country that you may not initially associate as a destination for emigrating Scots is Holland. This is where organisations like the Caledonian Society can be of real help, founded especially to help Dutch people with Scottish roots: www.caledonian.nl.

If you want to widen your understanding of emigration, immigration and naturalisation, one of the most comprehensive websites can be found at www.immigrantships.net. With over 14,000 passenger manifests listed, the countries covered and topics explored is vast. Dedicated volumes examine the Irish who emigrated to Argentina between 1822 and 1889, Second-World-War refugees and displaced persons who resettled in Australia, ship arrivals and departures in Nova Scotia over a twenty-year period from 1851; or step back in time and discover more about the immigrant ships that left Scotland during the Jacobite rising of 1745. The website is easy to navigate and allows you to use a number of search parameters depending upon what information you already have. For example you can search the site by date, by ship name, by the country and its port of departure, the port of arrival, or the name of the passenger or captain of the ship. Follow the numerous links and you will come to a page entitled 'The Compass', organised by the Immigrant Ships Transcribers Guild. Here you will find up-to-date information on the databases and resources both on and off-line that can assist you with immigrant related research.

EXAMINING EPHEMERA

If you want to get out and about, don't forget Britain's dedicated museums, whose archives and collections of images can really bring your own research to life. For those unable to visit in person, there is a whole host of holdings and exhibits viewable online.

The Merseyside Maritime Museum in Liverpool can be found at www.liverpoolmuseums.org.uk and is extremely beneficial for anyone with an ancestor who chose to work his passage or had a seafaring career. Examples of Mariners tickets, Discharge Papers, Certificates of Competency and Immigration Identification Certificates can all be downloaded and printed off, making them perfect visual aids to illustrate your story.

Never be disheartened if you do not possess personal ephemera relating to your ancestor's travels, as there is so much memorabilia in museums and archives that, with a little perseverance, you can find information, first-hand accounts and documentation that once belonged to those who had similar experiences to your forebears. The Liverpool Maritime Museum has a vast array of bequeathed personal collections that now form part of their holdings and could help you with your quest.

The Lockett Collection, which dates from the period 1853 to 1908, comprises of papers relating to arrangements made prior to its family members' emigration to Australia and Canada, including personal logs and correspondence. By comparison, the Battersby Collection consists of the letters of a Liverpool Irish family who emigrated to America and Australia and corresponded with family back home. Their thoughts and feelings make us aware of the problems faced by those who emigrated, how they adjusted to their new lives and their opinions of the country in which they decided to settle.

As we have already discovered, personal circumstances and events can prompt individuals to leave their country of origin. A perfect example of this is shown within the Cobham Collection, dating between 1863 and 1868, which includes the correspondence of a family member who escaped prison to flee with his family to start a new life in Pennsylvania, America, at a time when the country was in the grip of civil war.

Similarly, the National Maritime Museum in London holds a wealth of documentation and images relating to Britain's involvement with the sea from the 1500s right up to the late twentieth century. Visit the website at www.collections.rmg.co.uk to explore their charts, maps and extensive archive material relating to British vessels and their crews.

For a list of many other worldwide maritime museums and their specific archives, visit www.immigrantships.net/newcompass/maritime/mar_resources/maritime_museums_archives.html.

THE BRITISH EMPIRE

During the Victorian era, Britain was at its most powerful. It had numerous outposts across the globe, making up what was to become known as 'the empire'. Maps were dominated by countries highlighted in red to illustrate those under British rule, showing just how far its dominance stretched and coining the phrase that 'the Sun never set on the British Empire'. Reaching out in all directions, Canada, Australia, Kenya, Malaya and Southern Rhodesia (now Zimbabwe) were just some of the places where colonists found new homes and jobs.

When we look back at how the British Empire was perceived, it can appear as though it was simply home to upper-class gentlemen who either wished to expand upon their family wealth via a variety of lucrative business propositions or fulfil ambitions in their careers, but this was not the case.

Admittedly, the Colonial Administration Service – a British government department created to deal with the affairs of Britain's colonies and protectorates – was dominated by those with good educations and family backgrounds from the middle- to upper-class end of society, but to make Britain's ventures overseas a success required a much wider range of skills and talents that could be found across all walks of life. Below the high-ranking administrators were clerical staff in minor roles that ensured the Colonial Civil Service ran smoothly.

Officers and non-commissioned officers often joined the colonial armies (contact The National Archives to establish the medal rolls and information they hold on colonial units) along with other expatriates in police and prison services who helped keep law and order. On long postings and what for some would turn out to be lifetime settlements, they naturally brought their families with them making teaching posts, and doctors and nursing positions available to those who wished to fill the roles. Every aspect of civilian life required a workforce to create a home-from-home for the British colonists. Agricultural workers, traders and shop keepers, clerics and clergymen were all vocations that offered opportunities for those prepared to travel to some of Britain's furthest outposts.

Finding out specific details of those living the colonial life can sometimes be a tricky yet exciting quest. When trying to find the 'original' birth, marriage and death certificates of expatriates your best chance of success would be to contact the registration services in the former colonial territories. Depending upon the location you may find leads on the International Genealogical Index searchable at www.familysearch.org. (Note: from the 1880s until 1905 a number of African colonies were run by the Foreign Office instead of the Colonial Office. As a result, some births, marriages and deaths were considered as recorded in 'foreign' territories.)

On many occasions official publications produced by the colonial states were returned to Britain and are now housed in a number of repositories including university libraries. The 'Blue Books' were a set of records produced on a yearly basis by the individual colonies and contain a wealth of information for the family historian, including the names and job descriptions of those employed by colonial governments. Unlike the Colonial Office List, which only contains the names of the senior and more high-ranking officials, the 'Blue Books' detail those in minor roles and even those providing contract work. In the first instance contact the British Library (www.bl.uk) who will help point you in the direction of the most relevant documents. Cambridge University Library (www.lib.cam.ac.uk) can also help you to discover more about the 'Blue Books' and is home to the manuscripts, archives and photographs of the Royal Commonwealth Society Collection (www.lib.cam.ac.uk/deptserv/rcs/collections.html).

The British Library is also the place to find colonial newspapers or gazettes, focusing mainly on the lives and events surrounding the British community abroad. Expect to find information on the arrival and departure of expatriates in the country upon which the newspaper is based and details of appointments to official posts in not only the local government, but also the police and military. Other events connected with civilian life were reported just like any British equivalent, and disputes and legal matters in which your forebear may have been involved can provide interesting reading. These publications are an essential source for those wanting to understand more about everyday life in the colonies. Search at http://catalogue.bl.uk.

Although the majority of records connected to colonial administration have been kept by the governments who eventually took over the reins when each country became independent, The National Archives does hold an extensive amount of 'non-official' documents regarding expatriates who lived in the colonies which were later deposited in British archives. If you are able to find references to your ancestors, or to those who lived in the same settlements and worked in similar positions, you can build an extremely descriptive back story to their lives. Personal correspondence, photographs and papers contain details you couldn't expect to find anywhere else.

Over the years, a number of oral history interviews have been carried out with expatriates that vividly describe their lives and experiences in Britain's far flung outposts. Rhodes House Library (www.rhodeshouse.ox.ac.uk/page/library) in Oxford and the British Library are just two of the repositories where this kind of information can be found.

The National Army Museum and the Imperial War Museum have extensive collections relating to the Colonial armies – and police forces – within the British Empire, while Bristol Museum, Galleries and Archives have been gifted over 70,000 items from the British Empire and Commonwealth Museum when it failed to find a new home in London.

MARITIME CONNECTIONS

As an island nation, Britain has a long maritime tradition so it would be wrong not to include information on those ancestors who were mariners and whose experiences at sea and adventures abroad often led to them settling temporarily, or permanently, in foreign climes. Some chose to make a career on the high seas, while others worked their passage before seeking fame and fortune or employment opportunities on another continent.

Before the First World War, over half of the world's shipping was undertaken by the British Merchant Service, although it wasn't until their heroic efforts were acknowledged during the Great War that King George V issued a Royal Proclamation that renamed them as the 'Merchant Navy'.

The period in which your ancestor was employed will determine what information you are likely to uncover. From names, ages and date of birth to the possibility of a complete breakdown of their maritime career, a search through the records is well worth the effort.

It was not until 1747 that the Act for the Relief of Disabled Seamen was introduced, requiring ship owners or masters to produce a muster roll of their ship's crew and voyages. Those that remain are kept at The National Archives and arranged by port and year. Before 1800, the information only relates to Liverpool, Plymouth, Dartmouth, Shields, and Scarborough. After this date and before 1851, a variety of ports are mentioned. You can expect to find detailed lists that include the names of both the master and the crew, while others are much more minimalistic in the information they contain with some only providing a numerical figure of the crew on board.

The National Archives also holds Registers of Seamen, introduced under the Merchant Shipping Act of 1835, which aimed to regulate a seaman's working conditions as well as helping to keep an account of how many individuals were employed in this vocation and could be called upon in times of war. Expect to find name, age, place of birth, rank, name of the ship on which he was working, physical description of the individual, the year in which he first went to sea, the voyages undertaken and his ticket number. The amount of detail included will depend on the year in which he appears in the register. These registers date between 1835 and 1857 – the latter being when the system was abolished, not to be restarted again until 1913. Naturally, this makes

Right: The SS *Celtic*'s menu dating from 1902.

Below: Example of a purchased cruise ticket from 1902 for the SS *Celtic*, showing the shipping lines used and the cost of the voyage.

S.S. "CELTIC."

February 27th, 1902.

Celery Caviar

Hare a la St. George Consomme Printaniere

Broiled Blue Fish, Piquante Sauce

Calves' Feet a la Poulette

Ribs & Sirloin of Beef, Yorkshire Pudding
Haunch of Mutton, Red Currant Jelly
Turkey Poult, Cranberry Sauce

Cauliflowers Cabbage
Boiled Rice
Baked and Boiled Potatoes

Mallard Duck, Port Wine Sauce
Fried Hominy

Cold.

Cumberland Ham Braized Beef

Plum Pudding, Brandy Sauce
Russian Gaufers
Fanchonettes Trocaderos
Compote of Apricots

Lemon Ice Cream

Dessert

Clark's Cruise of the Celtic to the Mediterranean and the Orient, Feb. 8, 1902.

CERTIFICATE OF MEMBERSHIP 578

Berth *all*

Stateroom *334*
(The room is to be occupied by *2* passengers.)

111 Broadway, New York, *Jan 15* 1902.

Received of *Dr A. P. L. Pease + Wife* the sum of *Eleven hundred & Two* Dollars, being full payment for Membership in "CLARK'S ORIENTAL CRUISE," sailing per Steamer "Celtic" from New York, on Saturday, February 8th, 1902, at 3 p. m.

This amount includes transportation, hotel accommodation, and other items, as set forth in the printed programme, from New York back to New York.

This Certificate is issued subject to the conditions mentioned in the programme, and to the provisions applying to the transportation of passengers as set forth in the regulations of each of the various railroad companies and the White Star Line, employed in the conveyance of the passengers.

FRANK C. CLARK,
per *[illegible]*

$ *1102.00*

FRANK C. CLARK, Tourist Agent, 111 Broadway, NEW YORK.

researching an ordinary seaman between 1857 and 1913 a little tricky, but don't be disheartened, turn your attention instead to crew lists to try and track them down.

Within forty-eight hours of returning to a home port, the master of a foreign going vessel was expected to submit details of the crew that had been onboard ship and information about their voyage. Also included was information about when the individual joined and left the ship (this could well have been in a foreign port) as well as what ships he had previously worked upon and the next ship on which he was hoping to serve. This can help you to build up a resume of their working life and 'adventures'. Unfortunately, to access this information successfully it is important to know what ship your ancestor served on and what port it was registered in.

Home trade ships – those that operated around the waters of the UK or on voyages to Northern European and Baltic ports – also required the master to complete a form twice a year, giving the details of the crew he had employed during the last six months and the voyages he had undertaken.

Later crew lists are arranged by the ship's Official Number, which it retained for the whole of its working life. You can locate these in the Lloyd's Register or the Mercantile Navy List at The National Archives. Don't forget that crew lists and agreements are held in archives and maritime museums around the world so widen your search if you are trying to locate that immigrant ancestor who you believe to have previously had a career as a mariner.

When the Register of Seamen was reintroduced in 1913 more information about the individual was given, which sometimes included a description of distinguishing marks, i.e. tattoos, the name and address of his next of kin (extremely helpful when trying to connect generations) and on some occasions, even a photograph of the seaman. The 'Fourth Register of Seamen' covers the period 1918 to 1941 as, sadly, the records between 1913 and 1918 were destroyed.

To discover more about those ancestors who chose to work their passage before they settled in their new home countries we can find out about their working lives from tracking down diary entries, letters home and logbook entries which describe their experiences. These examples of ephemera do not have to relate directly to your individual ancestor for you to benefit and get an idea of what a 'working life' on the ocean wave was really like. Many recollections are given from the viewpoint of the immigrant passenger, so it is fascinating to discover memoirs or simple snippets of information from members of the crew.

T.J. Edwards kept his own notebook during one particular voyage which began in September 1875. His entries enlighten us as to the dangers and excitement faced on a daily basis as well as his first impressions of foreign lands. One of his tasks was to document the vessel's position at sea. He makes use of every spare inch of the paper and his tiny writing records the longitude, latitude and weather conditions they were experiencing. His free time seems to have been spent writing poetry or jotting down his favourite verses, giving us a glimpse into his own thoughts and feelings.

By comparison, a description in the 1891 diary of passenger George Russell Rogers gives us his perspective and tells of the sharing of provisions with the crew and enjoying improvised musical entertainment below deck in the evenings. He really seemed to enjoy the company of the midshipmen and apprentices, spending time in their quarters smoking pipes, singing and playing cribbage or whist. He writes:

> This berth contains 12 bunks where the Middies sleep, in the centre is a table of size sufficient to accommodate 12 people and each Middy has a large sea chest. I find these boys very jolly fellows and all gentlemen. Their language is certainly of a style which would astonish a Billingsgate Porter but they don't mean anything offensive and only adopt the traditional language of sailors.

There are literally thousands of letters, manuscripts and documents for sale on ephemera-based blogs and auction websites, it is just a matter of searching for the items and subjects that interest you. Try to concentrate your search by using phrases such as 'travel', 'voyage', 'naval', 'Maritime' or 'logbook'. Once purchased – or even if you have been lucky enough to inherit a particular written recollection – read the document through once to get the general idea of what it contains, and then reread it once again, scrutinising the details and making your own notes regarding names, dates and events mentioned that you can research at a later date.

Log books can be extremely revealing, showing us the wages, conduct and allowances that a crew member was given as well as a description of the voyage and conditions faced at sea. One log book entry from 1899 shows that 2nd Mate A.E. Taylor commenced sea pay from 30 December 1899, had cash when they reached Sydney and again upon arrival in Newcastle, that he bought cigars, tobacco and a pipe, and gave ten shillings to the Aged Seaman's Fund when they reached Falmouth. Where else would you find such interesting snippets of information to flesh out your family story!

MAKING IT MEMORABLE

There is nothing worse than future generations looking back through your lifetime's work only to find a whole load of dry, dusty facts portrayed through pages and pages of text. It is just as important to engage your reader in the family story as it would be to grip the audience with the opening of a thriller blockbuster. Novelists rely on the reader asking questions – what, why, where and who – and you should strive for this amount of interest to be shown in your own genealogical work. Yes … *you* will provide the answers – as far as possible – but in an interesting and imaginative way, broken up with visual elements that will want to make them read on and learn more. By including one simple postcard scene, a menu from on board ship, or a copy of an employment document, you can put a whole new spin on your ancestor's life and how they were perceived.

Consider what items you would keep to depict your life/travels for your descendants and think back to what your ancestors might have used to document their adventures in the past. Obviously, they would not have had access to the variety of devices for capturing images and videos of everyday occurrences that we have today, so try to be imaginative.

Before the invention of the camera, people used artwork to depict scenes or individual likenesses in the form of a portrait. To get a better understanding of the incidents in which your forebear was involved, why not look at museum works of art to see just what life was like during a particular period. Naturally, you are unlikely to be able to own these originals, but museums usually sell reproductions of their artworks as prints, postcards and greetings cards which make fabulous additions to any family history story.

Battles, Highland Clearances and immigrant ships have all been depicted, so although *you* may not have an image from the battlefields of Sebastopol or of the First Fleeters arriving in Australia, some of the world's art institutions may well have – it's just a case of tracking down those which are relevant to you.

3

AUSTRALIA AND NEW ZEALAND

'If we are always arriving and departing, it is also true that we are eternally anchored. One's destination is never a place but rather a new way of looking at things.'

Henry Miller

AUSTRALIA

During the seventeenth and early eighteenth centuries, Britain tackled its problems with crime by transporting the perpetrators to America, but when the American colonies called time on this agreement Britain needed an alternative option, so turned to Australia for the answer.

In January 1788 – after a voyage of over 250 days – the First Fleet of eleven penal transportation ships landed at Sydney Cove, Van Diemen's Land (Tasmania) to set up the initial convict colony. This fledgling settlement – the first European community in Australia – was instrumental in establishing the state of New South Wales. At this time, the country had an Aboriginal population of approximately 400,000 people, but between 1788 and 1840, the country witnessed the 'invasion' of 80,000 convicts from Britain and its colonies who were deported there for punishment.

For any convict – whether they had committed a heinous crime or a petty theft – the thought of being transported thousands of miles from home to a country with harsh landscapes and a hot climate must have been unnerving. Life in the penal colonies was extremely tough. Discipline was hard and often brutal and much of the way in which the prisoners were treated depended upon the governor in charge.

Those convicted could face transportation for a number of reasons. Poverty-stricken women pinching something as simple as a handkerchief were just as likely to receive a sentence of penal servitude as political prisoners attempting to overthrow British rule, although the severity of their crimes often dictated which colony they were sent to.

Despite the early reservations that the transportees must have had, once they had served their sentences, many never returned to Britain when they realised there were greater prospects to be had in Australia. After applying for land grants they settled, married and raised families in what was now their new home.

Transported Prisoners

One of the best places to locate convict transportation lists is on www.ancestry.com. Indexed by name, you can search for your criminal ancestor even if you are not entirely sure where their final destination was or on what ship they made the journey.

There are four main registers in which you can start your investigations – Australian Convict Transportation Registers covering:

- The First Fleet for the period 1787–1788.
- The Second Fleet from 1789–1790.
- The Third Fleet 1791.
- Other fleets and ships for the period 1791–1868.

If you are unsuccessful with the registers above, why not try one of the following collections:

- The New South Wales and Tasmania, Australia, Settler and Convict Lists covering the years between 1787 and 1834.
- The New South Wales and Tasmania, Australia and Convict Musters for 1806–1849.
- Perhaps your convict was pardoned? Try the New South Wales and Tasmania, Australia Convict Pardons and Ticket of Leave archive for the period 1834–1859.
- And finally ... how about the New South Wales, Australia Census for 1828?

CASE STUDY: A 'SUCCESS' STORY

Ephemera does not have to belong to, or relate directly to your ancestor for you to benefit from its historical importance. For example, to understand more about the methods used to transport Britain's criminals to Australia, we need look no further than the convict hulk *Success*, which until 1946, was the remaining survivor of England's fleet of vessels used for the custody of prisoners. For the latter part of its life it became a floating museum, portraying what life was like for those who faced the long voyage to penal servitude. As with all tourist attractions, leaflets, posters and postcards were produced for advertising – often with a sprinkle of artistic license – to attract visitors.

One in particular was a pamphlet printed in 1917 that revealed information concerning not only what life was like on board, but also the names of some of its 'inmates', the crimes they committed and the methods of restraint used to keep them in order.

This is the type of memorabilia that is priceless to us as family historians. Our forebears may not have been unfortunate enough to be holed up onboard the *Success*, but we can make comparisons and understand more about what convicts endured when transported on similar ships sailing at this time.

The pamphlet implies that the *Success* was built in 1790 at Moulmein in British India, but there is evidence to suggest that she was, in fact, built much later than this. At 135 ft long and with a 30-ft beam, she was constructed of Burmese teak to resist decay, initially making several journeys as a passenger and emigrant ship ferrying fortune hunters to the gold fields at the height of the Victorian gold rush. Early transportation vessels were known as 'Hell Ships' and you can see why when you read the reports of officials such as Colonial Surgeon, Dr White:

> Of 939 males sent out by the last ships (including the) 'Scarborough' and 'Neptune', 251 died on board, and 50 have died since landing, the number of sick this day is 450 and many who are reckoned as not sick have barely strength to attend themselves.

In a voyage often lasting nine months, he later documented the horrors he witnessed once the ships docked:

> A greater number of them were lying, some half and others quite naked, without bed or bedding, unable to turn for help themselves. The smell was so offensive I could hardly bear it. Some of these unhappy people died after the ship came into the harbour before they could be taken onshore. Part of these had been thrown into the harbour and their dead bodies cast upon the shore and were seen lying naked upon the rocks. The misery I saw amongst them is inexpressible.

To house the arriving convicts, five ships, including the *Success*, were purchased – refitted with cells for the lower decks to detain the worst criminals – and anchored permanently in Hobsons Bay, Williamstown as a receiving prison.

As if the voyage had not been enough, a number of devices were used to restrain and subdue the prisoners. Originally, they were branded with a red-hot iron in the shape of an arrow on their palms; this has become the well-known symbol of the convict and was repeated on prison uniforms in Britain from the 1870s. Leg irons – weighing from 7 to 56 pds – restricted their movements, while handcuffs ensured they could not strike the guards.

Punishment was cruel and there often seemed to be at least one official who enjoyed doling it out. Made from strands of untanned leather tied in knots or tipped

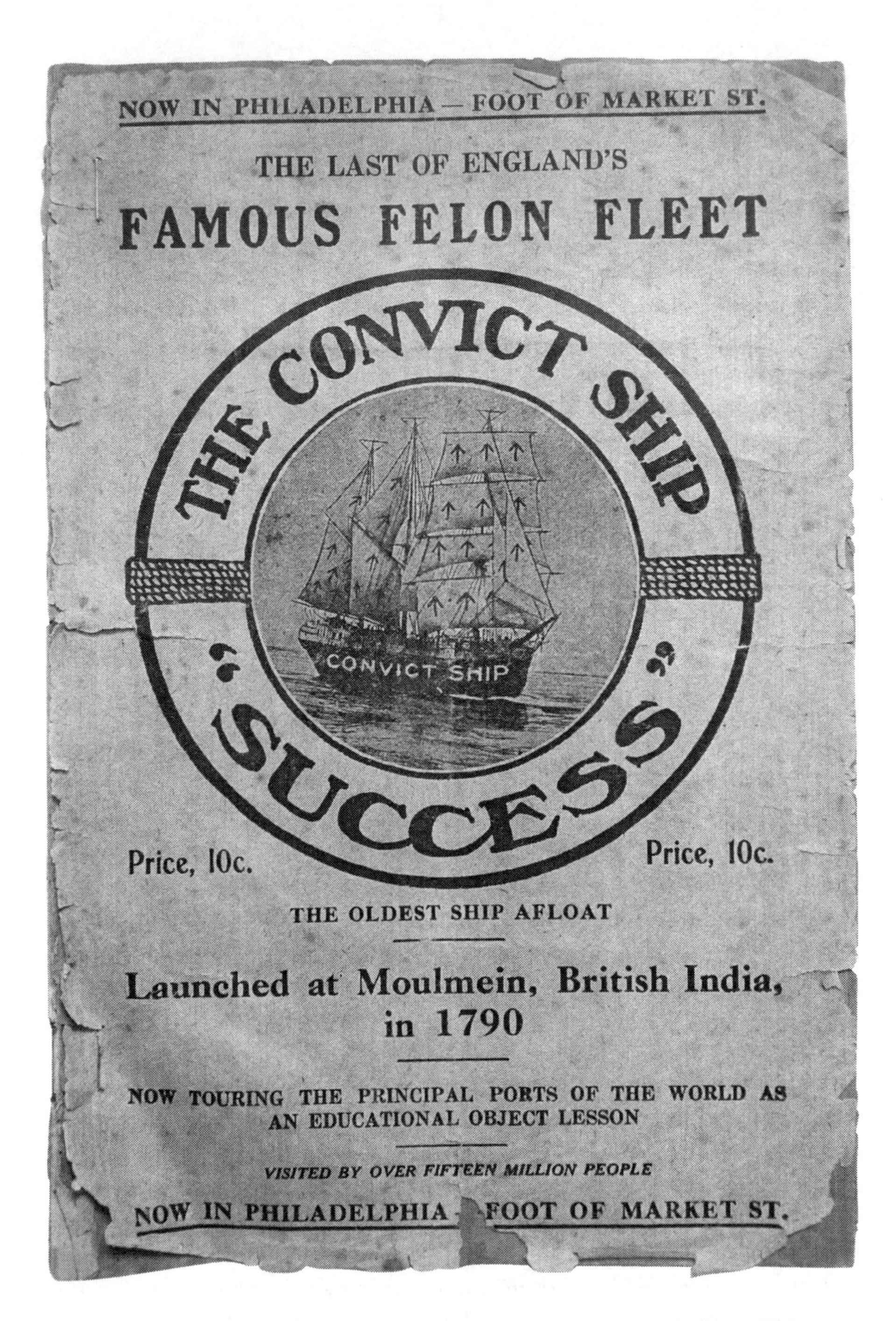

Tourist pamphlets give us an insight into what life was like during a particular era. This example was produced to encourage visitors to understand more about penal transportation, by using the ex-convict ship *Success* as a tourist attraction.

with pellets of lead, the Cat o' Nine Tails was a whipping device regularly used to flog the men into submission. The 72-pd iron punishment ball was strapped to the prisoner's belt before he was ordered to trail it up and down the upper deck for one hour each day, while spiked collars were used to stop the convict from stooping, but could in fact restrict their breathing. Many died from the cruelties inflicted, while those who survived must have, at times, wished for the release.

Anyone in breach of discipline was punished by solitary confinement, which could last from one to 100 days depending upon the offence. With no light and the minimum of air, the tiny torture chambers were dark and oppressive. The prisoner was chained up in such a way that he was prevented from standing upright or lying down, so was obliged to lean or stoop throughout his internment.

It was not until 1857 that the reports of the brutal treatment of prisoners created a revolt against the government and the abandonment of the prison hulk system. From 1860 to 1868 the *Success* was used as a women's prison before becoming an ammunition store. When a law was passed that all prison hulks should be broken up to sever Australia's ties with its harsh criminal past, the *Success* somehow managed to escape the order.

Although the vessel was later scuttled and sunk, it was decided that, despite the considerable expense, she should be raised and renovated to become an educational reminder of this period of penal history. The *Success* re-emerged as a travelling exhibition circumnavigating Great Britain, Ireland and the Australasian colonies. In 1917 – at the time the tourist pamphlet was produced – visitor numbers exceeded 15 million with famous faces including King Edward and other members of the English royal family, the German Emperor and the former Prime Minister William Gladstone all reported to have witnessed its exhibits and displays.

Perhaps most astonishingly, the *Success* had even taken its story across the Atlantic to America, a journey thought by many to be impossible considering the vessel's age. Within days of the ill-fated *Titanic* leaving Southampton, the *Success* set sail from Liverpool and, after 96 days, arrived in Boston Harbour before travelling on to share its history with the rest of the United States.

The *Success* finally met its end when a fire broke out on board while grounded off Port Clinton, Ohio. Despite the *Success* having become a tourist attraction, and the media hype and selective advertising used to increase footfall often overstepping the boundaries between fact and fiction, it helped to highlight a way of life that we now consider unimaginable. Like so much other ephemera, the items produced give us a glimpse into the past, raise questions and provide new lines of enquiry for us to follow.

Revealing Research

With over 170,000 references to convicts, settlers, soldiers, landowners and medical practitioners, the 'Free Settler or Felon?' website at www.jenwilletts.com/index.htm is a fascinating resource. Search the databases for free to find information about convict ships arriving in New South Wales between 1788 and 1840, Convict Ships Surgeon Superintendents and Captains' Indexes, and an endless list of detailed articles and news items taken from journals produced during the early Victorian era. The topics covered are vast and you will find a wealth of illustrated examples of original documents and publications from Australian almanacs to surgeons' gazettes. If you wish to read firsthand accounts of what life on the transportation ships was like, why not visit The National Archives website to read actual scans of the ledgers kept by the Ship's Surgeons.

Writing in 1828, ship's surgeon Thomas Logan described the conditions on board the male convict ship *Albion*:

> The Albion being at anchor in the afternoon, the convicts were all allowed to come on deck. Occasion was taken to clean the prisons out thoroughly by sweeping, partial scraping, and then swabbing. The wind being high, the ventilation of the prisons was complete.

He regularly explains the cleaning procedure for the convicts' prisons below decks and confirms that these holding areas were always thoroughly dry by the time the prisoners were readmitted at the end of the day. Logan treated the prisoners for their medical issues on a regular basis, tending to complaints such as diarrhoea, vertigo, sexually transmitted diseases and pneumonia. On 27 May he noted that twenty-seven convicts had received medical aid that day but 'the greater number were trifling affections, such as small sores and unimportant ailments not meriting a formal specification'.

Seasickness was naturally another problem but some of Logan's treatments for more serious maladies make fascinating reading, as he lists his remedies and the condition of his patients. He even includes the results of an autopsy carried out on one convict who, although he had previously been described as 'a robust young man of 18 years of age', did not survive all attempts to revive him when he had passed out on deck. More examples from this journal and many others can be viewed online at www.nationalarchives.gov.uk/documents/adm101-1-9.pdf and www.nationalarchives.gov.uk/surgeonsatsea.

Free Settlers

Since the start of European settlement in 1788, more British migrants have travelled to Australia than to any other country. As a result, a large percentage of its population today is likely to have ancestral roots originating in the UK.

Travellers preparing to go ashore for a day trip, disembarking from the ship onto smaller vessels. The introduction of the camera encouraged travellers to record their observations by photographing the sights en route. Perhaps you've inherited 'holiday snaps' which have tale to tell?

Obviously, not all early settlers were convicts, but they may have arrived under a bounty system that included indentured individuals tied to an employer for several years. Records of these Immigrant Applications and Bounty Tickets for Tasmania relate to the period 1854–1887. Others may have been hired to work for the immigration societies to encourage hard-working men and women to settle in the colony.

www.ancestry.com holds numerous data collections enabling you to search different periods between 1788 and 1930, in order to follow your ancestor's trail. Details of Immigrant Lists and Passenger Arrivals from 1841–1884 can also be found here. A search can reveal hiring registers, the name of the individual's employer, or who they were hired out to.

Attracting free settlers to fill the growing list of jobs was a difficult task, especially when the costs required for travelling were hugely inflated compared to those required to migrate to America. Some chose to use their own funds, but many others needed assistance resulting in a number of 'persuasive' schemes being introduced. By the 1840s, the British government had set out its terms for encouraging migrants to choose South Australia and produced posters explaining what was expected of them in order to qualify.

With the agreement of Her Majesty's Colonial Land and Emigration Commissioners, various companies offered free passage to South Australia as long

Left and above: Photograph of Victorian travellers in the Middle East preserved in a holiday diary.

Photograph of locals in the Azores captured by a western traveller and preserved in his travel journal.

as the candidates fitted specific criteria. After ensuring that all immigrants had been vaccinated or had previously had smallpox, certain requirements had to be met. An individual needed a particular trade or calling to be successful; these included agricultural labourers, miners, domestic servants and even blacksmiths and wheelwrights. If an individual had enough capital to buy land in the colony or to invest in a trade, they and their families were not eligible for free passage; neither were residents of a workhouse or those in receipt of parish relief. Age restrictions applied and no one above the age of 40 was allowed. It was preferred that the emigrants were married – and had to produce a marriage certificate to prove this – but they were not allowed to bring more than two children under the age of 7 with them. Single men, with the trades listed above, could be accepted if between the ages of 18 and 30, but it was essential they were accompanied (perhaps by sisters or unmarried relatives). As most domestic servants were single females, women aged 15 to 30 were entitled to apply as long as their lady employers were cabin passengers on the same ship or they were emigrating under the care of married relatives.

Upon arrival, each immigrant was at liberty to engage under whichever employer they chose. Posters published examples of the type of wages someone could expect to earn, further encouraging Britons to make the move. Miners had the opportunity to earn between 30 and 40 shillings a week, supplemented with an inclusive food ration, domestic servants might earn between £15 and £25 a year with the added bonus of their board and lodging, while blacksmiths and wheelwrights could expect between 3 and 5 shillings a day, depending on their skills and ability.

There was a vast array of positions to fill as colonies grew and developed in size. In 1895 a group of men were engaged to survey the region of Hampton Plains in Western Australia, who reported some of their findings and plans for the area via correspondence published in the *Illustrated London News*. Mr Julius Price explained:

> I told you in a recent letter of the many drawbacks attached to living in Coolgardie at any time, but more especially in the summer months, owing to the continual dust, the myriad of flies, and last but not least the insanitary conditions of the town.
>
> It was undoubtedly with this knowledge that the 'Hampton Plains Estate', a big English syndicate whose vast property, covering an area of over a quarter of a million acres, and reaching to within two miles of Coolgardie, had the happy idea of laying out a portion of their property nearest the town as a sort of suburban bungalow village – as a residence in summer; for although so short distance from the town itself it escapes entirely all that evil dust which makes life there a burden.

Creating new villages and towns in an area of previously uninhabited bush must have been a real challenge for our ancestors, requiring perseverance, as they faced the difficulties of setting up home in a land of conditions that were often completely alien to them.

What started out as Australia's need for labour was one of the reasons that transportation to Australia finally stopped. Thousands of free settlers had been making new lives there by filling jobs and helping improve the country, and so considered themselves and their families to be officially 'Australian'. Naturally, they were not too keen on the influx of convicts – many of whom were poor, uneducated and had obvious criminal tendencies – in what they now saw as their homeland.

When the British government was unable to use the excuse that Australia needed the convicts to help with the labour shortage, as the free settlers were now filling the jobs quite adequately, the last official transportation to the colonies took place in 1852, although convict labour was still used in Australia for another fifteen years.

Incentives and Improvements – Assisted Passengers

As most working-class migrants had to face the prospect of not earning wages for the length of the journey and the period of settlement once they reached their destination, the government schemes and grants were essential. Free passages were sometimes awarded to those who could not afford their own fare yet were specially requested for employment in the country; this could include married couples without children or female domestic servants. Stipulations dictated that applicants had to pay £1 for each adult and that they intended to reside permanently in the colony. Other schemes offered farmland in the 'new world' at a cheap rate. An example of this was proposed in New Zealand when the Canterbury Association was formed to establish an Anglican colony, resulting in a dozen immigrant ships leaving Britain to create the new settlement in the 1850s.

Those who had all or part of their passage paid for them became known as 'Assisted Passengers'. A naturalised migrant or citizen born in the colony could apply for a 'passage warrant' for a friend or relative in Britain to join them. Once presented with the warrant, the government could then arrange the immigration procedure – this was known as a Remittance or Nominated Passage. A similar process was arranged if an employer wanted a particular employee from Europe. He would pay the government a percentage of the fare, which would engage the labour on his behalf. Once the employees arrived they would be classed as Indentured Immigrants and be 'legally' bound to work for the employer for a set period of time. Visit the website www.records.nsw.gov.au and enter 'assisted passengers' in the search bar to be directed to their data collections. Expect to find dates of embarkation, ports of arrival and names of the vessels listed in these extensive indexes.

Surprisingly, no official application was required to emigrate from Britain and Ireland in the mid-nineteenth century. Permission in the form of a completed request was only necessary when the passenger needed financial assistance. Sadly, these application forms do not seem to have survived except those for the New Zealand Company between 1839 and 1850.

Liverpool was one of Britain's main ports of departure for passenger travel to the Southern Hemisphere, already well established due to its transatlantic trade. During the nineteenth century the dockside would have been continually bustling with activity. Clipper ships brought tea and spices from the Orient and valuable cargoes of wool and timber from Australia and New Zealand; the return journeys loaded with British goods, mail and passengers. Anxious and excited travellers would often spend an overnight stay in the city before their ship was due to depart, finding accommodation in one of a host of boarding houses that benefited from this constantly passing trade.

Immigrant ship companies operating from Liverpool included the Black Ball Line, which dominated Australian passenger travel with its fleet of Packet ships, set up by James Baines and Co in 1852. Carrying emigrants and cargo during the Gold Rush era, its first vessel, the *Marco Polo*, set the record for the quickest round trip, giving the company a reputation for fast passages. Shaw Savill and Albion ran cargo and passenger services to New Zealand from 1882 and purchased surplus White Star Line steamer ships to use on this route from 1883. Once you have discovered the vessel on which your ancestor sailed you will be able to establish the shipping company and research any additional information that survives at the Maritime or National Archives.

When a ship finally got under sail it was common for a voyage to Australia to take between three and four months. On board, the poorest passengers would be allotted the cheapest accommodation in Steerage Class. This was in the form of a crowded dormitory with bunks stacked around the outside walls, leaving the central area free for tables and seating. The damp and claustrophobic conditions meant that they chose to spend a great deal of their time huddled on deck, no matter what the weather situation was outside. With very little shelter from stormy seas and winds to extreme sweltering heat, the experience of a steerage passenger could be extremely tough.

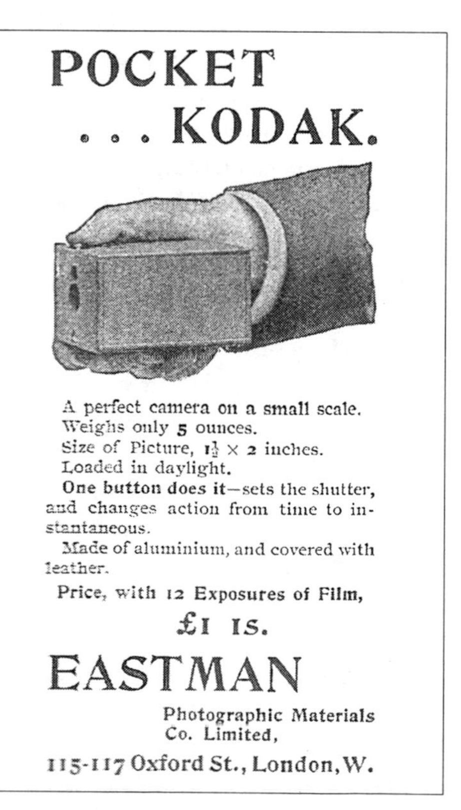

Essential photographic equipment advertised in the *Illustrated London News* of November 1895.

Lack of ventilation and sanitary conditions meant disease was rife. Cases of typhoid and cholera could quickly spread through these areas and although infected passengers were confined in an effort to control the outbreaks, many died without ever reaching the 'promised land'.

Conditions gradually began to improve with the introduction of the Passenger Act in 1855, which required minimum standards for ventilation, sanitation, the amount of space allotted and the food rations provided. Advancements in ship building meant that the magnificent clippers with their billowing sails – reliant upon the wind to complete their journeys – were replaced by steam ships that could accommodate an increasing number of passengers yet reduce the length and cost of the voyage. Companies began to offer the complete travel package to their customers, which included decent accommodation before sailing and better facilities when onboard. Despite this, it wasn't until the 1900s that steerage was replaced with third-class cabins.

Class Distinction – Unassisted Passengers

Barques, clippers and steamers all populated the waters around Britain and by the end of the nineteenth century London's Tilbury Docks – opened in 1886 – became a popular departure point for long-distance voyages. Two small (or one large) item of luggage was allowed per passenger. One was placed in the hold until arrival at the destination, while the other was used to store belongings throughout the journey. Look out for luggage labels such as the ones shown in our example, which would have been adhered to the cases advising the crew where the items were to be taken when they arrived on board.

Such was the length of the voyage to Australia that one 'well prepared' diarist wrote how he arranged his possessions and personal effects to make his cabin feel more homely:

> I found my small tool chest very useful as I had to draw out a good many old nails and screws and fix up new ones. This chest I bought at the Army and Navy Stores for 7/6 and it contains Bradawl, Chisel, Gimlet, Gouge, Hammer Mallet, Pincers, Turnscrew, Saw, Nails, hooks, Screws, etc. Now that my photographs are hung and my Portmanteaux arranged and made fast to prevent their falling about in a heavy sea, the cabin really looks very comfortable and smart and all the ladies have been to inspect it and have expressed their high approbation of my arrangements.

First-, second-, and third-class passengers travelled 'unassisted' – their finances dictating the accommodation they could afford. Stewards attended those in first-class cabins, while Messmen were elected to receive the provisions for the week from the purser to hand out to the passengers in the lower classes. This included daily allocations of three pints of fresh water to each adult, with a further three pints given to the cook to make each passenger soups, stews or hot drinks. Salt and molasses were used as preservatives and featured regularly in the menu as salt beef or porridge with molasses, while rationed oatcakes and bread were also provided. Mealtimes were strictly adhered to, with intermediate passengers required to supply their own utensils and dishes.

A greater awareness of hygiene, sanitation and ventilation helped to keep passengers healthy during the voyage. Each day from 6 a.m. the doctor would complete his rounds to ensure all passengers had risen – the hot weather and humid climate could prove difficult to cope with for some that were only used to the cooler British weather. Specific days were set aside for washing clothes – a mammoth task when you consider the many layers and heavy, detailed ensembles worn by some of the ladies. In the days of sail these freshly laundered items were hung from the rigging to dry, which must have been quite a sight!

Each decade brought improved conditions and procedures, but compared to their 'assisted' counterparts, wealthy 'unassisted passengers' were in a league of their own. Those with means often chose to travel for their health, to visit relatives already settled in the colonies or to pursue employment opportunities. Their accommodation varied, with some passengers even able to 'choose' their cabins before departure.

Built in 1874 by pioneers of the South Australian passenger trade – Messers Devitt and Moore – the SS *Rodney* was a full-rigged clipper. Competition between shipping companies was intense and speed of the essence when providing a trouble-free and efficient service to encourage both repeat and potential customers. The *Rodney* had a good reputation and made her best passage to Sydney in 1887 in just sixty-eight days. Three years later her voyage from Sydney to London took seventy-seven days, just behind the *Cutty Sark*, which had arrived four days earlier. At the mercy of weather and sea conditions, these voyages relied on the skills of the captain and crew. Tugs and pilot boats would help guide the clipper ships in and out of the docks creating a great spectacle for the passengers on deck.

The *Rodney* was constructed from iron and fabricated for the comfort of its passengers. An Australian newspaper, reporting in 1874, declared that: 'the intending voyager can step on board ship and find his cabin carpeted and fitted up with almost all the accessories and appointments of a bedroom in a hotel.' By 1891, a *Rodney* passenger could expect the vessel to accommodate sixty people in two-berth first-class cabins of up to 10 ft square. These compartments were equipped with fitted lavatory basins and chests of drawers – regarded as extreme luxuries for the day. Communal bathrooms had the added selling point of both hot and cold water – itself a novelty, as previously only cold water had been available in the washing facilities. An 80-ft saloon provided a place to socialise and relax and a sanctuary where women could read or sew, sheltered from the weather outside. In most ships of this type, the saloon was well lit and decorated to a high standard, often with images of the destinations where the vessels were bound, stained glass, carved woodwork and plush upholstery. A piano was accessible to provide entertainment and the furniture could be pushed back to allow room for dancing. The male domain of a smoking room was located near the companionway, where men could enjoy their cigars and discuss events of the day. Well-ventilated areas between decks were set aside for second-class and steerage passengers, with a galley able to feed 500 people when necessary.

En Route Observations

The journey to the other side of the world was undoubtedly a long one. Both passengers and crew were fascinated by the sights and sounds they experienced along the way, which were so far removed from what was familiar to them back in Britain.

The maritime world was steeped in history and superstition, so on lengthy voyages it became customary to mark the crossing of the Equator with a little light hearted fun. Once this point had been passed, it was traditional for sailors to adopt the nickname *Son of Neptune*, or *Shellback*, while those who had not yet had the privilege were termed Griffins or Pollywogs. Equator-crossing ceremonies were held on deck, initiating new recruits, and later passengers, into the 'Mysteries of the Deep' by performing a series of entertaining tasks presided over by everyone onboard and a person in the role of 'King Neptune'.

Captain Fitzroy of HMS *Beagle* thought the proceedings were a real boost to morale, breaking up the monotony and hardships faced at sea. Petty Officer John Bechervaise wrote of wearing a grey horse-hair wig and beard for his role of Neptune when overseeing the ceremony on board HMS *Blossom* in 1825, and even Charles Darwin noted in his diary how he was initiated from novice 'Griffin' upon approaching the Equator in 1832!

By the mid-1890s, those travelling to Australia by steamer found that the route via the Suez Canal would take them past the Seychelles. The conditions onboard had improved dramatically and these late-nineteenth-century passengers were much more fortunate than their predecessors, giving them chance to enjoy and experience the beauty of the Tropics. The largest island of Mahe became a British colony in 1812 and remained under our control until 1976, when it became an independent nation. These beautiful and exotic islands were a sight to be seen for the British traveller, who was used to a much less humid climate back home. Tropical fruit, palm trees, lush mountains and clear blue waters – even with its plentiful array of sharks – made this an idyllic break in the journey. One nineteenth-century observer shows just how fascinated Europeans were with documenting various fruits, flora and fauna in their natural setting:

> A great part of the heavy green foliage that one sees is due to the curious tree whose home is here, and here only – the 'Cocotier de Mer' – or double

> cocoanut palm, the leaves of which reach the length sometimes of 18 feet. The curious feature of this tree is its fruit, two nuts being found in one husk. It is so-called because the fruit had been found floating about in the sea before it was known that it came from these islands; and, as no place on earth was known which produced such fruit, it was concluded by the wholesalers that it was a product of the sea. The growing of this double coconut is now one of the most important industries of the place, as the coconut is a very useful tree in many ways, not only the nut and its milk being valuable, but also the husk and fibre, and most of all, the oil.

Perhaps your ancestor passed through on this (or a similar) route but left little in the way of memorabilia, letters or journals describing their adventures? This is not a problem as we can utilise the observations of others to get a feel for our forebear's experiences. The lengthy journeys required the ships to gather new supplies from different ports of call to ensure that there was a full and varied menu for the passengers on board. Mahe, it seems, had an endless supply of natural produce to tantalise the taste buds of the foreign travellers:

Image from the *Illustrated London News* of 1895 depicting workers surveying the land territories of Western Australia. Did your ancestor make their contribution to establishing new colonies within the British Empire?

> Among the many products of the island are chocolate, vanilla, pepper and various spices, cinnamon, and coffee [writes Lawrence Liston][...] Sugarcane is also grown, but there is no sugar industry, the canes being sold for sucking as a sweetmeat. As many as sixty varieties of bananas can be found and you will be sure to take some on-board your ship for dessert during the voyage. They are taken on board in a green state, and allowed to ripen off the tree; but you should take the opportunity of tasting them in their fresh ripe state. Other fruits which you will find taken from these islands are pineapples, of which two kinds grow here, the red and the golden.

Liston even feels the need to describe the difference between lemons and limes to his British readers who may never have seen, let alone tasted such an exotic fruit:

> Lemonade is made from limes, which are a sort of small green lemon, very full of juice, and having a very distinct flavour. There are plenty of oranges of various kinds [...] Mangoes and tamarinds. The cabbage palm, which is found here is utilised on board, the pith being made into a kind of salad named 'Choux des Palmistes'. The celebrated breadfruit of storybooks also grows here, and is cut up and fried as a substitute for potatoes.

It is also interesting to read about practices that would not be accepted today, but as the island lacked any sheep or bullocks and, at this time got its meat supplied from passing ships, a substitute, alongside fish, had to be found:

> At one end of the town you will notice a large pond, wherein are placed a number of turtles; these creatures are caught and placed in the pond to be kept until required, the flesh selling at the rate of six pence per pound.

Liston sums up his experiences of the island of Mahe as he is rowed back in a little boat towards the steamer to continue his journey to Australia:

> There it lies in its perpetual summer, unconnected by telegraph with the rest of the world, no railways to disfigure its surface, the only advance of modern communication visible always being the post office, which now boasts a set of stamps of its own, very pretty design and having Her Majesty's image upon them.

Expanding Your Ephemera Archive

Your initial interest in foreign research may have been sparked by an item you have discovered in your ancestor's belongings, passed down through the generations, which revealed reasons for permanent migration or short-term travel plans and adventures.

To help conjure up a picture of the past you can expand upon your own knowledge and understanding by collecting various period items from antique, book, collectable and ephemera fairs, or from auction sites, helping visually to illustrate a specific period or episode in your family history.

You would be surprised at just how much memorabilia relating to people's travels and emigration overseas still exists. Naturally, we are not all in the position to have inherited specific pieces from our forebears, but we can still track down items that, in turn, help us to get a new perspective on their thoughts, feelings and observations during one of the most important decision making moments of their lives.

For those with ancestors who emigrated to Australia in the twentieth century, leaflets, posters and paper ephemera can give us an insight into what they initially experienced when they arrived on foreign soil. A pamphlet issued in the mid-1940s includes a message of welcome from Arthur Calwell – Minister for Immigration and Information at that time. It also includes a cautionary note that states: 'the immigrant will find in Australia neither gold in the streets nor fortunes to be had for the asking – but there are riches in health, happiness and security to be won by conscientious endeavour.' This is followed by a whole host of information covering how to register at local employment offices, how the state educational systems work, traffic laws, banking and taxation information as well as explaining the currency in use and the transportation services available. Although this is only a brief outline, all important considerations have been covered and addresses provided to enable new arrivals to settle in as quickly as possible.

In the 1940s Australia planned to increase its population by many millions and had an objective of encouraging 70,000 people each year, but actually welcomed many more than that. After the shortages of the war, production and manufacturing created thousands of jobs which needed filling so they initially turned to the British and former members of the United States Forces, mainly G.I.s who had served in the Australian region during the war against Japan. The program was designed to be mutually beneficial – the new settlers sharing in a life opportunity while helping develop the country.

You may be lucky enough to have already discovered leaflets of this nature (explaining immigration procedures) within your ancestor's belongings – perhaps kept as a memory of the path they had chosen, or even as an opportunity they were considering but which didn't come to fruition? Although archives and libraries have immigration documents within their holdings, many will have found their way into the personal possessions of the public, so look out for similar examples at ephemera fairs, specialised auctions and even car boot sales.

A fantastic site to view images online is at the Australian Government Department of Immigration and Citizenship website, www.immi.gov.au/about/anniversary/memorabilia.htm. Here you will find leaflets and handbooks detailing everything from what the new settler could expect to earn in a variety of occupations to an explanation of the political voting system for British migrants. Food, clothing and household essentials have all been classified to give an idea of the cost of items likely to be purchased by an average working family.

There is also a 1929 booklet on what Australia can offer the British 'boy' and encourages those between the ages of 15 and 18 to consider the employment prospects on offer – mainly agriculturally based – in what was termed 'The Land of the Better Chance'. Perhaps this was one of the opportunities that your ancestor decided to take advantage of?

Other Sources to Try

- The 'Making Australia Home' project was set up by The National Archives of Australia (TNAA) and provides access to digitalised items and over 7 million records of people who resettled in Australia in 1901. This dedicated website enables you to search for digital copies of original migration documents by the name of the person, their place of birth and the date of their migration, enabling you to confirm in your family timeline exactly when they arrived in their new home country. For more details go to www.naa.gov.au.
- Released in July 2008, the Newspaper Digitisation Programme was introduced by the National Library of Australia (www.nla.gov.au/content/newspaper-digitisation-program). Providing free access to digital papers published in Australia between 1803 and 1954, it covers a whole array of editions including the *Sydney Gazette*, the *Adelaide Advertiser* and the *Northern Territory Times*. Initially concentrating on major titles, regional and local editions have also been added. Ensuring that out of copyright newspapers are digitally preserved, they allow you to search for snippets of information about people, places and events relevant to your family history, helping you to get a feel for the area in which a person/family lived during a particular period.

Location, Location

From Bosnia to Brazil, Switzerland to Sweden, the website 'Origins – Immigrant Communities in Victoria' (www.museumvictoria.com.au/origins) is a must for anyone trying to trace ancestors who they believe initially emigrated to Victoria in Australia. Created by Museum Victoria, it is one of the most detailed compilations of data on immigration to a specific location and not only guides us through the history of why immigrants from a whole selection of countries ended up in Victoria, but also gives overview graphs of their ages, genders, languages spoken and occupations – all extremely helpful when trying to understand why our forebears chose to move in the directions they did.

In 1854, there were just under 237,000 people living in Victoria. When the government census was collated it found that 97,943 of these citizens were English born, closely followed by those of Irish and Scottish origin. Might your ancestor have been one of them?

Previously, with the influx of arrivals disembarking to try their hand at gold prospecting, new communities sprang up throughout the state. As the towns grew, major institutions were built to accommodate the needs of the population. In that initial census year (1854), the University of Melbourne was founded along with the National Museum of Victoria and the State Library. When the first steam-powered railway was established in Australia it ran from South Melbourne (Sandridge) to the Railway Pier (later known as Station Pier), which became the arrival point for thousands more new immigrants. *The Age* newspaper had its first print run, helping to provide news for the locals and preserve history for future generations.

Could your ancestor have kept up with current affairs by reading this publication; perhaps they left diary entries recording visits to the National Museum or wrote letters to family back home explaining the development of Victoria and the new cultural facilities that were being built? They may have even encouraged relatives to come and visit them, stating that they would meet them at the Station Pier as soon as they arrived.

Researching more about the local history of a particular location can help you to piece together the jigsaw puzzle of events that may have happened in your ancestor's life. Remember – local history and family history are inextricably linked – often the resources used can overlap, helping to provide answers to your genealogical questions.

NEW ZEALAND

New Zealand is made up of two islands – North Island and South Island. Although they had first been charted in the seventeenth century, it was not until the eighteenth century that a small number of Europeans settled here.

Populated by between 100,000 and 200,000 Maoris, these 'locals' were initially suspicious of the newcomers, but they built up a rapport with the British colony of neighbouring New South Wales in Australia and enjoyed the benefits of trading their timber and flax.

In 1826 two shiploads of immigrants arrived in New Zealand, hoping to make their first attempt at colonising the country, but they were unprepared for the harsh terrain and many left to make their homes in Australia instead. Fourteen years later, the Maori chiefs agreed to accept British sovereignty in return for the promise of protection of their lands and rights. This enabled the floodgates to open for new settlers to arrive and there was a slow and steady rise in the number of European inhabitants until a defining moment came in the late 1850s when gold was discovered on the islands.

Fortune hunters arrived by the shipload, pouring into the port of Dunedin in their thousands as news spread and prospectors disembarked ready to find the productive land and stake their claim. By 1867 there were over 200,000 Europeans living in the colony – a number which rose considerably to three-quarters of a million when assisted passages were introduced. The appearance of so many new residents ultimately had a detrimental effect on the indigenous people, and although huge numbers died during the twenty-eight years of Maori Wars that had been raging since 1844, they had no immune systems to combat the new diseases that the immigrants brought to the islands, which saw many perish through ill health. By the end of the nineteenth century, there were less than a quarter of the original indigenous population left.

Civil Registration

Voluntary registration of births and deaths began in New Zealand from 1848 but it was not made compulsory until 1856. The registration of any European marriages had been introduced two years earlier in 1854 but Maori marriages, and birth and death registration, did not become compulsory until 1911 and 1913 respectively. Early birth entries included the name, date and birthplace of the child, its parents and the occupation of the father. From 1876, the additional information of the age and birthplace of both parents and their marriage date were included, providing far more details than the UK equivalent and enabling you to trace the previous generation back even further.

White New Zealanders of European descent are known as 'Pakeha', but are unlikely to have more than five or six generations of ancestors before they revert to the nationality of their forebear's country of origin. It is worth remembering that the marriage records of Maoris and those of the Pakeha were indexed separately until 1952, as were birth and death registrations until 1961. After these dates the indexes were combined.

DID YOU KNOW?

Genealogy is just as important to the Maori culture as it is to us. Known as 'Whakapapa', it is taught very early to young children who learn the names of their forebears off by heart. The tribal elder would have made it his business to have known information about all those in the tribe he governed. There is great importance set upon the oral history and reciting family facts to ensure all of the ancestral details are passed down through the generations.

Church Records

Before the introduction of civil registration, you can use church records to establish links within your family. Roman Catholics arrived in New Zealand in 1838, and prior to that, Wesleyans had established a following in the colony. Check to see what records have been deposited in the local archives, or follow the trail back to the appropriate parish church to see if they still hold the original registers. Remember to enquire if any of the early registers have been transcribed – they may even have been published online.

The New Zealand Society of Genealogists at www.genealogy.org.nz, which has branches across the country, should be able to point you in the direction of any other transcribed records within their collection and it may be worth taking out membership to gain access as well as their knowledge of genealogical information on the islands.

Electoral Rolls

Although the first Parliament was not called in New Zealand until 1854, electoral rolls were already being compiled in the year previous to this. Originally, only men over 21 years of age were allowed to vote, which was also dependent upon them having specific property requirements. By 1879, all adult men who were resident in the county for more than one year – except the prisoners and non-British citizens – were given the entitlement to vote.

No matter where you were in the world, the 'Rights of Women' was a hot – and volatile – topic during the late nineteenth century. Any changes in legislation naturally prompted news coverage and in 1893, when New Zealand led the way in allowing women to vote signalling a real coup for the female sex, a paragraph in the *Illustrated London News* from September of that year gives us a taste of just some of the difficulties faced and challenges won on their long hard road to equality:

> New Zealand is the first important part of the British Empire (only the Isle of Man having preceded it) to admit women to full citizenship. The Women's Suffrage Bill of the colony has now become an accomplished Act, and has just received the sanction of the Governor [...] The measure was passed by the small majority of two [...] But this did not represent the full majority in favour of the emancipation of women as some who voted against the bill were in favour of its principal, but wished to have women record their votes by proxies, while the majority desired to see the female voters placed in all respects on the same footing as the male ones; and the latter is the course adopted finally.

Each country eagerly watched the developments of its neighbours, with the author explaining that:

> there is one of the states of the American Union (Wyoming) where women are now allowed to vote. This right was given them when it was a sparsely peopled territory; and when the population justified the admission of Wyoming to the Union, with representation in the United States Senate, the question of excluding the women from voting in future was raised. But the women had votes themselves, and they refused to vote for any candidate for local Parliamentary office except such as were in favour of the retention of the political representation of both sexes in the new state; which was accordingly achieved.

Remember – many towns and small communities in the colonies were originally founded by emigrants. As pioneers of their time, their tales and endeavours have often been preserved by future generations or local history groups and published as pamphlets, or even books. These can be invaluable to the family historian and include snippets of information that you couldn't hope to get from an official document or record.

Enquire at living history museums, local archives or contact history groups in the area where your ancestors settled. You might be surprised at what you uncover. If you learn of a publication title which is now out of print, try to track it down using websites like www.abebooks.co.uk, which provides information on millions of used, rare and out of print books on sale through independent booksellers around the world.

Despite being oceans apart, Britain and Australasia have strong historical connections. The topics I have covered are literally just the 'tip of the iceberg' and as their record keeping mirrors our own it makes researching this part of the world and its inhabitants, a fun and often productive experience.

4

AMERICA

'Remember, remember always, that all of us, and you and I especially, are descended from immigrants and revolutionists.'
Franklin D. Roosevelt

The crossing of the Atlantic in 1620 by 102 forward-thinking individuals in search of a better life, undoubtedly ranks as one of the greatest emigrant sea voyages of all time. It is hard to believe that this small group of brave souls, who risked their lives on the high seas aboard the ship, the *Mayflower*, would 400 years later have literally tens of millions of descendants. Many are unaware of their connections, while others are genealogically obsessional about their illustrious roots, eager to discover more and honour the memories of the early pilgrims.

During the reign of King James I, this group of English people, seeking religious freedom, made the decision to leave Britain and take the long voyage to America with hopes of settling in North Virginia. Their story was to change the face of history and with thousands of emigrants following in their footsteps in the coming years, they helped create the foundations for the democratic country we know today.

REVEL IN THE RESEARCH

Rough seas forced the pilgrims to put ashore at Cape Cod and it was in this region they built their first plantation. The six New England states comprise Connecticut, Vermont, Rhode Island, Maine, Massachusetts and New Hampshire, and there is a wealth of genealogical information available if you find you are connected to the families of the early settlers. Each state in New England gained its status at different times. As a result, the vital records and documents of each state were also created at different times.

EAST SIDE OF SALT LAKE CITY.

East Side of Salt Lake City from *Harper's New Monthly* magazine, 1884.

In later years the main port of entry for immigrants to New England was Boston. Begin your search at www.ancestry.com, which allows access to a variety of Boston and New England databases relating to 18th-century passenger arrivals.

While Boston passenger lists between the years 1820 and 1891 can be searched for free at www.familysearch.org, a wider timeframe of 1820 to 1943 can be viewed if you subscribe to the Ancestry US and Worldwide package. But don't be disheartened if you are unsuccessful in locating a specific individual on the Boston lists; consider that they may have arrived in the United States at one of the smaller ports such as Portland, M.E. or New Bedford, M.A., or even that they entered the country via Canada.

Once you have confirmed their arrival, the census is vital for establishing where your ancestors decided to set up home. Available every ten years from 1790 to 1940, each census records detailed household and family information, searchable online under subscription at www.ancestry.com.

Accessing genealogical records in Rhode Island is easier than in the rest of New England, as all the vital documents are kept at the relevant town or city hall. Although records are more complete after 1700, they do have some birth, marriage and death records from as far back as the 1630s.

The Rhode Island Historical Society at www.rihs.org is well worth contacting once you have confirmed your links to this area, and if this state provided your forebear's final resting place, try searching online at www.rootsweb.ancestry.com to access the Rhode Island Historical Cemetery database.

The Great Migration Study Project aims to compile both genealogical and biographical accounts of approximately 20,000 English men, women and children who crossed the Atlantic to settle in New England between 1620 and 1640. This is a mammoth task but could not be more fascinating for those with connections to early immigrants.

SAVE THE DATE

By establishing religious freedom and, in turn, creating an American democratic country, the celebration of Thanksgiving has become an annual national holiday, its roots tracing back to a feast held by the pilgrims in 1621 to give thanks for their first good harvest. Thanksgiving Day always falls on the fourth Thursday of November and it is traditional for families to gather together and enjoy a meal of roast turkey and vegetables followed by pumpkin pie.

THE CHURCH OF THE LATTER-DAY SAINTS

All genealogists are aware of the amazing work and record keeping achieved by the Church of the Latter-day Saints, and there are very few of us who have not used their extensive website https://familysearch.org to help us with our own research. The Latter-day Saints practice the Mormon faith and they have a long and intriguing history, which has impacted on the lives of many converts since their conception in the 1820s.

Were your forebears looking to escape the hardships of life in Britain? If they suddenly disappeared from the census, perhaps the Mormon faith provided the answer?

In order to understand more about this religious group and their beliefs, the timeline below briefly explains the key events which helped to establish their membership, and the theology that they continue to live by.

Following the Faith

1820s Joseph Smith is believed to have been visited by God and given the power to translate an ancient language that revealed a document – equal to the Bible – and regarded as the true scripture written by a man called Mormon. This was named the Book of Mormon and published in 1830.

Mormons believe in a religion and cultural existence that relates to this book as another testament of Jesus Christ.

1830 A Church is established and named the Church of the Latter-day Saints in 1834.

1844 Upon the death of Joseph Smith, Brigham Young is elected leader.

1847 The majority of Mormons leave Nauvoo, Illinois, driven from their homes by conflicts and disagreements with other settlers due to their beliefs. They head west with Brigham Young to establish themselves in the Great Salt Lake Valley. New converts arrive from around the world between 1847 and 1868.

1852 The doctrine of plural marriages is announced.

1853 Brigham Young instructed fellow church member, Lorenzo Snow, to create a self sufficient community in Box Elder County, which was later named Brigham City.

1860 The church is reorganised with Joseph Smith's son Joseph Junior as First Prophet and President.

1877 Death of Brigham Young.

1893 Completion of Salt Lake Temple dedicated to President Wilford Woodruff – named the Fourth Prophet.

1895 Utah becomes America's 45th State.

1898 Woodruff dies and Lorenzo Snow becomes Fifth Prophet.

1900 The Latter-day Saints enter a new century with members continually increasing. By 1982 there were over 5 million members worldwide growing to 10 million by 1996 and a reported 14 million by 2012.

Between 1847 and 1868 over 60,000 Latter-day Saints followed the Mormon Trail with the help of 250 'travel' companies especially organised to aid their journey. These converts included English, French, Germans, Scandinavians and many other nationalities. If you believe your ancestor made this expedition, visit http://history.lds.org/overlandtravels/home to find out which company they travelled with, while the website www.xmission.com/~nelsonb/ship_list.htm gives more details about the Mormon Emigrant Companies and their leaders, the vessels used, their departure and arrival dates, along with the duration of the passage.

CASE STUDY: TRAILBLAZERS – A TALE OF MORMON PIONEERS

Family historian Kath Jones explains how her own ancestors emigrated from Derbyshire in a quest to start a new life in Utah as devotees of the Mormon faith. Their journey was a difficult one and mirrors that of thousands of others during the nineteenth century:

> Isaac Allen was my 2nd cousin 5 times removed – together we share a common ancestor in my 6th Great Grandfather, but it was Isaac's conversion to the Mormon faith and emigration to Utah to escape the hardships of life as a miner that I found fascinating. To learn more about Isaac's journey it was important to widen my net with a little background research.

Kath Jones discovered that on 5 June 1810 in Harefield, Middlesex, George Edward Grove Taylor was born to parents Joseph Taylor and Martha Grove. George, a tailor by trade, met and married Ann Wickes – who was ten years his senior – in February 1830, with their first son, Joseph Edward, arriving in December of that same year. After a move to Lincolnshire they eventually settled near London, where they came into contact with the Mormon missionaries. In July 1848 George, Ann and 18-year-old Joseph were baptised in the Mormon faith. George and Joseph were extremely active members, becoming dedicated missionaries converting many others across the country to the doctrines of The Latter-day Saints.

George's reputation eventually led him to Derbyshire where, on 30 March 1851, this well known recruitment leader was recorded by the enumerator in Chesterfield at the home of Kath's ancestor – Isaac Allen. 'Although listed as a Tailor, we now know George's main purpose was to recruit Isaac with a promise of a better life in the United States compared to the one he led as a miner in the local colliery,' Kath explains.

The Mormon religion freely accepts the taking of several wives – known as polygamy – but not all relationships survive this arrangement. George Taylor went on to marry Jane Baxter, ignoring the disapproval of his wife Ann, which sadly resulted in the couple separating.

Their son Joseph had previously left for the United States on the long journey to Salt Lake in Utah, where the original American Mormons had settled. With news of his mother's distress, Joseph sent for Ann to join him. On 4 April 1854 Ann left for New Orleans on the ship *Germanicus* to be reunited with her son.

The Journey Begins

Kath Jones's research into her ancestors also led her to discover that:

> Back in Britain, Isaac – like many others – had been persuaded to leave for the United States and went on ahead of his family, with the intention of earning enough money for them to follow later. He boarded the same vessel as George's first wife Ann and is listed five names above her on the ship's passenger list. With many of these arranged Mormon passages, a representative was chosen to take charge. On the *Germanicus* Richard Cook was the company leader of 220 'saints'.

The passage took a colossal ten weeks due to the ship spending several days in the virtually motionless waters of the Caribbean. Onboard the travellers suffered from the excessive heat with temperatures reaching a sweltering 120°F between decks. Despite these conditions and the water shortages, only four deaths occurred en route, but just short of reaching dry land, the ship was quarantined due to an outbreak of cholera resulting in twenty-four deaths both on board and during the subsequent journey.

The *Germanicus* finally docked in New Orleans and after a torturous voyage the pioneers faced a further hazardous journey across the American Plains to their ultimate destination of Salt Lake City. Some stayed in St Louis for a year to earn enough money for the trip, where it's probable that Isaac worked as he waited for his wife and children to arrive. Kath learned that:

> When Isaac's family followed exactly a year later, they travelled from Liverpool to New York on board the 1,167-ton ship, the *William Stetson*. Even though the number of passengers was greater than on the *Germanicus*, the passage was considerably shorter, taking only thirty-one days from their date of departure on 26 April 1855. Although this route was faster by sea, the journey by land was by no means easy.

Kath continues:

> It's recorded that wagon trains led by oxen – sometimes up to thirty-nine wagons long – began to make their journey across the plains: so determined were they to reach their goal that those with very little finance made the journey on foot.

As a result, the LDS Church established a revolving fund, known as the Perpetual Emigration Fund, to enable the poor to emigrate, and even created a system of handcart companies allowing people to travel more cheaply, pulling their belongings behind them. By 1869 the first transcontinental railroad was completed, allowing the Mormons to travel by train and helping to alleviate some of the deprivations previously endured. Kath goes on to explain:

> At first, the Allen family followed the Mormon trail to what was then called Great Salt Lake City and are recorded on the 1860 US census as farmers with a personal estate estimated at $150 – a far cry from their lives in Derbyshire. On 9 July 1869, Isaac became an official US citizen and was sworn in, in Brigham City – a settlement named after the Mormon founder Brigham Young. By the 1870 census, the Allen family were well established in the town of Portage, Box Elder, in Utah, where Isaac's real estate was valued at $200 and his personal estate at $150.

There were several communities which made up Box Elder County and they all seemed to have developed during the same era. Men and their families were chosen for their trades, using their expertise to establish new settlements. The attempts to industrialise Utah with a sugar mill and a pottery industry using the knowledge of the skilled craftsmen brought in from Britain initially failed. Surprisingly, the industry that was destined to do well was the manufacturing of woollen goods.

One of the first residents of Portage was Isaac Allen and his family, who joined another dozen families working hard to build the community in which they were to spend the rest of their lives. Initially, they attempted to establish roots on the east side of the Malad River – known as Mound or Oregan Springs about 6 miles from the Idaho border – but the commune only lasted a few years when their crops were destroyed by grasshoppers and the inhabitants were plagued with the threat of Indians.

While discovering the southern Salt Lake Valley, the pioneers met several parties of Indians – Shoshonis from the north and Gosiutes from the south and west. They shared their skills and taught the Mormons how to harvest sego lily, sunflower seeds and other roots to make a meal. One delicacy was to combine honey and crushed crickets to make a cake. Not surprisingly, this strange concoction didn't appeal to the new settlers!

Although they traded with the Indians, the Mormons also disrupted their lives by attaching their permanent settlements to the Native American land. Consequently they spread illnesses such as smallpox and measles to the Indians who had little or no immunity, resulting in the death of many of their numbers. The Mormons insisted that the land was owned by the Lord and could only be distributed by the priesthood. Even though the Indians had lived in Salt Lake for many years, the settlers did not recognise that the land belonged to the Native Americans and expected them to convert to Mormonism, which naturally, did not go down too well.

The settlement finally uprooted in 1872 and moved to the west side of the valley so that they could tap irrigation water from the Samary Lake and construct a 12-mile canal using hand tools. Once again the Mormon folk worked closely together to erect a schoolhouse, which was to serve all public purposes. The surrounding mountainsides provided natural resources from which they built log cabins and forts.

A TYPICAL MORMON FAMILY.

A Typical Mormon family depicted in the *Harper's New Monthly* magazine, 1884.

All their food was grown and harvested in the fertile soil, which had been provided by the mountain streams producing adequate water supplies for domestic and agricultural needs. Even adjoining native grassland wasn't wasted – the cattle and horses had all the food they needed to survive.

Isaac's home, like that of so many of the early pioneers, would have been sparsely furnished and very plain, but a central fireplace would make it comfortable and warm contributing to their happy and healthy wellbeing. Pork was scarce at times so the families would have stocked up on the game they killed throughout each season. Along with chickens, their meat was cooked on a wire spit over the fire and the grease kept for use as candles. They would twist a button in a piece of rag to form a taper, place it in some grease on a saucer, and light it on a dark evening.

The women would do all their baking in a brick oven built in the side of the chimney, although they only had a limited stock of corn, wheat, pork, chicken and potatoes to cook. The only available fruit were the wild berries and plums from the woods. Coffee, tea, sugar and butter were often in short supply and so substitutes were used. A herb called tea-weed, which grew wild, was steeped in hot water and drank, while coffee – known as crust coffee – was made from browned grains, but in taste it didn't replace the real thing. The women also worked hard making clothing from wool or flax by spinning yarn, weaving the cloth and then sewing the garments together.

Sadly, in 1874, Isaac's wife Christina passed away and was buried in Portage Cemetery. Isaac went on to open a general store in the town, where he worked – with the aid of a clerk named James Matthews – until his death in 1891. His son Joseph established himself in the area and worked hard to provide a home for his growing family under the Mormon faith. His headstone is featured on the www.utahgravestones.org website – a fabulous resource for anyone with links to this part of Utah that provides a huge amount of detail about the families who lived and worked in this area, as well as information on their original birthplaces, a large percentage of whom were from England and Wales.

Although many Latter-day Saints lived outside Great Salt Lake City it was still the central location for those of the Mormon faith. The first transcontinental telegraph linked the area to lines in the east and west in October 1861, giving the City greater communication with the outside world. By January 1868, the name was changed to Salt Lake City and in 1893, the Salt Lake Temple, which had taken forty years to build, was finally complete.

George Taylor, the man who had persuaded Isaac to emigrate to America, continued to work as a tailor in the city; his son Joseph became one of the first Morticians and Embalmers in Salt Lake and ended up making the pine casket for the great Mormon leader Brigham Young.

THE IMMIGRANT ANCESTOR'S PROJECT

Between 1821 and 1924, approximately 55 million Europeans emigrated to the New World. The growth of the British Empire encouraged a whole cross-section of people – from the wealthy to the poor – to migrate. This included everyone from soldiers and colonial civil servants to miners, cabinetmakers, engineers and entertainers.

While the men sought work in varying occupations, single females also took the opportunity to try domestic work overseas. Some simply sought adventure – perhaps following global events such as the discovery of gold which made them eager to seek their fortunes – others had no choice but to escape their current existence due to religious or political issues back home. Many went on to settle in their new countries, prospering, and for the most part, having happy lives; others found that life in a new location was not necessarily for them and returned to Britain at the earliest opportunity.

There were also thousands of Europeans, West Indians and Africans who thought that our own country was the Promised Land, emigrating from all points of the globe to try and carve out a better life here.

The Immigrant Ancestors Project is sponsored by the Brigham Young University and its Center for Family History and Genealogy. This is a free online index that uses emigration registers to locate the details of individuals' birthplaces and their native countries of origin, information which is not found in the naturalisation documents of destination countries or the port registers, helping to give us a broader perspective of emigration and providing more understanding of individual stories.

Initially focusing on the immigrants of England, Ireland, France, Germany, Italy and Spain, more nations will be added in order to complete what is a mammoth project. The documents used to provide these specific pieces of information include port of departure records such as passports, passenger contracts, certificates of personal identification, certificates of completion of military service and British and Irish Pre-departure Records.

After arrival in their recipient countries immigrants also appeared on various other documentation, including consular records, emigrant lists and hometown censuses – all helping to provide the Immigrant Ancestors Project with a well rounded study of an individual's journey. Find out more at http://immigrants.byu.edu.

GOLD FEVER

Ancestors frequently disappeared off the UK census during the Victorian era for a number of reasons, but have you ever considered that they may well have been struck down with gold fever? For the majority of our forebears, the search for a better life was paramount. This could involve trying to master a new job, achieving a successful harvest, or even improving their education, but others set themselves much higher goals. As gold deposits were discovered in countries as far afield as Argentina, Australia, Canada and the United States, for some, the lure proved too great and they set off to seek their fortune.

California Dreaming ...

The United States' first significant gold rush took place in Georgia in 1829. Despite this initial breakthrough, further gold deposits became harder to find until in January 1848, when James Wilson Marshall discovered nuggets of the mineral at Sutter's Mill in Coloma, California. News of the breakthrough spread rapidly with some of the early Georgia miners moving west to join the thousands of other prospectors, who soon began to arrive from all four corners of the globe.

It's believed that 300,000 gold seekers made the journey to California – 150,000 by land and 150,000 arriving by sea, initially by ship but travelling the final arduous distance by covered wagon. From Britain, Europe, Australia and Asia, these prospectors became known as 'forty-niners' in reference to the year 1849, when the mining here was at its peak.

As with other towns located near 'gold fever' hotspots, the huge influx of people put a massive strain on resources. Soon it was realised that goods needed to be imported to meet the demands of flourishing towns like San Francisco and its surrounding settlements. As ships arrived with cargoes of porcelain, fine silks, ale and fancy goods, new problems had to be faced when the crews abandoned their vessels in an effort to try their luck in the goldfields. People made homes in wooden shanties made from the timbers of the deserted ships, or pitched their tents wherever they could find a vacant area of land.

But it was not only the men who took advantage of the Gold Rush era. Astute women became entrepreneurs in their own right, opening businesses to cater for the hundreds of prospectors who came into town. Some arrived with their husbands, while widows and single women came in search of adventure and the possibility of a new life in a thriving city. Those who had little money turned to prostitution as a way of making ends meet and, with an endless stream of potential customers, ended up opening smart brothels for those who could afford their services.

Wives whose husbands had died on the trail – either in accidents or by contracting cholera – gained an independence they'd previously not known, enabling those women who were confident enough to break free from the mould, to make the most of a variety of opportunities.

Flash in the Pan

Before the more sophisticated methods of mining developed, a simple technique known as 'panning' was used by the prospector, who spent hours trying to extract tiny specks of gold from within the gravel of the riverbed. His main piece of equipment was a steel pan measuring between 12 and 15in in diameter, which he darkened over a campfire enabling him to see any flakes of gold more clearly and helping to coin the phrase, 'Flash in the Pan'. Initially he would stake a claim to a particular area. A gravel bar in the middle of a river or stream was sought from which he would first begin his search but an understanding of the flow of the river was needed, as well as a knowledge of the spots where gold could become lodged, such as in cracks along the riverbank near the waterline or around submerged tree roots. A pan full of gravel was scooped up and sifted of any large stones or lumps of mud and clay. Keeping the pan just under the water at all times, a swirling motion was applied, allowing the heavier pieces of gold to separate from the sand and gravel and sink to the bottom. The debris was gently washed over the rim and the process continued until nothing remained inside the pan except tiny minerals and flakes of gold.

Mining Life

Throughout the Victorian era there were several major global gold discoveries with each location experiencing the similar highs and lows of mining life.

It was said that for many, religion was abandoned on the trail, with the arduous journey robbing them of any belief they may have previously had in God. But inside the mining camps were those who tried to spread the word of the Lord as missionaries, renting rooms in the growing towns and building a congregation.

The prospector's diet often did little to lift their spirits. Malnutrition and scurvy were not uncommon and a combination of bread, beans, rice, molasses and a little meat was all that was available. Along with tea, coffee and water to drink, it was little wonder they sought out the alcohol offered by the saloons.

When the towns began to prosper, improvements were made. Permanent cabins were constructed and hotels sprang up offering imported fine wines and food to those who could afford it. Forward-thinking entrepreneurs opened venues for entertainment, encouraging actors and dancers to brave the dangers and discomforts en route to prise the gold dust from the successful prospectors' pockets.

Negative Nuggets

Growth of trade, the development of the towns and cities and the construction of the railroads, were just some of the positive aspects of the Gold Rush, but there were also many adverse effects. Native Americans were pushed off their lands in order to make way for new settlements and violence erupted as they defended what had been theirs for generations. When the easily retrievable gold became less plentiful the Americans began to begrudge the foreigners who had come to take what they saw as *their* gold and organised attacks on these 'invaders' broke out in an attempt to drive them out. A new Californian State Legislation, in the form of a foreign miners' tax, was finally introduced, requiring a levy of $20 per month in an effort to control the trouble.

At the start of the rush when gold was abundant, miners had been able to stake their claim to a plot of land and even leave their tools unguarded overnight, but as stocks depleted and rivers became crowded, other problems arose. Desperate miners turned to stealing, fights broke out over claims, and hard-earned gold dust was lost to professional gamblers in the saloons. The early judicial systems of the frontier towns were swift. Impromptu mob trials were held with punishment dished out in the form of whippings, hangings or banishment. These scenes were witnessed in all countries that experienced the rise and decline in the amount of gold available.

By 1851, the focus had shifted to Australia, where gold fever hit Victoria in Melbourne. Again, the discovery indirectly helped bring settlements and economic development to the nation with the introduction of railroads and telegraph wires, the mixing of multicultural societies as well as seeing the end of penal transportation. Gold fields continued to be found throughout Southern Australia and into the western regions by the 1890s. During the glory days between 1881 and 1892 more than 17,000 gold licences were granted in South Australia alone. When river and surface gold finds had been exhausted, the focus changed to hydraulic mines, which then became the chief sources for extracting this highly coveted mineral.

In subsequent years, new discoveries were found during the 1860s in Central Otago, New Zealand, in South Africa at Witwatersrand in the 1880s, in Chile and Argentina in the 1890s with the Tierra del Fuego Gold Rush as well as the Klondike and Alaskan Rushes between 1896 and 1914. If family hearsay talks of one of your ancestors being in these regions within this particular timeframe, you could well have a potential prospector in your family tree!

For many, the first sign of 'golden roots' will come from a family story handed down through the generations. Take advantage of this and ask as many questions of living relatives as you can to establish dates, details and which gold rush your forebear was involved in. You may be lucky enough to discover mementos, letters, stock certificates and even journals describing their experiences. Use this information to read up on the relevant area during that era to build up background knowledge of the conditions endured at the time.

Before your ancestor went off to seek his fortune, try to find out what their lives were like before they left, perhaps revealing a reason that would prompt them to go on what was often an epic journey overseas. Was it a quest for adventure or the chance to escape from a poorly paid existence? Depending upon the period, clues may lie in the census returns or BMD certificates which could help identify a previous occupation or even sad events such as the loss of a child or spouse which could have led to their change in situation, and may help to give an idea of your forebear's frame of mind as they left their wider family for pastures new.

A TURN OF PHRASE

When forty-niners left for the California Gold Rush they used the expression that they were 'Going to see the elephant'. Upon their return they would state that they had 'Seen the elephant's tracks' or 'the elephant's tail'. This curious turn of phrase actually originated before the Gold Rush, when a farmer was desperate to see an elephant when the circus came to town. Sadly, when he encountered the circus parade his horses were terrified and bolted, overturning his wagon of vegetables, but he concluded, 'I don't care a hang, for I have seen an elephant.' The gold prospectors adopted this expression as the elephant symbolised the high cost of their endeavour both on the trail, and in California, as well as being an exotic sight and the adventure of a lifetime!

If you're fortunate enough to have 'forty-niners' in your tree, then why not visit 'California's Most Wanted' site, dedicated to those ancestors who were lost in the California area during the Gold Rush period. Crammed with articles, mailing lists and tips on how to research a mining claim, www.californiagenealogy.org/goldrush should definitely be your first port of call.

Prospector's Picks:

- Those who travelled to the Yukon region for the Klondike Rush could well be tracked down at www.yukongenealogy.com/content/database_search.htm but follow this up with a visit to Cyndi's Mining List, which will help you to identify other gold mining regions and related databases (www.cyndislist.com/mining.htm).
- The Alaskan State Library provides a thorough online guide to researching those who were connected to the Klondike Gold Rush. Visit http://www.library.state.ak.us/hist/parham.html to find out where the repositories are located, and the records, databases and indexes that they hold, or that are available for viewing online.
- If Australia was the destination of choice for your fortune-seeking forebear, take a look at the Australian Government's Culture Portal at http://australia.gov.au for a glimpse at how the spreading of 'Gold Fever' affected the nation. Consider using the Message Boards at www.ancestry.com to question likeminded researchers who may be able to help you with your particular mission.

Following the Paper Trail

Even the smallest newspaper cutting can explain to us what a town, region, or country was like at a particular point in history, shedding light on how an event, or circumstance, can change an area and its inhabitants forever. For example, a headline in the *Illustrated London News* of August 1863 announced, 'Gold has been found in the Hudson's Bay territories.' The short article, copied from the *Toronto Globe* of 28 July, would have been of huge interest to adventurers eager to seek their fortune in this part of the world, explaining that:

> For some time it has been known that gold was to be found on the Saskatchewan River, near the Rocky Mountains, and it was presumed that it had been washed by the river from the gold bearing rocks of these mountains, and would consequently be found only in the beds of the rivers and not anywhere else in the territory. Recent discoveries indicate that this view of the matter is not correct [...] Gold has been discovered at Fort Ellice, and also on branches of the Qu'Appelle River. It is not only communicated by letter from Red River, but Governor Dallas, of the Hudson's Bay Company, who has recently arrived from the territory, is personally cognisant of the discovery. We see no reason to

> doubt that the whole of these vast plains will very soon be covered by a busy population [...] The new Hudson's Bay Company contemplates a very speedy opening up of the territory.

Today we have reporters based in countries all over the globe with special correspondents able to fly to a specific destination at a moment's notice, but this has not always been the case and the newspaper companies made good use of anyone willing to act as their 'eyes and ears' in foreign climes.

For those who chose to accept a position of employment overseas, they would undoubtedly broaden their horizons from the sights they witnessed en route. Depending upon the role they had undertaken and the length of time they expected to be away, some would take the opportunity to make a little extra money by acting as 'foreign correspondents' by sending regular journalistic contributions to newspapers back home. The speed of emails and development of instant photography was still a long way in the future so alternative methods had to be found. In 1888 Mr Melton Prior was sent to Australia from England by what he called a 'somewhat indirect and lingering route [...] across two oceans'. His skills as an artist also enabled him to make sketches which were used for illustration within the newspaper. His journey was a long one and after visiting the West Indies and making sketches of the Panama Canal works, he proceeded to New York and then Montréal, with the purpose of crossing the North American continent by the Canadian Pacific Railway. His purpose in Canada was to visit the gold mines in Denison. After alighting from a railway freight train he had to walk 3 miles in pouring rain – through forests and swamps along a path to get to his destination. His recollections enable us to understand the enthusiasm and hope experienced by those emigrants who chose to seek their fortune in the various goldmines that attracted so many prospectors in the nineteenth century. Discovered in 1887, 'the Vermillion Mine Company is expected to be one of the richest anywhere, but which is certainly remunerative to its fortunate owners,' writes Mr Prior. He continues:

> The Company have put up a few shanties and a house, and are now sinking shafts and crushing the quartz, still on quite a small scale; but the whole township of Denison, so rich in gold, will soon be full of stamping and crushing mills; and no doubt a town will spring up in this wild and forest wilderness.
>
> Everything is very primitive at present; the shaft is about 32 feet deep, and only two men can work at a time, filling the bucket which is then carried over to the crushing machine, and for washing. So great is the excitement about this particular district that people of all classes are flocking to the spot. Men who have bought lots in the township are to be seen and heard of all over the place. I made a sketch of the party of prospectors starting from the Ranger Lode hut in search of the precious metal.

We can only begin to imagine the number of men living on little or no wages, in poor sanitary conditions back home, who were prompted by articles similar to Mr Prior's to pack up what little belongings they had, in search of what they hoped would be a better future via the bounty that awaited them in the gold fields of Canada, America, Australia and beyond.

Remember – no traveller, adventurer or explorer worth their salt would leave home without a map of their intended destination. Perhaps they might acquire one en route, or for those who, due to their circumstances, could not afford a printed version, would instead create their own in a notebook or journal.

Maps can be fascinating in their own right, showing changing boundaries and place names as well as providing clues as to a journey undertaken or an intended destination. Make full use of these handwritten maps and compare them to today's versions by following a person's route, working out their means of transport and the length of time it would take them to complete the journey, helping to build a bigger picture of the lengths some travellers were prepared to go to, especially when for necessity and not simply just for pleasure.

The Roaring Days by Henry Lawson, 1889
The night too quickly passes
And we are growing old,
So let us fill our glasses
And toast the Days of Gold;
When finds of wondrous treasure
Set all the South ablaze,
And you and I were faithful mates
All through the roaring days.

FEMALE ADVENTURERS

It was not only the menfolk who sought adventure – there were women who enjoyed the thrill of travelling to new destinations. Not all intended to settle in the new countries, they simply wished to take on the challenge, see the world, and gain from the experience.

Nellie Bly was the pen name of New York journalist Elizabeth Jane Cochrane, who emulated the journey of Jules Verne's character Phileas Fogg by taking a record-breaking trip around the world. An article in the *Girl's Own Paper* of June 1890 reports on her trip, focusing on the length of the journey, transportation taken and destinations visited, showing us that despite it being a 'man's world' at this time, women were beginning to come into their own and were both recognised and celebrated for their achievements:

> The circuit of the Earth was made in seventy two days, six hours and eleven minutes, leaving New York on November 14, 1889, and reaching the city again on January 25, 1890 – two months and eleven days. Her route was from New York to Liverpool, London, Dover, Calais, Brindisi, Port Said, Aden, Colombo, Singapore, Hong Kong, Yokohama, across the Pacific, and San Francisco. Then she went by train to New York.
>
> Her competitor, Miss Elizabeth Bisland of *Cosmopolitan* magazine, went the reverse way, departing from San Francisco, leaving the passage across the Atlantic, always rather doubtful in the winter season as to the time it occupies, to the last, and this apparently is what caused her defeat, for she was only able to catch a slow boat to Liverpool, and arrived in New York some few days after her rival.
>
> Miss Bly went from Calais to Amiens, en route, to visit Jules Verne, the well-known author of *Around the World in Eighty Days*, where she consulted that distinguished Frenchman on the possibilities of her accomplishing her journey round the Earth in even a shorter time than his vivid imagination had allowed.

Despite this amazing detour to visit a historical character we can now only read about, publications at that time were also captivated by the small amount of luggage Miss Bly managed to take with her. Women from the upper and middle classes were universally known for requiring an excessive amount of cases and trunks to house their wide selection of garments and accessories, but this particular report shows that even on the longest trip exceptions can be made:

> This remarkable journey was accomplished with no other luggage than a handbag containing the need for changes of linen and brushes and combs, her railroad and steamer tickets for the entire route, and Bank of England notes for £500. Only one gown – and that on her back – a warm cloak and rug; but nothing that she could not carry with comfort herself, thus securing that no delays should arise from taking luggage or from the loss of it.

This reduced amount of clothing prompted reporters to comment in a variety of articles, but as family historians it also shows us that the world was changing and meeting the demands of the female traveller:

> The story of Miss Bly's luggage shows conclusively how much the efforts of the reformers in women's clothing have done for her in that way by the introduction of the combination garment and coloured petticoats and stays, as well as in other ways, in which fashion has gone hand-in-hand with common sense.

They even speculated as to the contents of her 'good sized handbag':

Gold miners examining a gold nugget, taken from the *Illustrated London News*, 1888.

Stamping machine used to crush the gold bearing quartz.

Gold miners washing and testing the panned gold.

The entrance to a traditionally constructed shaft mine.

> Four combination garments, three nightdresses, two pairs thick and two pairs thin stockings, a dozen handkerchiefs, a pair of house shoes, two blouses, one of cambric, one of silk, two pairs gloves and a flannel dressing jacket.

A host of articles began to appear to aid the female traveller starting with suggestions as to the type of luggage she might require:

> The fitted 'Gladstone bags' – with the fittings on a kind of relief in the centre – are very convenient, and some of these are now sold at very moderate prices. Perhaps the brushes and combs might be of a little better quality, but that might be altered by giving a few shillings extra when purchasing. If you are not quite well enough off to purchase a bag ready fitted, the next best thing is to fit one up yourself. This is easily done by taking your empty bag and a piece of broad elastic, and sew it onto the side of the bag in loops which are large enough to hold what you most require in travelling. These would be a soap box, a bottle, or a small flask for eau de Cologne, and another bottle for your glycerine, or a small pot for cold cream, either of which you are sure to need on your journey. If you choose, you can also make places for other articles – a button hook, clothes brush, comb and brush, nail scissors, and toothbrush. For a sea voyage it is unquestionably a capital plan for carrying your little toilette necessities. You can unroll and spread it out on your sofa or berth, and have all that you need before you.
>
> Many ladies prefer a good sized sponge bag, into which they put their soap wrapped in a piece of oil-silk, along with the nail and toothbrushes, a tooth powder box and also a little bottle of ammonia for insect bites.

CASE STUDY: STUDYING THE FACTS

As you can see, newspapers and journals are essential for adding atmosphere and interest to our facts. The story of a migrating ancestor can be passed down through the generations, but the newspaper obituary of an individual who travelled, or settled far from their country of origin, for example, can provide a whole host of details that you might be hard pushed to find anywhere else. Even the obituary of the second or third generation migrant may offer details of their parents' or grandparents' past – especially if their journey had been a hazardous or an eventful one.

Most countries are proud of their early pioneers and local publications love to share their stories, so this is an area well worth investigating when trying to find interesting ephemera – even if it is a photocopy of the original cutting – to add to your family biographies. Take for instance Barbara McNabb (née Park), whose obituary in the US-based *Petersburg Observer*, published 31 March 1950, tells a fascinating story:

> Mrs Barbara McNabb, 93 years old and one of the country's oldest residents, died at 11.15 PM on Thursday, March 23, 1950 [...] Mrs McNabb was the daughter of John and Catherine McCray Park, both natives of Scotland, she was born on board a ship bound for America, from her parents' homeland. They landed at New Orleans and came up the Mississippi and Illinois rivers by Steamboat, to Havana where the family lived for a short time, and then came to Menard County, living for many years in the Curtis community North East of Petersburg.

This cutting is evidence of the family emigration and further continues to tell their story. Packed with details about her early life and her surviving children, it concludes with the arrangements for her funeral service. But it is a previous newspaper cutting published to celebrate her 85th birthday that gives even more clues, not only about her life but also events in the lives of her sons:

> Mrs Barbara McNabb, who resides east of this city, will observe her 85th birthday anniversary on May 16. Mrs McNabb was born on the Atlantic Ocean as her parents were en route from Scotland to the United States. They were six weeks crossing the ocean, landing at New Orleans. On Mrs McNabb's birthday in 1918 a son, Hugh Toohey, was crossing the Atlantic Ocean going to the World War and on her birthday in 1919 another son, John Toohey, was crossing the Atlantic Ocean en route home from the World War.

These are fascinating facts that were truly important to this family which prompt questions and help to provide further avenues of research. Always scour local newspapers around family events to see what gems you can uncover.

IMMIGRANT ENTRY

Did your ancestors choose the United States as the country in which to make a fresh start? Advances in transatlantic travel and the developing rail networks that began to criss-cross the American interiors not only made the prospect of travel more affordable and easier to navigate, but offered adventure and employment: consequently, to 'outsiders', America was seen as the 'land of opportunity'.

Between 1855 and 1890 New York State and New York City collaborated to make Castle Garden America's first official immigration centre. Today this area is home to the Castle Clinton National Monument situated in a 25-acre waterfront park at the tip of Manhattan. With information on over 11 million immigrants, you can search the free database at www.castlegarden.org.

By January 1892 arrivals to the United States were moved to Ellis Island, a small portal located in New York harbour. For over sixty years, until 12 November 1954, it processed 12 million immigrants and is likely to have been the place where your ancestors first set foot on American soil. Its archives have now become one of the major resources for family historians tracing their migrant forebears. Crammed with detailed information on all arrivals between the above dates, its website (www.ellisisland.org) can help you trace a person's origins and perhaps provide the next clue as to their onward journey. Included in their holdings are thousands of passenger lists, ships' manifests and details of shipping companies. By completing a simple name search you could be well on the way to discovering your forebear's age upon arrival, their country of origin, how much money they had with them, and where they intended to travel to.

The ability – in some cases – to print out an image of the ship on which they travelled provides a fabulous keepsake to add to your family files, and may even enable you to track down other ephemera relating to that particular vessel to enhance your ancestor's story. Shipping lines and their vessels often appeared on postcards, which make a great addition to a collection. You may discover ship's stationary, advertising leaflets, or come across letters or a journal written by someone who might have travelled on the same ship, or by a similar vessel in the same shipping line. The likelihood of this is not as fantastical as you might think. There are literally hundreds of thousands of pieces of written ephemera out there, just waiting to be found. Items sell at auctions, specialist fairs and online sites every day. Each little detail and extra piece of information you can uncover can help you to seek them out.

You may have already been aware that your ancestor emigrated to the US in 1902. Using the Ellis Island search options you can use this information to try to track them down on a ship's passenger list, discover their intended destination, the name and identity of the vessel upon which they sailed, and possibly view its image. This website is a potential goldmine for capturing those 'migrant manoeuvres'. It is free to use and simply requires you to register your details in order to view the records.

Don't forget to visit www.archives.gov/genealogy – the National Archives of America – which has a section especially tailored to immigration and naturalisation records. Here, you can search their 'Access to Archives Database' in order to find the location of all the documents and records held in repositories across the country.

Understandably, not everyone can afford to travel the globe in the name of family history – however much we'd all love to – but why not take advantage of the research services that these institutions offer? My top tip is to investigate online first, covering every conceivable eventuality that you can think of, as this will help you

Postcards depicting various vessels and shipping lines or advertising leaflets, clippings and even stamp sets can help us to build a bigger picture of the type of voyage our ancestors might have taken and the conditions they faced while on board.

to keep the cost of hiring an independent researcher to a minimum, and in turn make full use of their skills and knowledge to seek out alternative sources to find the information you require.

POTENTIAL AND POSSIBILITY

The smallest piece of ephemera could give a clue as to your ancestor's 'travelling' past. Share certificates for gold prospectors, emigration advertisements viewed by Highland crofters, ships' logs from those who worked their passage, travel journals from explorers and adventurers and ship ephemera from those who travelled during a period of luxury – all have their own story to tell.

If your ancestor emigrated with their family to America during their childhood, perhaps you've uncovered a Reward of Merit showing their progress at school in a new country? Trade cards given out by merchants and shopkeepers could describe services and products not available in the UK. Prices for the items might be listed in dollars; the fashion, style and design of the product helping to date the period in which your ancestor was overseas, adding a new line of enquiry to your research. Consider that the trade card – and business that it promotes – could in fact be part of a business set up by your ancestors when they started their new life abroad. Ask yourself was there a skill, craft, or particular business that has been handed down within the family? Once you begin to look for ways to illustrate your genealogical journey, the possibilities are endless!

5

CANADA

'Do not follow where the path may lead. Go instead where there is no path and leave a trail.'
Ralph Waldo Emerson

Comprising ten provinces and three territories, the North American country of Canada stretches from the Atlantic to the Pacific and north into the Arctic Ocean. Up until 1867, it was split into Upper and Lower Canada and did not become a unified country until Newfoundland joined as a province in 1949.

Although it was the early French settlers who founded Quebec City back in 1600, British explorers also led expeditions, creating new settlements along the country's Atlantic coast. Britons began migrating to Canada in earnest mainly due to the formation of the Hudson's Bay Company, which dominated the fur trade and was instrumental in the exploration and settlement of some of the remotest regions in the world. The opportunity to work for the company, join exploration teams and settle in new communities attracted merchants, pioneers and those seeking adventure.

THE FUR TRADE

The Hudson's Bay Company holds the distinction of being the oldest commercial corporation in North America bearing its own heraldic coat of arms since 1671. Established in the latter part of the seventeenth century, the company provided strong links between Britain and the New World. Today, their headquarters is based in the Simpson Tower in Toronto.

In the late sixteenth century, one of the main reasons for continued exploration of the western hemisphere was to find easy access and a more direct route to the Orient. This was believed to lie through the North American continent via what was to later become known as the Northwest Passage. After numerous attempts to find this fabled route, other areas were discovered, including the great saltwater sea region of Hudson's Bay – named after its founder – Henry Hudson.

By the 1630s, explorers realised that Hudson's Bay did not hold the key to the Orient but that the area surrounding it was populated by some of the best fur-bearing animals in the world. There were many hurdles to overcome, but it was two Europeans – Pierre-Esprit Radisson (1636–1710) and Médard Chouart, Sieur des Groseilliers (1618–96) – who thoroughly surveyed this region and negotiated with the inhabiting Cree Native Indians to establish a business based on trading this natural 'commodity'. Their initial commerce with the Cree enabled them to export the furs back to France, but landed Des Groseilliers in jail for trading without a licence. Upon his release, and disappointed with the restrictions placed upon them, Des Groseilliers and Radisson travelled to Boston to try to interest a 'backer' in their venture. It was not until they became associated with Englishman Colonel George Cartwright that a subsequent trip to Britain led to a meeting with King Charles II. By 1667, the King's cousin Prince Rupert was persuaded to sponsor the venture, and the loan of two vessels – the *Eaglet* and the *Nonsuch* – was provided for the explorers and their crew by the Royal Navy. Although the *Eaglet* was damaged by storm and had to return to base, the *Nonsuch* continued on her quest and nearly four months after leaving England the vessel arrived at its destination. Via a 'League of Friendship' established with the First Nations, land was purchased and a fort – Charles Fort, later known as Rupert House – was erected at the mouth of the Rupert River in James Bay. When the harsh winter weather broke, trading began in the spring, enabling the furs to be loaded onto the *Nonsuch* for the journey back to Britain (through the melted ice) with a cargo estimated to be worth £1,380.

On 2 May 1670, the success and excitement created around this venture enabled a Royal Charter to be granted by the King to the extensively titled 'Governor and Company of Adventurers of England trading into Hudson's Bay', confirming Britain's monopoly over the fur trade commitments in this area of the New World.

Supply and Demand

The First Nations had caught animals for food and clothing long before the traders 'invaded' and many of their techniques for preparing the animal pelts were initially used by the newcomers. Most animal trapping was carried out in the winter months, when the fur had grown to its thickest and best condition in order to protect the animal from the cold conditions. A combination of 'baited trap' – where food is left to coax the animal into a confined space, a 'deadfall trap' where a heavy weight would fall upon the creature and kill it, or a wire noose method known as a 'snare', were all used to capture the hunted animal. The trappers had to constantly check their baited traps to ensure that any creature held captive was not eaten by another animal before they had chance to acquire the much sought after pelts.

Originally, the women's role was to prepare the pelts. They not only had to pull out all the 'guard hair' – a rough first layer that protected the inner, soft, velvet-like hair beneath – but also had to ensure that the inner skin of the pelt was clean of animal meat and fat, washed and rubbed until smooth in texture.

By the time the fur trade had become a hugely profitable business, springtime would annually signal the shipping of the pelts to manufacturers in Europe. Here they would grade and sort the cargo using thick-haired furs to line hat interiors, which were varnished to make them waterproof, while the finer hairs were used on the exterior. Specific furs were fashioned into beautiful coats, garments and accessories ready for sale in the coming European winters, whereas the skins were put to good use in the manufacture of suitcases and gloves.

But the term 'trade' means to sell or exchange one item for another so while the furs found their way into Europe, numerous other items made the return journey to North America. The First Nations preferred goods to money, needing commodities that they were unable to make themselves and that would be useful in their everyday lives. Scissors, kettles and pots were popular, alongside buttons, blades, bayonets, tobacco, gunpowder and bullets. Surprisingly, one of the most popular items – made by the Hudson's Bay Company (HBC) – was the Point Blanket. Not only were they good for camouflage but the wool used to weave them helped keep their wearers warm in winter. To determine each blanket's size and weight it was graded by 'points' – hence the name 'point blanket'.

Scottish Connections

The severe winters and rough terrain of this part of the world required the Hudson's Bay Company to find employees who were prepared to live and work in these conditions. As a result the majority of its early workforce was made up of Orcadian men from the Scottish Hebridean isles of the Orkneys, or inhabitants of the Shetlands. This location made them ideal candidates for the harsh climate they would face in Canada and their boat-handling skills as fishermen gave them a distinct advantage. When the HBC ships called in at Stromness for supplies they also recruited a local workforce. Initially the men took five-year contracts but many extended them or settled permanently in Canada. In 1799, out of 530 men working for the HBC in North America, 416 were Orcadians. The Stromness Museum houses many unusual artefacts which connect the islands to the HBC and its fur trade; these include decorative items made by the Aboriginal First Nations and personal mementos brought home by the employees.

Canadian Bruce Watson is researching Orcadians who worked on the Pacific Slopes of Canada for the HBC prior to 1858. There is a huge amount of his information gathered to date at http://www.genuki.org.uk/big/sct/OKI/canada.html, where perhaps you might discover more about your own ancestor's involvement or even be able to contribute new findings.

The journey from Scotland to Canada took several weeks and upon arrival the men and supplies would be unloaded only to be replaced with furs to take back before the bleak winters set in; it was a quick and efficient turn around and made maximum use of each voyage.

The men would be taken to their new posts overland by dog-sled or by canoe and led by Aboriginal trackers. Over time relationships were formed between the men and Aboriginal women – despite the company trying to forbid it – and many men never returned to Scotland, choosing to create new lives in Canada.

By the 1830s new settlements were built with better living conditions and the company finally allowed its employees to bring their wives and families from Scotland, so the dynamics changed once again. Life for the European wives was difficult and many struggled to cope with the isolation and long periods of loneliness, but gradually social conditions improved and families made their own entertainment with outdoor activities, musical evenings and get-togethers with others within the community.

For the men, the work varied considerably depending upon their role. From clerks and fur traders down to the 'servants' who were skilled labourers and craftsmen, there was always a task to complete, from unloading cargo and dealing with correspondence to repairing buildings, tools and guns, or hunting and fishing for provisions. The Europeans and Aboriginals worked alongside each other at every outpost, calling upon their individual native skills to perform the numerous jobs required. This working relationship was essential to create a smooth and mutually beneficial operation of the fur trade industry.

Finding Out More

Perhaps you're lucky enough to have ancestors connected to this fascinating part of our trading history, if so the Hudson's Bay Company Archives (HBCA), located at Winnipeg, Manitoba in Canada, should be your first port of call. Their extensive website provides help on how to start your search 'from a distance' using their online resources, or the services of a professional researcher, and explains how best to get the most from your findings. The Keystone Archives Descriptive Database http://pam.minisisinc.com/pam/search.htm is an online catalogue that helps you to locate records in their holdings.

Tracing an Employee's Career

At the HBC Archives employee records are broken down into categories – commissioned officers (chief factors and traders), clerks and postmasters, and servants. Depending upon where the information lies, it is possible to trace a career using the variety of correspondence in their holdings from letters of application and recruitment embarkation, to contracts and abstracts of engagements. Other paperwork such as company ledgers, documentation and even wills could hold details of your

Images portrayed on postcards can help us visualise a specific location, event or, in this case, even an occupation or trade. Here, employees of the Hudson's Bay Company are shown delivering furs.

ancestor's involvement within the company, how long they were employed and in what capacity, their full length of service, and the wage they received.

A fabulous resource which can be searched and viewed online is the Biographical Sheets compiled by HBCA staff to record employees. Search the alphabetical listings at http://www.gov.mb.ca/chc/archives/hbca/biographical/index.html and you may be amazed at what you find. For example, a James Cowie – born in 1853 and died in 1913 – was apprenticed to the company between 1876 and 1879. He went on to have a long career as a clerk and accountant in the Lake Superior area before retiring and ending his days in British Columbia. The document also gives details of his uncle, who was an agent for the company back in Lerwick in the Shetlands, and of his brother who was employed by the HBC. These sheets of biographical information could open up a whole new line of enquiry for you if your ancestor is listed.

To learn more about Canada, its fur trade and those employed within it, visit: http://www2.canadiana.ca/hbc/intro_e.html, which covers everything from the new colonies formed to land claims and personal biographies. This 'Exploration' site lists primary and secondary sources which can be referred to for information, explains where the records are held and gives an overview of a country that was influenced dramatically by what was then, a sought after trade.

Although much of the information referring to the Hudson's Bay Company is centred on its own archive, there are alternative places to track down details that could help you find out more. Perhaps your ancestor settled, or eventually married into a local family within an area, resulting in you having deeper Canadian connections? Why not visit the Archives of Manitoba directly (http://www.gov.mb.ca/chc/archives/family_history/index.html)? There you will find advice on how to find private documentation on early Manitoba families, the area's settlement census records, Hudson's Bay Company engagement registers and personnel files, alongside wills and estate records which may mention your ancestors and their descendants. This link – http://www.gov.mb.ca/chc/archives/probate/index.html – provides a guide to searching the probate records of the region.

The Orkney Family History Society and the Orkney Library and Archive may be able to help you to trace the lives of the island's inhabitants before they left for work overseas. Contact them at:

Orkney Family History Society
Website: http://www.orkneyfhs.co.uk

Orkney Library & Archives
44 Junction Rd
Kirkwall
Orkney
KW15 1AG
Scotland, UK
Telephone: 01856 879207
http://www.orkneylibrary.org.uk

For an overview of the connection between the Scottish and the Aboriginals involved in the Fur Trade visit Material Histories created by the University of Aberdeen (http://www.abdn.ac.uk/materialhistories/index.php).

CHANGING TIMES

When the Seven Years' War broke out between Britain and France in 1754, it was not long before the troubles escalated into a worldwide conflict. Many of the great powers became involved in the dispute over their conflicting interests, which affected their territorial, colonial and trade empires. After the signing of the Treaty of Paris in 1763, the governing of Canada was passed to Britain and her interests in the colony only increased. France surrendered Canada to England and the territories were reorganised through royal proclamation under the leadership of King George III. The governor was appointed and English criminal law replaced the rules of its French predecessors. Despite some adjustments regarding religion and civil law, peace under British leadership was gradually established and Canada was seen by many as a land of opportunity.

DID YOU KNOW?

Newfoundland was England's first overseas colony claimed under the Royal Charter of Queen Elizabeth I, establishing connections with the country long before the 'British Empire' was formed. Such were its connections with British migrants that it became Canada's most English province with the 2006 Canadian census statistics recording that 57 per cent of its people could claim British ancestry, 43 per cent of them having at least one English parent. Even St George's Day – honouring England's patron saint – is declared a public holiday in the province.

Free passages and land grants were offered when the Land and Emigration Commission was set up in 1833, and such was the success of this promotion that thousands more migrants flooded into Canada throughout the nineteenth century.

At this time, England was becoming rapidly industrialised and as machines replaced agricultural labourers and tradesmen, many found themselves out of work and on the poverty line. Those from rural areas took the opportunity to escape the downturn in the agricultural economy back home, and after the long voyage, set up farmsteads and new lives on Canadian soil. Their occupational histories attracted them to New Brunswick, Prince Edward Island and Québec where they could use their skills to great success in the country's flourishing timber trade, while others took advantage of the good farmland on offer in Ontario and Nova Scotia. But it wasn't only farmers that were drawn to the better prospects on offer, and fishermen – especially from the south-west regions of England – headed to Newfoundland to put their traditional family trades to good use and work in the cod fishing industry.

QUARANTINE IN QUEBEC

For those immigrants heading to Canada, many had one last stop after their long journey before they reached the 'promised land'. Between 1832 and 1937, Grosse Ile – an island in the St Lawrence River, 30 miles upstream from Québec City – was home to a quarantine station and became the official gateway into Canada.

Québec City was founded by Samuel de Champlain – a French explorer – back in 1608, but it wasn't until 1759 that it became part of the British Province of Québec and later the main port of entry for immigrants to Canada, and for those who chose to make their onward journey into the United States.

With the majority of newcomers arriving from the British Isles and Europe, the outbreak of disease on the Continent was a worry to the North Americans who

An advert for Canadian Pacific.

wanted to avoid, or detain, similar outbreaks in their country. Initially, a small quarantine station was set up across the St Lawrence river from Québec City at Pointe Levis, but in 1832, when a cholera epidemic rapidly escalated in Europe, a larger facility needed to be found to cope with the potential threat of infection that the new immigrants could bring.

At just over 1½ miles long by half a mile wide, Grosse Ile was the perfect location, and once it had been requisitioned by the British Army from the farmer who worked the land, a new quarantine station was established and became a regulation stop for all vessels destined for Québec City. To ensure that the ships stopped for inspection, guns were positioned at regular lookout posts on the island with orders to fire upon those vessels that tried to ignore the procedure. Once this system was in place, the captains' soon complied.

At Grosse Ile doctors would examine each passenger and hospitalise those who were sick. Those who remained healthy – but had been in contact with the sick – were housed separately and their condition monitored to see if they developed any illness. The ships were disinfected, and in the early days, the procedures required the passengers to wash themselves and their belongings in the river. This was later replaced with a purpose-built shower stall which sprayed each user with disinfectant.

Quarantine lasted for up to fifteen days before the ships were allowed to continue with their journey. Although many of the sick recovered, there were hundreds that died. During the twelve months of 1847, the death rate was at its highest. The potato famine in Ireland sparked the mass migration of close to 95,000 Irish in search of a future in Canada, but many were already weak from lack of food before they had even begun the long journey north. Hundreds fell prey to typhus and diphtheria on board ship, so that by the time they reached Grosse Ile, the number of infected cases had reached epidemic proportions. As the head count of those in need of hospitalisation increased, the quarantine station could not cope and many had to remain on board ship. The sickness spread to those who tried to help, with doctors, nurses, island workers and clergymen succumbing to this devastating disease. Thousands of victims were treated and over 5,400 were buried in that one year alone. Previously, each deceased passenger had been buried separately, but the death toll was so great that a mass grave was required, stacked deep with coffins.

In 1909, the Ancient Order of Hibernians erected a 40-ft Celtic cross on the island as a memorial to all those who died during the fateful year of 1847–48, inscribed with the words:

> Children of the Gael died in the thousands on this island having fled from the laws of the foreign tyrants and an artificial famine in the years 1847–48. God's loyal blessing upon them. That this monument be a token to their name and honour from the Gaels of America. God save Ireland.

One positive aspect of the tragedy was that the layout of Grosse Ile was strictly reorganised in order to prevent any such disasters occurring in the future.

The western sector became reserved for those immigrants under observation while the eastern sector was turned into the hospital area and home to twelve large sheds known as 'lazarettos'. This division helped stop the spread of infection and contamination, with the belief at the time that the westerly winds would blow any germs out over the river and away from the healthy people.

There were three cemeteries on Grosse Ile – one aptly named the Irish Cemetery in recognition of the nationality of those buried within it, another created in the eastern sector and in use until the late 1860s, while a third burial place was created in the central sector, divided into separate areas for Protestant and Catholic burials.

By 1881 a brick building known as the Marine Hospital had been constructed, and from 1886 a system of disinfecting and fumigating the incoming ships was set in place. By 1893 a purpose-built disinfection area was completed to handle the passengers and their baggage, and when the shipping companies started to suggest that accommodation should be provided for passengers, a hotel was constructed for cabin passengers with a third-class, less expensive accommodation option erected in subsequent years. Surprisingly, electricity did not reach the island until 1902.

To man the facility the island also had its own village called Saint Luc de Grosse Ile, which was home to the people and employees who worked at the quarantine station. Along with medical staff there was a cook, laundress, interpreter to help translate between the foreign immigrants and the nationals, and even sailors to row the passengers back and forth between the island and their ships. To cater for the islanders themselves, there were teachers, bakers, policemen, postmasters, and clergymen to officiate in the Catholic and Protestant churches and presbytery.

The majority of immigrants to Québec City undoubtedly originated from the British Isles, and many met their fate at Grosse Iles. During the 105-year operation of the quarantine station, there were 7,553 burials of those who died in the hospitals, on the quarantine ships and among the island employees and soldiers, with over 31,000 of the 4 million-plus immigrants receiving hospitalisation.

In the end, it was world events that impacted on the future of Grosse Ile. The Great War of 1914–18 and the economic downturn resulting in the Great Depression of the 1930s reduced the number of immigrants on the move. Coupled with the developments in medical science and the massive improvements in transatlantic crossings, the requirement to monitor the spread of disease into North America was greatly reduced. Grosse Ile continued to monitor minor cases but finally closed its doors as a quarantine station in 1937.

IRISH INVESTIGATION

The Strokestown Park Irish National Famine Museum in Roscommon, Ireland, is a fabulous resource for the family historian, enabling one to appreciate the full extent of the devastation caused by the potato blight of the late 1840s. Strokestown was pivotal in the events surrounding what is now considered the greatest social disaster of nineteenth-century Europe, as it was home to Anglo-Irish landlord Major Denis Mahon. On 2 November 1847 he was assassinated by several local men who carried out the act in response to the removal of starving tenant farmers from the estate lands.

The *Cork Examiner* of 5 November 1847 reported the incident and explained that the people were displeased with his system for clearing from his lands of 'what he deemed the surplus population'. The newspaper also explained that Mahon 'chartered two vessels to America and freighted them with his evicted tenantry.' Unfortunately, the major's death did not halt the evictions and over 11,000 tenants were removed from the estate during the potato famine.

Home to numerous archival evidence, it has one of the most extensive nineteenth-century estate collections in Ireland, comprising of 40,000 documents that include maps and plans, property deeds, books and papers relating to the Irish famine between 1845 and 1851. There is an online learning zone, where you can examine examples of both primary and secondary resources prior to arranging a visit. For more information go to www.strokestownpark.ie.

Delve into the Databases

The majority of records relating to Grosse Ile are held by the Library and Archives of Canada and can be searched at www.collectionscanada.gc.ca. The database includes details of 33,026 immigrants who appear on the surviving records of the quarantine station between 1832 and 1937. You can also expect to find information on:

- The 135 people born on ships during the Atlantic crossing between 1837 and 1913.
- The deaths at sea, on the quarantine ships at Grosse Ile, or on the St Lawrence River, of 4,936 people between 1832 and 1922.
- The hospital registers relating to 12,196 people who were treated at Grosse Ile between 1832 and 1921.
- The baptisms of 554 people on Grosse Ile between 1832 and 1937.

- The forty-six marriages on the island between 1832 and 1937.
- The burials of 4,871 people on Grosse Ile between 1832 and 1937.
- Details of 8,339 people of various nationalities who were buried in the Grosse Ile cemeteries between 1832 and 1937 and whose names appear on the Grosse Ile and Irish Memorial erected in 1997 to commemorate those who died on the island.
- Details of the 1,431 tenants who, in 1847, were evicted by Major Mahon, landlord of the county of Roscommon, Ireland (see Box Out – Irish Investigation).

Recommended Reading

First published in 1848, the diary of Robert Whyte records his personal journey on the ship *Ajax*, which set sail from Dublin harbour on 30 May 1847. After a six-week crossing of the North Atlantic, it arrived in what promised to be a land of hope and optimism. His vivid recollections and descriptions allow us to imagine what it must have been like to flee the famine and its aftermath, and to arrive in Canada via the St Lawrence river and the Grosse Ile quarantine station. The book has since been reprinted under the name of *Robert Whyte's Irish Famine Ship Diary 1847: The Journey of an Irish Coffin Ship* by author Patrick Conroy, and is essential reading for anyone with Irish immigrant ancestors who made this long and difficult voyage during the mid-1800s.

IMMIGRATION ESSENTIALS

As with all ancestors who emigrated overseas during the nineteenth century, you should first check the British census to clarify in what decade they stopped appearing – this will help you whittle down the timeframe you need to research within. Once you've established that their destination was British North America, try cross-referencing your information by searching the Canadian census records. Luckily, these are readily available to search online. Each province created an individual census and maintained vital and immigration records separately, so it is worth considering exactly where your ancestor settled before you begin your research. The 1901 and 1911 returns also include a year of immigration for those not born within the country.

Canadian vital records contain extra information compared to their British counterparts. As well as giving the full names of the parents on a birth record, on many occasions you can also find the parents' dates of birth, birthplaces and occupations. The parents of both the bride and groom tend to be listed on each marriage record, while death records can provide a date and place of birth of the deceased and even details of their parents. These extra snippets are invaluable in your family history research and can help you to link back to another generation purely off the information given on one well researched certificate.

The Library and Archives of Canada, which can be searched online at www.collectionscanada.gc.ca, is an extensive site literally jam-packed with research aids, articles and advice to help you discover more about British forebears who settled on Canadian soil. By heading to their Immigration and Citizenship section, you can find out exactly how to access everything from passenger lists and passports to border entry records and 'Home Children' documentation. Many of the 'top tips' you will find here can help simplify the mass of information, making research that little bit easier.

For example, it explains that: 'passengers from mainland Europe usually sailed to Great Britain, where they boarded transatlantic ships at ports such as Liverpool, London and Glasgow'; that 'immigrants from Europe destined for Western Canada landed at ports on the East Coast, then continued their journey by train'; while 'some immigrants to Canada arrived at American ports'. It also points out that, for the period between 1865 and 1935, 'the Government of Canada did not keep records of people leaving the country; there are no passenger lists for departures from Canadian ports.' Vital snippets of information when trying to follow a migrant's trail!

OFFERS OF ASSISTANCE

Although the granting of free or assisted passages overseas was sometimes restricted to individuals with specific trades or occupations of interest to a particular country, parishes also had schemes in existence where they would pay the fare for paupers and their families to emigrate, realising that it would save them more money than having to financially support them within the community.

The Poor Law Union's correspondences are held at The National Archives at Kew, but also check the County Archives in the area where your ancestor lived for local Poor Law Union papers and Board of Guardian records. Each union was run by an elected Board of Guardians with day-to-day administration carried out by paid officials. Any minutes of meetings, decisions made and relief offered (either monetary or through the workhouse) would be written within these documents and could provide a clue as to whether your ancestor was eligible for free or assisted passage.

The acquisition of land at a reduced rate was also an option for some immigrants. Information regarding options offered to new settlers can be found at The National Archives of Canada (www.archivescanada.ca). Here you can expect to find original correspondence from those intending to settle in the country and their applications. The Land and Emigration Commission Papers list the names of emigrants who arrived between 1833 and 1894.

CASE STUDY: KNOWLEDGE AND KNOW HOW

Today we take the ease with which we can access information for granted, but in the nineteenth century, finding answers to questions required a lot more effort than putting your details into a search engine. As we have previously discovered, correspondence columns and letter pages were the ideal way of querying any subject, and for those intending to emigrate these were the perfect places to begin your enquiries. A response in a journal dated August 1892 gives advice, essential top tips and explains in what trades an individual can find employment when considering moving overseas:

> After consulting the circulars from the Emigrants' Information Office, Westminster, just issued [...] Spring is the best season for going to Canada. There will be, it is believed, a good demand for farm labourers, general labourers, navvies, and mechanics in the building trade. The Canadian government is now offering bonuses of $5–$10 a head to those who take up land (free grant) in the north-west or British Columbia. In New South Wales and Victoria, mechanics are not wanted, except in a few districts, and in the last named Colony the depression is great. The Queensland government withdrew their free passages last February, so now all excepting nominated and 'indented' emigrants have to pay full fare. This withdrawal is the most important fact that has happened during the last quarter. Western Australia offers free and reduced passages to certain classes, but the free passages are just suspended for farm labourers. There is some demand for navvies, miners, and labourers in the building trade. In Tasmania, the chief demand is for farm labourers, miners, and a few country blacksmiths. In New Zealand there is a demand for the same classes.

This information – taking up less than two column inches – provides fascinating reading. This may explain, or at least give clues, as to why your ancestor decided upon emigrating to a particular country, the job they found themselves in, and how they paid their passage. As you can see, situations, assisted passages and land-grant opportunities were changing all the time. Another miscellaneous published response explains the facilities available to women emigrants who arrived in Canada in the mid-1890s – could your ancestor have taken advantage of this service?

> A fully organised home is now inaugurated at Montréal by the Women's Protective Immigration Society, where women and young girls of good character are received on their arrival in Canada. Board and lodging is free for the first twenty-four hours. Suitable employment is found for them in the first instance, and a home of rest and protection is there afforded to them in the

> future, if required. This society is supported by the Dominion and Provincial Governments. You would be met on arrival of your steam vessel at Montréal by the Resident Secretary; and should you land at Quebec and continue by railroad to Montréal, you should send a notice of your proposed arrival, when you will be met at the station.

Further details as to travelling and rates of wages could be obtained by writing to an included address.

The Women's Protective Immigration Society was established in 1881 by a group of prominent Montréal women and worked on the principle that single female immigrants required protection against the physical and moral dangers they might encounter when travelling. By 1882, the first Canadian hostel – ran by women for women – opened for non-denominational single female immigrants, and by the 1890s played a major part in the British female settlement programme.

BORDER CONTROL

The close geographical links between Canada and the United States meant that immigration records between the two countries were perhaps not maintained to the best possible standards. With such an extensive border there were numerous occasions when people lived in Canada but worked in the United States, naturally passing back and forth across the border became regular occurrence. From the 1850s onwards, thousands of Canadians emigrated to the United States in search of employment, so although Canada may have been your ancestor's intended destination, economic circumstances may have led them to move again. You can search the database of Border Crossings between Canada and the US from 1895 to 1956 at http://search.ancestry.ca/search/db.aspx?dbid=1075.

MILITARY MESSAGES

Any information we require today can be accessed at the touch of a button, whether this be via our mobile phones and computers or by turning on the TV or radio. For our ancestors the main media source was the newspaper, which was avidly read and scoured for details about what was happening in other parts of the world. For those with families living and working overseas or involved in military activities in the latest global conflict, a fragment of information in a weekly newspaper seemed like a lifeline.

A note added to a diary – originally taken from the *Illustrated London News* of 25 March 1865 – shows us just how eagerly our predecessors sought up-to-the-minute facts to help them build a bigger picture of what was going on, and the scale of particular events and incidents:

> A Canadian journal states, information which it has reason to believe is correct, that the number of Canadians who have enlisted in the United States Army since the beginning of the war is 43,000. Of this number 35,000 were French-Canadians, no less than 14,000 of whom have died on the battlefield.

For Canadians with loved ones involved in the American Civil War, the statistics were pretty grim. Your ancestors may have emigrated from Britain earlier in the century and become Canadian citizens; their descendants could well have been caught up in this conflict. Use this information to ask yourself:

- Why did the diarist keep this particular cutting? Did they have a son, father, husband or brother who had signed up?
- Can you research the close relatives of the diarist to see if they were engaged in military service during the period of the American Civil War between 1861 and 1865?

There are a number of websites which can help you track down those Canadians who played their part. The Canadian Military Heritage Project can be found at http://www.rootsweb.ancestry.com/~canmil, while the website www.pastvoices.com/usa provides an extensive collection of letters from individuals who enlisted in the civil war and other conflicts. One, penned by a William Brown in November 1863, tells of the terrible difficulties and emotions that these men faced:

> I will tell you of an instance which happened three or four days ago. Two men were shot to death for desertion. There was an old man and the young man. They both followed the conference to the place of their executions. They were lifted off the wagon and were placed on their coffins. The sentence was read to them and that they were blindfolded. The general with a flag would signal to

> them when to shoot, for there was no command given by the mouth. A squad of about 20 men fired on them. They both fell, one rolling off his coffin, the other laying crossways on the coffin. It was indeed the hardest sight I ever saw. The screaming of the wounded on the field of battle was not so hard. Neither of them appeared to be alarmed in the least – the young man, especially.

Imagine the thoughts going through this soldier's head, and that of the relative to whom the letter was addressed back home.

MIGRATIONAL MISDEMEANOURS

Instead of using child migration as a last resort in times of war or conflict, it's a sad fact that Britain is the only country in the world where removing children from their families to ship them thousands of miles to a new home has been a major part of their care strategy. Understanding child resettlement schemes may form the basis of your family research if your ancestors were affected.

Child migration from Britain first began in 1618 when 100 children from London were sent to Richmond in Virginia to supply labour to plantation owners. The practice continued in earnest from the 1800s and it was only after the Second World War that numbers started to decline.

During the mid-Victorian era, Britain was experiencing a difficult period in its history as people flooded to the cities from rural areas and Ireland in search of work. The economy began to buckle under the strain as too many people fought for too few jobs, and the unemployment problem soon began to have a knock on effect. Housing and food was scarce and many families lived in squalid conditions of overcrowded tenements and courtyards where diseases like cholera, tuberculosis and smallpox were rife. The situation prompted some parents to abandon their offspring, while others forced their youngsters into a life of crime in order to survive. Increasing numbers of children lived on the streets and gradually officials started to think of a way to protect them from the hardships that were presenting themselves on a daily basis. Poor Law Unions were already sending some adults overseas as a way of populating the new colonies, so it wasn't long before the idea was extended to children as a way of improving their chances in life.

Despite the work of pioneers such as Annie MacPherson (who established her first home in the East End of London in 1867) and Leonard Shaw (who created children's homes in the Manchester area), it soon became a case of supply exceeding demand, and there was just not enough space to house all those in need: the idea of relocation quickly became a serious option.

Church and philanthropic agencies believed that they were offering these children a new start in life filled with opportunities that they wouldn't have access to at home, but this was not always the case. Many youngsters were taken – sometimes without their parents' knowledge or consent – and an uncertain future lay ahead of them.

Abandoned and Alone

Over 130,000 children between the ages of 3 and 14 were sent to the countries of Canada, New Zealand, Rhodesia (now Zimbabwe) and Australia, chosen by specialist agencies (such as the Fairing Society as well as the Salvation Army, the Catholic, Methodist and Church of England) with the purpose of populating the empire with what amounted to 'British stock'. Like his contemporaries, Dr Thomas Barnardo founded a series of successful children's homes but was responsible for the largest numbers of migrants sent to Canada from all over Britain.

How these youngsters were perceived depended on where they were placed. In Canada, most were housed with farmers and so were thought of as cheap agricultural labour, carrying out tasks without training, preparation, or little supervision. In Rhodesia, their arrival was thought to be a way of preserving the 'elite' white race, while in Australia they would boost a diminished post-war population.

Despite the process of child migration being thought of as a way to give underprivileged youngsters a better start in life, for many their future was not always a happy one. The system was plagued by scandals, with reports of physical and sexual abuse, child labour and lack of education. The promise of a 'land of milk and honey' where they would lead fantastic lives and want for nothing was often a myth and a world away from reality. Many were sent to educational institutions which were impersonal and overcrowded, while others were directly put to work as labourers. Throughout this living nightmare, they must have wondered what they had done wrong to deserve this treatment and be completely rejected by their families.

Their past in Britain had been completely erased, as they left without full birth certificates for identification, passports, or information about their real family. Not content on separating these children from their parents, those with brothers and sisters were often separated by gender at the dockside on arrival and sent to different parts of the country with little hope of making contact with their siblings again. The pain and emotional trauma this must have caused for these 'lost souls' would have been unbearable and truly heartbreaking for all those affected.

It has to be said that not all children suffered the same fate and some migrants are known to have made positive comments recalling happy memories of their relocation overseas. They benefited greatly by the resettlement, later serving in the Canadian and British forces during both world wars and developing contented and successful adult lives which may not have been achieved had they remained in the urban slums of their birth.

THE ILLUSTRATED LONDON NEWS, Aug. 10, 1907. [illegible]

COUNTING HIS FLOCK.

SKETCH BY S. BEGG, OUR SPECIAL ARTIST ON BOARD THE "EMPRESS OF BRITAIN."

THE CANADIAN PRIME MINISTER'S RETURN TO CANADA: SIR WILFRID LAURIER WATCHING THE EMIGRANTS ON BOARD THE CANADIAN-PACIFIC ROYAL MAIL-STEAMER "EMPRESS OF BRITAIN."

Sir Wilfrid Laurier returned to Canada on board the "Empress of Britain," one of the finest mail-steamers of the Canadian-Pacific Railway Company. The vessel conveyed a very large party of emigrants; and our Special Artist, who sailed on the same vessel, has sketched the Prime Minister of the Dominion watching, with the deepest interest, the people who were on their way to seek their fortune in the country of the future.

Newspapers are ideal for providing us with images of global events. In 1907, the Canadian prime minister observes the new arrival of immigrants on-board the *Empress of Britain*. Did your ancestor choose Canada as the place to start a new life?

Canadian Connections

Over a fifty-year period between 1870 and 1920, 80,000 children are believed to have been evacuated via government schemes to Canada. In the majority of cases those chosen were the neediest from the poorer classes, orphans housed in institutions and workhouses, and even those who lived on the streets, in the belief that *they* would benefit most from resettlement overseas.

If your ancestor was sent to Canada, why not take a look at some of the data extracted from the Government of Canada Sessional Papers, Passenger Lists and Government Immigration Reports compiled on Marjorie Kohli's website at http://retirees.uwaterloo.ca/~marj/genealogy/homeadd.html. There are links to helpful databases and a vast array of online content referring to the institutions, homes and agencies that were involved in the migration procedures. The British Isles Family History Society of Greater Ottawa (www.bifhsgo.ca) are locating and indexing the names of these Home Children found in different records held by the Library and Archives of Canada www.collectionscanada.gc.ca/index-e.html. The Society's database is searchable online and there are thousands of references to Home Children records which may hold the key to your ancestor's past. Names of children were sent to Canada from England between 1886 and 1916 by Boards of Guardians. These Guardians were locally elected administrators of Poor Relief for each Union – or group of parishes – which administered the help and built workhouses in each area. This database is also searchable for those children who were sent overseas from the workhouse.

Consider tracking down the outbound voyages from Britain between 1890 and 1960 available for viewing at www.findmypast.co.uk or visit www.ancestry.ca for indexed Canadian passenger lists.

Australian Administration

In order to keep all child migration under one heading, I have included Australia's information in this section.

The second biggest wave of migration took place after the Second World War when up to 4,000 children were sent to Australia. Unfortunately, little had been learnt from previous forced migrations and stories later began to emerge of hardships and abuse taking place.

The effects of the war had made Australians realise that they needed to strengthen their defences against the threat of invasion if there was ever to be another conflict. The way to achieve this was to encourage families to have more children and to accept child immigrants from overseas – who had a long, working adult life ahead of them – via a scheme with the slogan 'Populate or Perish'. This was not only beneficial to the Australians but also to the British, who were relieved of the burden of looking after their poor, destitute or orphaned children as they had little in the way of finance available in the post-war economy.

At the time, both the Australian and British governments had welcomed the scheme and encouraged outside organisations with the promise of grants and subsidies to get involved in the resettlement procedures. It must be said that many of these organisations were formed with good intent and the benevolent belief that this was the best option to provide help. The Fairbridge Society had started off this way, arranging training in 'farm schools' in order to provide Australia with its next generation of agricultural workers and a bright future for the children, but sadly, by the 1950s their standards and optimistic vision was a long way from their original plan.

Similarly, the Catholic order known as the Christian Brothers managed four Western Australian orphanages and had a long history in child migration, but a track record soon began to emerge of cruelty and abuse. Towards the end of the twentieth century, the Christian Brothers apologised for the devastating traumas caused in their homes and funded travel costs for former migrants to make family reunions, but for many this may well have been a case of 'too little, too late'.

In later years, as the children grew into adulthood, numerous other claims of mistreatment began to emerge and public enquiries were made. In a parliamentary report produced in 1998 entitled 'The Welfare of British Child Migrants', it was found that some children – many of these from Catholic agencies – had been told that they were orphans and that there was nothing left in Britain for them when, in fact, one or both parents were still alive. Upon arrival in Australia, only the shortened version of their birth certificates was kept, which omitted the names of their parents and all ties were cut with any remaining members of their families. The report stated that these children were then placed in 'inadequately supervised, monitored and inspected' institutions without 'any real nurturing or encouragement' and found both the Australian and British governments to blame.

With time running out for those with surviving parents who would be in extremely old age, help was put in place to make as many reunions as possible. This was thanks to the Child Migrants Trust (established in 1987), which had put pressure on the government to provide funding and also counselling.

By 1999 the Christian Brothers, Sisters of Mercy and Poor Sisters of Nazareth set up a database known as the Personal History Index (PHIND), detailing the location of records held in Australia for former child migrants to Catholic Homes between 1938 and 1965. The first group came from Britain in 1938 with the last arriving from Malta in 1965. To find out more, visit http://www.cberss.org/archive/phind.asp.htm.

Help is now at hand to ensure that these children who were once abandoned and alone are not forgotten, that their stories and recollections are heard, and that all of those who wish to be reunited with any remaining family get all the assistance they need.

Where Can I Find Out More?

You too may have found gaps in your own family tree with missing relatives seemingly untraceable. Perhaps it's worth considering that they may have been part of Britain's mass child migration exodus? Others may already know that their ancestor (or living relative) was chosen for the scheme and want to discover more. Below is a list of useful contacts to help you with your quest.

As always, start with what you know, work backwards and confirm your facts. When making contact with individuals directly connected to this sensitive area of our history, always tread with caution and consider that feelings may be very raw. Tact and diplomacy are needed, and also the acceptance that not everyone will want to talk about this part of their past.

Sadly, there is also another line of enquiry that you must make if you are having difficulty finding your 'home child' ancestor listed in any official records within their new country. The voyages overseas were notorious for overcrowding and below deck had very little in the way of adequate ventilation. As a result, diseases spread rapidly and many migrants died. To discount this theory – or to confirm your suspicions – check with The National Archives, which houses records of those passengers who died at sea between 1854 and 1972, or search online at www.findmypast.com. Those offering assistance and further information include:

Action for Children
Access to Records Service
12a Hackford Walk
Hackford Road
Stockwell
London
SW9 0QT
Tel: 07921 404195
Website: http://www.actionforchildren.org.uk/our-services/adoption-fostering-and-children-in-care/records-and-support/former-child-migrants

Child Migrants Trust
124 Musters Road
West Bridgford
Nottingham
NG2 7PL
Tel: (0115) 982 2811
Email: www.childmigrantstrust.com

Child Migrants Trust Inc.
169 Riversdale Road
Hawthorn
Melbourne
Victoria 3122
Tel: (03) 9347 7403
Email: www.childmigrantstrust.com

Banardos
Visit their website and fill in a contact form to find out more: www.barnardos.org.uk/who_we_are/history/child_migration
Tel: 0208 498 7536

The International Association of Former Child Migrants and their Families
P.O. Box 1319
Fitzroy North VIC 3068
Australia

CLICK FOR CLUES

The website www.goldonian.org provides a useful timeline of child migrational history from 1607 to 1998. An informative site detailing the plight of those youngsters shipped to Canada – known as the British Home Children – can be found at http://freepages.genealogy.rootsweb.ancestry.com/~britishhomechildren. Virtually every question you've wanted to ask about this area of migration is answered here along with a searchable online database with over 57,000 records.

6

FRANCE

'If you reject the food, ignore the customs, fear the religion
and avoid the people, you might better stay at home.'
James Michener

France has a rich and intriguing past. The Hundred Years' War, the Napoleonic Wars, and the reign of its infamous kings and queens are just some of the events and people that have shaped the country into what it is today. For this chapter I have chosen two major incidents that had the greatest impact on the migration of its citizens and, for some of us, resulted in the Anglo-French connection in our ancestry.

HUGUENOT HISTORY

The term *Huguenot* is alleged to be the Gallicised version of a combined Flemish and German word. It became the 'badge' used to describe those whose faith in the Protestant religion brought them into conflict with the King of France and the Catholic Church, who looked upon their beliefs as an act of heresy.

In the mid-sixteenth century, Huguenots in France came from all walks of life, choosing to be guided by the Bible rather than the edicts of the Pope. Their Protestant beliefs meant they were outnumbered by those of the Catholic faith by at least eight to one, so trouble between them was never very far away.

In 1562, a massacre at Vassy in Normandy led to the death of over 160 Huguenots, the violence escalating to devastating proportions a decade later with the infamous St Bartholomew's Day Massacre, when 100,000 people were killed in just a matter of a few weeks. The Huguenots' continued persecution led to survivors seeking refuge overseas with an initial wave of immigrants fleeing to England. The Edicts of Nantes was issued when King Henry converted to Catholicism, giving protection to both Catholics and Protestants alike … but the reprieve was shortlived.

By 1627 Louis XIII and his ally Cardinal Richelieu ordered a siege at the Huguenot city of La Rochelle and the troubles surfaced once again. In all, 80 per cent of its population died over the following year, many from the aftermath of famine and disease. When Louis XIV came to the throne in 1661 he revoked the Edict of Nantes, making Protestantism illegal, starting another period of upheaval and renewed persecution. At this point, approximately half a million Huguenots had already fled France from fear.

For many Huguenots, England and Ireland had always been a place of sanctuary – even more so after 1687, when Catholic monarch James II issued a Declaration of Indulgence, allowing the freedom of religion whatever the denomination. With France literally on our doorstep, it is not surprising that the majority of them took refuge in Britain, greatly increasing the population and resulting in later claims that a large percentage of Britons have Huguenot blood.

Early immigrants headed to the London areas of Spitalfields and Soho, seeking employment in trades in which they excelled, such as hat and felt making, gold and silversmithing, silk weaving and cabinet making, bringing with them new techniques and design styles influenced by their French roots. At first, they were welcomed wherever they settled within the country. They tended to live and work in Huguenot-based communities, utilising their skills in weaving, dying, bookbinding, jewellery making and glassblowing, but all was not plain sailing and some resented the newcomers and their craftsmanship, seeing them as competition in the work market.

But Britain was not the only country where Huguenots found safety, and many were attracted to other areas of Europe, with the Netherlands, Germany and Denmark seeing a swell in the number of immigrants arriving. Priscilla Mullins was one of the original 1620 Mayflower Pilgrims and numerous others after her saw America as a new place that they could call home. Settlements appeared in Virginia, Pennsylvania and South Carolina. In the city of New York, one of its oldest streets – New Paltz – was founded in 1678 by twelve French-speaking families. Today, seven unique restored stone houses, a stone church (dating from 1717) and burial ground remain, all in their original Huguenot village setting, making this area a national historic landmark district. Visit the website www.huguenotstreet.org to find out more. Note – along with our own British ties, it is even said that one-third of America's presidents have a Huguenot link within their ancestry.

It cannot be denied that their artisan skills and cultural traditions had a direct effect on the countries in which Huguenots settled. In South Africa, for example, they found it easy to blend in with the already Protestant congregations; they influenced the Dutch language with their own French dialect to create Afrikaans, and helped establish the region's winemaking industry, bringing tips and techniques with them from France.

WALLOONS

When researching Huguenot ancestry you may come across the term 'Walloon'. Wallonia is a French-speaking area of southern Belgium – traditionally Protestant – whose refugees came to England in the late 1500s to escape the Catholic Inquisition. Once arrived, they naturally settled in existing Huguenot communities, making homes in the Kentish and Canterbury regions and establishing weaving businesses that not only helped them to earn a living, but also provided employment for the local women. Gradually, the records of the Huguenots and the Belgian Wallonia became intermixed.

Due to the large settlement of Walloons around Canterbury, it is well worth searching the online catalogue to the collections of the Canterbury Cathedral Archives at http://archives.canterbury-cathedral.org/Default.aspx. Here you will find links to the early Walloon congregation and quarter session papers, which may help you establish a settler's place of origin.

Huguenot Research

Following the trail of French Protestant ancestors can be a daunting task, but not impossible. Initially, look for unusual names, name changes, or references to foreign places of birth on birth certificates and censuses back to the start of civil registration in 1837, before turning your focus to parish records and Bishops' Transcripts. Establish where your ancestors settled – they would often try to recreate their own communities, attempting to fit in with the locals while continuing to uphold their own traditions and customs, as well as finding the means to support themselves. Despite their religious persecution they still upheld their faith. The French Protestant Church of London (www.egliseprotestantelondres.org.uk) was once a place of worship for early settlers, while churchyards across this region became the final resting place for those who adopted this country as their own.

It is said that most people with London ancestry will eventually discover a Huguenot ancestor. Founded in 1885 and renamed a year later, The Huguenot Society of Great Britain and Ireland is the ideal place to advance your search. All the registers that are known to exist in England and Ireland have been published by the Society; consequently, the Huguenot Library is the largest dedicated collection of related documents in the country. Their registers of French Protestant communities in England and Ireland give details of Huguenot settlers in London, Norwich, Canterbury and Dublin. By becoming a member you will gain free access to their extensive archives as well as to journals devoted to Huguenot genealogy, and the opportunity to attend informative meetings held throughout the year. Visit their website at www.huguenot-society.org.uk.

The National Huguenot Society (www.huguenot.netnation.com/general) provides more information on the history of these refugees and offers useful advice on how to track those who settled in other countries besides Britain.

As always, The National Archives (www.nationalarchives.gov.uk) may prove fruitful with naturalisation records available for viewing online, as well as records of baptisms and marriages from Huguenot churches, which will help establish a person's place of origin. One of the most important collections released in 2013 by www.thegenealogist.co.uk included more than 150,000 naturalisation and denization records created between 1609 and 1960. At the time of release, 5,000 Huguenot records were also added with even more expected to be incorporated into this data set in the future.

With the aid of a search engine you can find Huguenot Museums, not only in France, but in various locations around the world. The Huguenot Museum in Franschhoek, South Africa (http://www.hugenoot.org.za/huge3.htm) documents the lives of those who arrived at the Cape of Good Hope in the late seventeenth and early eighteenth centuries, while the Hugenottenmuseum in Berlin focuses on the emergence of the French congregation in the German capital.

The main focus of French immigrant life in London can be found both at the Huguenots of Spitalfields website (www.huguenotsofspitalfields.org) with its numerous links to related places of interest within the capital, and at www.19princeletstreet.org.uk – a rare, Huguenot silk weaver's house now run by a small charity who aim to preserve the building as a permanent exhibition to 'tell the stories of the many diverse peoples and cultures who created our society'. Built in 1719 and occupied by the Ogier family after they had escaped persecution in France, the attic windows of Princelet Street were altered to allow in more light to enable the weavers to work.

THE REVOLUTION

The French Revolution of 1789–1799 was one of the most turbulent times in the country's history. The need for social and cultural change around the globe kick started the demand for democracy across the British Empire and resulted in a bloody and violent revolt.

On 14 July 1789, when the people of Paris stormed the Bastille – thought to be the symbol of a corrupt monarchy – little did anyone realise the full impact their actions would have. The revolutionists were fighting for elected assemblies, and as a result they bought about the end of feudalism and serfdom in France. The Declaration of the Rights of Man was later issued, which recognised that all men are born and remain free and equal in rights, and a new constitution was adopted. Those who

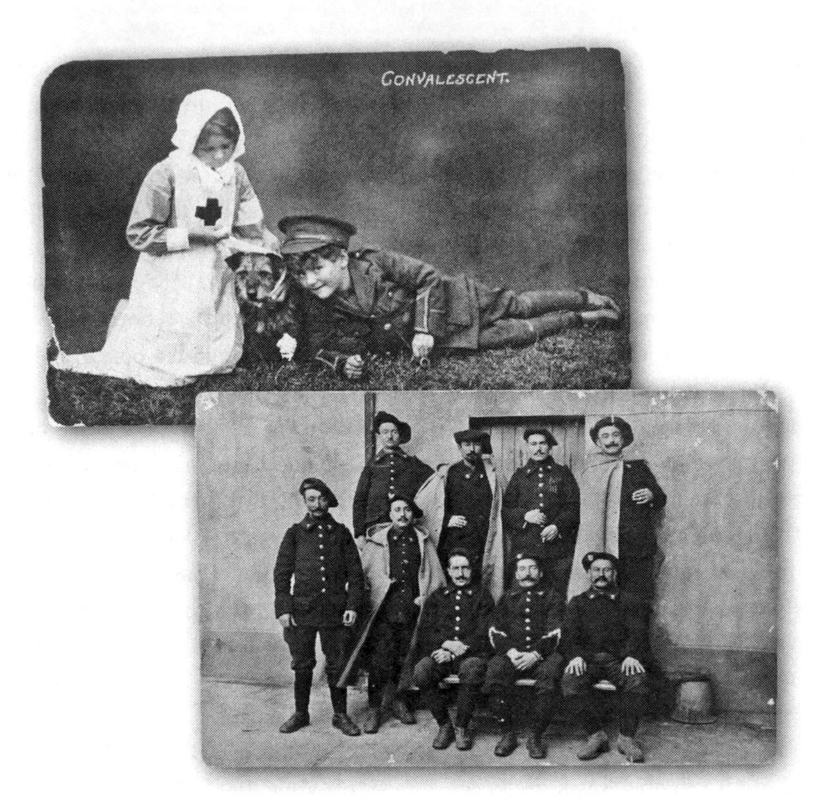

First World War postcards depicting military personnel.

were enemies of the revolution were spared no sympathy and were dealt with swiftly, finding they had their own personal appointment with Madame Guillotine. Between 20,000 and 40,000 people were executed between 1793 and 1794 alone.

Queen Charlotte – the third great-grandmother of our own present Queen – had a close acquaintance with the French Queen Marie Antoinette and prepared apartments so that her friend could take refuge in Britain during the troubled times. But even Charlotte realised the severity of the situation when King Louis XVI was executed in January 1793, with his wife Marie Antoinette meeting the same fate in October of the same year.

Revealing Records

In 2009 www.ancestry.com released a huge collection of over 13,000 records detailing the executions of people from all walks of life during the period 1792–96 and known as the 'Reign of Terror'. The individuals included within these documents show that no one was safe from the guillotine, and money, wealth, social standing and intellect could not save you if you were considered an enemy of the revolution. The youngest victim was just 14 years of age; the oldest were two women of 92. Thirty-seven nuns met this gruesome end along with an unbelievable 247 people on Christmas Day of 1793. Even the most influential figure of the revolution and the father of the 'Reign of Terror' – Maximilien Robespierre – met his end on the scaffold and perished by the guillotine.

These fascinating details have been indexed from a six-volume work created by French journalist and newspaper publisher Louis Marie Prudhomme, who in 1796 created the aptly named *Dictionary of Individuals Condemned to Die During the Revolution*. A further compilation, entitled *The French Deaths by Guillotine, 1792 to 1796* (searchable online at http://search.ancestry.co.uk/search/db.aspx?dbid=1409) includes the name, age, occupation, place of residence and date of execution of each victim and also includes those condemned to death by firing squad, hanging and drowning. For anyone with connections to this bloody period in history, this unique set of records could help prove your link to an aristocrat who died in the most gruesome of circumstances, or a revolutionary who was prepared to meet his maker for the cause he believed in.

Keeping the Peace

It wasn't long before the repercussions were felt across the Channel in Britain. Naturally, our own royal family were worried that if the French revolutionists could try, convict and execute their monarchs and aristocrats in such a brutal way, then the same thing was possible on British soil. In an attempt to quell unrest and keep his own nation happy, King George took the preventative measure of lowering taxes to ease the burden on his own people.

After the execution of King Louis XVI of France, Prime Minister William Pitt the Younger knew it was time to act; concerned with the impact and spread of social unrest he decided to introduce a legislation to record the arrival of immigrants into the UK.

During this period, 32,000 French citizens – mainly aristocracy and clergy, whose ultimate fate would have been death if they had remained in their homeland – fled to England to seek refuge and avoid the revolution. As a direct result, it is thought that over 6 million Britons have French ancestors in their family trees.

Revolution Research

The Bouillon Papers are a collection of letters, documents and other correspondence relating to the émigrés who began fleeing from France from 1789. These papers were named after Philippe d'Auvergne, Prince de Bouillon, who served as a naval officer defending the Channel Islands while gathering information which would help the French royalist refugees to escape the tyranny that was sweeping their nation. He was supported by the British government which provided finance to help those who intended to emigrate to Britain.

This fascinating resource can be found at The National Archives and dates from 1794 to 1814. If you believe your ancestor may have escaped from France at this time, it is also worth consulting the archive which refers to the French Refugees Relief Committee set up in 1792. This collection not only includes the names of those involved, but also letters, accounts and memorials from its inception to 1823.

CHANGING PLACES

But it was not only the French who migrated to Britain, there were numerous British citizens who made the trip across the Channel for a fresh start on the Continent.

During the Napoleonic Wars, Napoleon's inability to defeat Britain led to his attempt to cut us off from the rest of Europe and limit our trade. When Napoleon was eventually imprisoned, many British workmen took the opportunity to travel to France in search of employment.

At this time, France's textile and iron industries were desperate for machinery and employees who knew how to work them, so it wasn't long before British immigrants found well-paid jobs that could support them and their families. Lace makers from Nottinghamshire, Derbyshire and the East Midlands were just some of those who relocated to factories in Calais.

Until 1824, British law did not allow the export of machinery so initially it was down to the workers to smuggle items with them until they could build their own in situ. Back home in Britain, these workers were not always looked upon kindly and in some areas even considered traitors for their migration. The sad fact was that in France's textile industry, whole families could be offered employment, so they had little choice but to leave their homeland and go where the money was.

Although many eventually returned to Britain, there were those who settled and became French citizens, but the turning point came in 1848 when they became caught up in another revolt. Known as the February Revolution and sparked by the economic depression, banks closed, work stopped and food was hard to find. Some French nationals blamed the British immigrants for their situation, forcing the workers to flee back to Britain, despite living for many years on the Continent and bearing their children on French soil.

GETTING YOUR BEARINGS

To understand French record keeping it is important to familiarise yourself with the country's regional administration system. *Before* the French Revolution, France was divided into provinces, which we now refer to as regions. *During* the Revolution, the government reorganised the territorial divisions into *départements*, of which the

Paper ephemera made the ideal keepsakes to collect from places of interest, such as this religious memorabilia collected from a trip to Lourdes or this 1898 French theatre ticket from the Orchestra.

majority are within the French borders, while the others are in overseas territories such as Guadeloupe, Martinique and Mayotte. Each *département* has its own archive where genealogical records are kept separate from those of the national government. You may also find similar records kept at local town halls known as *Mairies.* The three largest cities in France – Paris, Lyon and Marseille – are also divided into areas known as *arrondissements*, with each of these having their own town hall and archive, making it extremely important to first confirm exactly where your ancestor lived to avoid wasting time with unnecessary research.

Finding Out More

From the seventeenth century to the French Revolution, information known as 'BMS' – *baptêmes* (baptisms), *mariages* (marriages) and *sépultres* (burials) – were entered by the parish priest into registers. These are stored in the town where the event occurred with a copy sent to the departmental archives.

Decennial tables are ten-year alphabetical indexes to births, marriages and deaths starting from 1793, which have been registered by the Mairie. They provide a date on which the event was registered, although this is not necessarily the same date that the event took place.

Civil registration began in 1792. Depending upon the time period, some birth records also included the age of the parents, the father's occupation and the birthplace of the parents.

Before a couple could wed in church, marriages had to be performed by civil authorities. Although the church ceremonies usually took place in the town where the bride resided, civil registrations could take place in any locality. Interestingly, these registers often gave the names of any children born before the marriage, making this extremely useful when trying to determine parentage or previous relationships.

Death records not only included the deceased's name, date and place of death, but also their age and birthplace, and the names of their parents. In later years, these records included the name of the spouse and whether they were still alive.

GLOSSARY OF TERMS

When deciphering French civil registration records, the following translations may prove useful:

Baptism	*baptême*
Birth	*naissance*
Burial	*sépulture, enterrement*
Civil registry	*registres de l'état civil*
Death	*décès, mort*
Name, given	*prénom, nom de baptême*
Parish	*paroisse*
Year	*an, année*
Mother	*mère*
Father	*père*

N° 1588 (31e année) 26 novembre 1925

Le Noël

Abonnements
LE NOEL
France et Col. 28 fr.
Belgique 29 f 50
Etranger fr.

LE NOEL - LA MAISON
France et Col. 40 fr.
Belgique 42 fr.
Etranger fr.

Abonn. Combinés
LE NOEL
avec L'ÉTOILE NOËLISTE
France et Col. 48 fr.
Belgique 50 f 50
Etranger fr.

LE NOEL - LA MAISON
avec L'ÉTOILE NOËLISTE
France et Col. 60 fr.
Belgique 63 fr.
Etranger fr.

• REVUE HEBDOMADAIRE ILLUSTRÉE •

5, rue Bayard. PARIS. Chèque postal, 1668, Paris

Cliché Bonne Presse.

LES PIFFERARI — L'HOMMAGE A LA MADONE
(Tableau de MARY BENNER, au Salon de 1925.)

Creating a scrapbook was a popular pastime for many Victorians, providing a method of preserving precious souvenirs for future generations.

Prior to the introduction of French Civil Registration, the only means of recording births, marriages and deaths was in the parish records. As the state religion was Roman Catholic until 1787, these would be Catholic parish records. Those that have survived can usually be found in the departmental archives, or in some smaller parishes, at the church in which the registers were created. Those produced after 1793 are likely to be held in the parish, with a copy also in the Diocesan archives.

Remember, you can start your search online and access advice regarding civil registry at www.acte-etat-civil.fr/DemandeActe/Accueil.do. The site automatically translates into English and is concise and easy to follow.

Although the first census was taken in 1801 (under Napoleon's rule), from 1831 they were taken every five years; the exception being the census of 1871 (which was recorded in 1872), and those of 1916 and 1941 (abandoned altogether due to the world wars). As in Britain, France does have some examples of earlier census records but this would require you to investigate in your chosen area to establish whether those pertaining to your forebears still exist.

These records have not been indexed so it can be a little difficult to locate a surname, but the results are worth the effort, providing the name of residents at an address, their age, birthplace, occupation and nationality. If an individual resided in a particular location for a number of years, or set up home in a small village or community rather than a larger town or city, you may have more success. It is also worth checking to see if a specific census has been made available in digital format online. For an overview of searchable French databases, follow the extensive list of links at http://genealogy.about.com/od/france/tp/France-Genealogy-Records-Online.htm.

Anne Morddel has been writing a blog for a number of years, aiming to help those who wish to do their own genealogical research in France. From heraldry to Huguenots, her fabulous site is in English and is packed with useful information, fascinating facts and hints and tips on how to get the most from the information you discover (http://www.french-genealogy.typepad.com).

A FORCE TO BE RECKONED WITH

Although we often use military records to follow the trail of our male ancestors' lives, it should be noted that the equivalent documents in France are kept confidential for 120 years from the date of the soldier's birth. This can make genealogical research extremely difficult but you should contact the archivists at the Army and Navy Historical Services in Vincennes (http://en.chateau-vincennes.fr/index.php) to see what help they can provide. Remember, men were required to register for military service and the conscription records are usually held within the local departmental archives. The French have been involved in many conflicts from the Thirty Years' War to the Franco-Prussian War, as well as those within living memory, so it is essential to seek all possible assistance to acquire information if you wish to chart a foreign military career. During the wars, émigré units were formed from refugees from countries occupied by France, along with prisoners of war from the French armies; this can add even more fascinating complications to the mix if you discover that a forebear who served in a French unit actually originated from another country on the Continent!

Top Tip – you may not have a photograph of your ancestor in military attire, but period postcards were often produced depicting men in their uniforms. These were extremely popular during the First World War.

7

SOUTH AFRICA

'A journey of a thousand miles must begin with a single step.'
Lao Tzu

From its first permanent European settlement by the Dutch in 1652, South Africa's indigenous people have lived side-by-side with a whole host of refugees and immigrants who have made their home at the Cape. This diverse cultural mix has resulted in the country having a rich, yet turbulent history.

Before becoming a union in 1910, only two nations had governed the colony – the Dutch and the British. Since Britain's initial occupation of the Cape in 1795, its links have meant that many British people continue to have ancestral ties to South Africa.

THE 1820 SETTLERS

In 1819 the British government introduced the Cape Emigration Scheme. The aim was to install British families who were prepared to settle in the eastern frontier regions of the Cape Colony and act as a deterrent to the Xhosa tribes, who were attempting to cross the colonial boundary.

Naturally there were hazards involved for the families agreeing to take part but the scheme was well timed. Britain was in its post-Napoleonic-War period and unemployment was high. People were looking for new opportunities and ways of making money, so the offer of free passage and 100 acres in South Africa was an attractive proposition despite the dangers. The possibility of prosperity overseas was extremely appealing and in 1820, one thousand families left the shores of Britain for good, heading for the Eastern Cape. Their arrival was to leave a lasting legacy on South Africa's history.

Consisting of approximately 4,000 individuals arriving on twenty-one ships between 6 April and the end of June 1820, the immigrants were divided into approximately sixty individually led parties. They settled at Albany, expecting to have land of fertile soil on which to cultivate their crops and rear their cattle, but they were bitterly disappointed when their crops failed. Some persevered, adjusting to the new environments, while others tried to seek alternative employment in the growing townships.

Details of 'Permissions Granted to British Settlers' between 1820 and 1824 can be found at the Cape Town Archives Repository (www.southafricanfamilyhistory.com/the-western-cape-provincial-archives-and-records-service), along with a list of the immigrants who arrived in that first year. Try to seek out *The Settlers Handbook* by M.D. Nash, which paints a vivid picture of the 1820 immigrants and uses documents from the Cape Town Archives Repository and The National Archives at Kew to provide names of individuals, the ships they arrived on and the parties into which they were grouped.

IMMIGRATION SCHEMES

Immigration to the area known as Natal began in earnest at the end of the 1840s when it acquired colonial status, and coincided with the exodus of the Dutch from the colony and the economic downturn in Britain.

One particular Irish entrepreneur – Joseph Byrne, a native of Dublin – took advantage of the situation and organised a private scheme to bring settlers to the region. For 2,200 Brits, the opportunity was too great to miss, and between 1849 and 1851 they signed up for the proposal offered by Byrne's Natal Emigration and Colonisation Company. The pamphlets that he produced outline what the migrants could expect from the scheme. Along with their passage, each adult would be provided with dietary provisions for the sum of £19 or if funds were limited, they would have the option of a steerage passage for £10. He even went so far as to explain that each passenger would need to take with them a knife, fork, tablespoon, teaspoon, metal plate, hook pot, mug and bedding, outlining the amount of food each individual would be given depending upon the fare that they had paid. Upon arrival in Natal, they would also have 20 acres of freehold land secured for them. All monies for the journey were expected to be paid in advance.

Byrne's scheme allowed would-be migrants to travel from around Britain with fifteen ships sailing from London, three from Liverpool and two from Glasgow. The first arrived at Natal on 12 May 1849, with nineteen other ships following in the coming months. The vessels were mainly low-tonnage brigs and barques but were adequate to get the passengers, their possessions, and their agricultural equipment to their destination. Although small, these ships had to comply with the 1849 Passengers Act, which required a doctor to be on board. Sadly, there were some deaths on the long voyage but the majority survived the journey and the hazardous Atlantic storms, and arrived safely.

To find out more, visit Shelagh Spencer's website (www.shelaghspencer.com), which gives a detailed account of Byrne's scheme and a Biographical Register of the Settlers in

Natal between 1824 and 1857, covering approximately 2,800 individuals. Along with the database there are maps and pictures of the region and articles regarding the settlers' lives which make essential reading for those with ancestors in this part of the world.

It must be noted that Byrne was not the only individual to organise immigrant arrival in Natal. John Lidgett and Richard Hackett brought Wesleyans on the ships *Hebrides*, *John Bright*, *Herald*, *Nile* and *Choice*. W.J. Irons organised the Christian Emigration and Colonisation Scheme bringing 400 Wesleyan Methodists to settle at Verulam on the Natal North Coast, while Henry Boast brought Yorkshire migrants over on the ship *Haidee*. These were just some of the settler parties that helped populate this area of the South African colony.

FEMALE SETTLERS

One thing that all Victorian females had in common was that their lives were – on the whole – dominated by the decisions of men. For many women, they had little choice when it came to emigration. Those who were married had to follow their husbands, while single women found their only option was to emigrate due to the circumstances they found themselves in. Unmarried females of middle or working-class were required to find a job that supported them – the alternative was to face poverty, the workhouse, or a life on the streets. When the chance of emigration – assisted or otherwise – arose, there were thousands who were eager to see what a new country could offer them.

South Africa was one of the places chosen by settlers during the mid-1800s. The report of Her Majesty's Land and Emigration Commissioners showed that in the year 1851 alone, 1,864 British nationals (some of which were single females) emigrated to the Cape Colony and 2,710 to Natal.

The sea voyage could take between three and four months with little privacy below decks. The outbreak of an infectious illness, which had the potential to spread throughout the ship, was a constant worry. There were numerous instances – not only on voyages to South Africa – where the husband of a young family had died during the journey. The wife would then be left in desperate circumstances. Not only had she got the grief of her husband's passing to deal with, but she was now en route to a new country, often with small children to care for and no means of supporting them, or herself. Unless she had other adult relatives or friends travelling with her, or she intended to live with existing family who had already settled, her future was bleak. She may have swapped a bad situation back home for an even worse one abroad – all through no fault of her own.

Despite these dire circumstances many women became strong through adversity and life was hard with, or without, a husband for support. Most chose to make the best of what the experience offered them, and while some fell by the wayside, others prospered.

AGAINST ALL ODDS

One such story was that of Mary Boast. Her husband – Henry Boast – had charted the ship *Pallas* from Hull ship-owner Joseph Rylands, in order to help a group of Yorkshire families reach Natal. As the emigrants converged on the quayside, the official emigration officer condemned the *Pallas* as unseaworthy. A court case ensued where Boast was found liable. Left with 240 stranded passengers, he was required to find them accommodation and food while Rylands searched for a new vessel.

Eventually, the ship *Haidee* passed inspection, but shortly before they were about to leave, Henry Boast suddenly died. The strain of organising the venture was thought to have been a contributing factor in his death. Mary – along with their three young daughters – resolved to continue with their intended plans. It would seem that her decision was one of fate, as later, once settled in the colony, she met and married widower John Moreland, who himself had been a settlement agent on the Byrne emigration scheme. With the families combined, they went on to make a success of their new lives in Natal. Search for Haidee Settlers at www.geni.com/projects/Haidee-Settlers-Project/10500.

Setting up Home

If the settlers made it through the arduous voyage they still faced a long wagon journey to their final destination and many months living in tents until they could afford to build and complete their future homes.

Wives tended to the day-to-day housework, although many had very little furniture when they first arrived and cooked their meals over an open fire outdoors. Despite fencing off their properties, they were still open to the threat of dangerous animals that roamed the bush and could carry off their domestic livestock. Settlers had to be wary of snakes, which could bite them or their children – their poisonous venom having the potential to be fatal – and they were constantly under attack from all manner of insects, from ants and mosquitoes to locusts that could destroy their crops.

Even the climate took some getting used to. The excessive heat during the day was not only exhausting to work in but could parch their land and make growing certain crops extremely difficult; the torrential rain and thunderstorms brought its own problems.

Although the menfolk were relentlessly occupied building their homes, sowing and tending crops, and constantly maintaining their buildings, land and equipment, the women's lives were equally full. Caring for the children, the upkeep of the home and ensuring food was on the table were their obvious priorities, but with little in the way of shops and supplies for the early settlers, the women had to sew and repair their clothes, adapting those they had bought from Britain to fit the circumstances in Natal. Tending to, and feeding the livestock was another of their tasks as well as maintaining the garden and helping their husbands and sons with planting and harvesting on their land. There was very little time for leisure.

Single women took on similar roles to their married counterparts. Some took jobs as domestic servants to assist those families that could afford the extra help, while others, with a good education, enrolled as governesses to teach the children of the wealthier settlers.

GOLD AND DIAMONDS

When gold and diamonds were discovered in South Africa, hundreds of miners from across Britain made the trek to South Africa in a bid to seek their fortune (see Chapter 4 regarding gold mining procedures). Some were successful, settling in the country never to return to Britain again. This left their families back home without husbands, fathers and sons, not knowing if they were dead or alive, while the miners themselves took the opportunity to make new lives, often remarrying and starting second families in the Cape. Today's online access to records and civil registration documents makes the world a smaller place, helping to finalise those questions left unanswered within many family trees more than a century or more ago.

MILITARY MANOEUVRES

It didn't take long to realise that the Cape of South Africa was strategically positioned halfway along the sea route between Europe and the East, with the Dutch discovering that it was the perfect refreshment and refuelling stop for their ships.

By the late eighteenth century, Britain had installed thousands of troops to prevent the Cape falling into French hands. Married soldiers brought their families with them, while single men often married local girls before deciding to settle in the region. This in itself created new communities near the garrisons and, in time, the construction of churches where baptisms, marriages and burials took place. If your military ancestors settled here, try to establish the garrison camps where they were stationed and the churches that were located nearby to help you locate any relevant records.

BOER WAR, 1899 TO 1902

Despite the politicians believing that the Anglo–Boer War would be over in a matter of months, this was not the case. Of the 450,000 British and Empire troops that served in the Second Boer War in South Africa, the War Office reported that over 21,000 were dead or missing. Furthermore, in excess of 52,000 officers and men were wounded in combat and sent home as invalids.

When Britain took control of the Cape area from the Dutch in 1814, the Boers – the Dutch term for 'farmers' – were completely opposed to British colonial rule. Migrating first to Natal in the North before establishing two independent republics – the Transvaal and the Orange Free State – the problems between them only escalated, culminating on 11 October 1899, when war was officially declared between the two nations.

Lasting nearly three years, the Second Boer War was a long and bloody battle. Britain called upon reinforcement troops from the Empire from as far afield as Canada, Australia and New Zealand, but still suffered numerous casualties as the soldiers were unprepared for the unfamiliar environmental conditions and terrain. The conflict finally ended on 31 May 1902 after the signing of the Treaty of Vereeniging.

The National Archives in South Africa (http://www.national.archives.gov.za) houses the records relating to those regiments that were established locally. www.ancestry.com also has a rich resource in the form of the data collection entitled 'The Casualties of the Boer War 1899–1902', containing information on over 54,000 soldiers who were wounded or died from their wounds in conflict. Expect to discover the force, regiment, battalion, battery/corps, rank, name of the individual, the casualty type and date and place upon which the incident took place, all helping to further your knowledge of the military campaigns in which your ancestor took part.

Contact The National Archives at Kew (www.nationalarchives.gov.uk) to help discover the fate of your British ancestors who fought the Dutch settlers in South Africa. Those men who volunteered would have joined the Imperial Yeomanry and are likely to be listed in an index known as 'Aspin's Roll'.

REGIONAL RESEARCH

When Jan van Riebeeck founded Cape Town in 1652, the influence of his Dutch compatriots was to have a lasting effect on the South African way of life. Along with their traditions and customs, the Dutch brought with them their skill and understanding of record-keeping and it is thanks to them that the earliest civil records were established in the Cape in 1700. Initially these only included marriage registrations; births and deaths were not officially recorded until nearly 200 years later in 1895.

Natal's marriage records were established in 1845, but their births were registered from 1868 and their deaths recorded from 1888. The Orange Free State has birth and death records dating from 1903, while their marriages were first recorded in 1848. The Transvaal also lists births and deaths from 1901, their marriage records dating from thirty years earlier in 1870. Each province is responsible for housing its own records in their various archival repositories.

In order to begin your research you must first familiarise yourself with the 'archival' layout of the country. There are six major National Archive repositories that are responsible for organising the documentation relating to the province in which it is situated. These are located in:

- Cape Town in the Western Cape.
- Port Elizabeth in the Eastern Cape.
- Pretoria in the Transvaal.
- Durban in Natal.
- Pietermaritzburg in Natal.
- Bloemfontein in the Free State.

The National Automated Archival Information Retrieval Service (NAAIRS) at www.national.archives.gov.za is extremely useful for anyone with ancestors who immigrated to all areas of South Africa. It is designed to help identify and locate archival material wherever it is housed within the country and has in its collections a wide variety of genealogical and public records including mortgage bonds, estate files, divorce records, certificates of naturalisation and residential permits, as well as lists of immigrant ships, employees of the civil service and private collections which can contain family trees, letters, photographs and diaries.

Your initial visit to the website should start on the NAAIRS 'Help Page' to assist you in finding your way around. There are a number of acronyms used to identify the various repositories, helping you to narrow down the location of the records you wish to find.

KAB – Cape Town Archives Repository
NAB – Pietermaritzburg Archives Repository
SAB – National Archives Repository (public records of central government since 1910)
TAB – National Archives Repository (records of the former Transvaal Province and its predecessors)
TDB – Durban Archives Repository
TBE – Port Elizabeth Archives Repository
VAB – Free State Archives Repository

Military keepsakes and ephemera from a serving soldier in the Boer War.

You can search the NAAIRS online databases using these acronyms and others relating to audio/visual/oral sources, while those hoping to find the location of ancestors' gravestones should try the GEN database, which refers to the 'Data of the South African Genealogical Society on Gravestones'.

Don't expect to find the vast amount of downloadable documents that we are used to having access to on The National Archives website at Kew, but this resource will at the very least help you to locate the available records you seek. The section on recommended Professional Freelance Researchers at South Africa's public archive repositories could prove invaluable when trying to find information from a distance.

Remember, before 1795 – and the British governing of the colony – early official documents were written in Dutch. For a short period between 1795 and 1810, both languages were used, but after this period the documents were written in English. You should bear the language change in mind if you need to translate any early finds.

DEATH DILEMMA

When researching the death of an ancestor in this country, take a moment to get an understanding of the difference between the Death Certificate and a Death Notice.

The Death Certificate is a civil document first introduced in 1895. It requires a person who is legally competent to certify death – although this is not always a doctor – and lists the cause of death of the deceased.

Death Notices were first introduced in 1834 as a legal document to be sent to the Master of the High Court who oversees the estates of the deceased. They are used to inform the authorities of the death of an individual and although completed soon after death, this is not always by the next of kin. The information contained on current death notices includes the date and place of birth of the deceased, the name of the spouse and children – as well as the married names of any daughters – the date and place of death and place of residence, and details of any property or assets left by the deceased. Although this document can provide a fascinating insight into the life of the individual, the information contained relies solely on the accuracy of the informant. Surprisingly, these can sometimes be easier to find than the death certificates, but you should always try to cross reference any information you discover with other documentation to confirm your facts. Start your search at NAAIRS.

UNCENSORED

The largest disappointment when researching South African ancestors is that there is no detailed census returns; sadly, once the information had been extracted, they were destroyed. This rules out the enjoyment of investigating household information, relationships and occupations all on one document, but don't be disheartened, to overcome this hurdle you need to focus on an alternative source.

The next best option is to turn to the Voters' Rolls, which were documented every year from 1853 and are available for viewing at The National Archives. The only problem being that the criteria used to enable a person to be eligible for inclusion on the Rolls were details such as property ownership, income, age and race – so it is not necessarily guaranteed that your ancestor will be included. For those that were, expect to find a person's initials and surname, while in larger towns their first names and occupations would be listed.

Vintage viewfinder cards can provide photographic scenes of locations and events around the world.

PASSENGER LISTS

Although the majority of immigrants to South Africa arrived by sea, the country's Passenger List records are few and far between. There is no central resource and without the name of the ship on which your ancestor travelled, finding any information can be a little hit or miss.

Start by visiting the Genealogical Society of South Africa website at http://www.eggsa.org/arrivals/eGGSA%20Passenger%20Project.html. This dedicated bunch of volunteers has embarked on a project to transcribe all the existing passenger lists in the South African Archives. At present the Natal Immigration Board's lists of immigrants recorded between 1850 and 1911 has been transcribed, along with twenty passenger lists of ships from the Emigration schemes of 1859–64 and 1873–84. Also underway are lists of departures from British ports between 1879 and 1881 from the monthly newspaper the *British Mail*, and from the weekly *Colonies & India* newspaper from 1883 to 1888.

While random listings can be searched at individual archives, why not consider scouring the newspapers where, from the 1800s, passenger lists were published on a daily basis. These are located in the National Library and you may just strike it lucky.

The *South African Weekly Journal*, for example, published many first- and second-class passenger arrivals and departures from 1889 onwards – those in steerage were rarely listed.

The *Natal Witness* is another publication – found in the Pietermaritzburg Archives – where passenger lists were published, or why not try the Cape Town Archives, where government gazettes are housed and may just provide you with another lead to follow?

EPHEMERA – FORWARD THINKING

It is very easy when you start your family history research to presume your forebears came from a certain county, were known for working in a specific trade, and with very little money were likely to have stayed in the same area for generations. As you discover more about their lives, you can often find that this was not always the case. Understanding what was going on in the world during a certain era had a huge effect on the choices and decisions that people made, impacting upon their beliefs, ideals, occupations and even their freedom.

For instance, have you ever wondered why one individual is missing from the census during a particular decade? Ask yourself was there a war on in the world at this time? Maybe they joined up for military service and travelled overseas to 'do their bit' for queen and country?

Perhaps a whole family disappeared from the censuses altogether with no records of death to account for their mysterious departure. If so, this is the time to further your research, to check passenger lists, overseas censuses and electoral rolls, and to chase up those family whispers that referred to a set of relations who left home for far-flung shores.

Just like today, photographs were greatly treasured by travelling Victorians and provided a way of keeping the memory alive of the loved ones they were leaving behind. Dating them can even help pinpoint a period in which your ancestor moved overseas.

You only have to look on www.ancestry.com's 'Family Trees' to see that there are numerous cases of photographs existing many thousands of miles away from the subject's native homeland. Despite the wish for adventure and a new life, thoughts of loved ones were never very far away and migrating relatives took portraits abroad that were easily packed and lightweight within their luggage; these precious images later to be passed down through the generations. Emigrants requested up-to-date photographs when they wrote letters back home, preserving a likeness of family members to maintain the connection. Those employed in the military and stationed abroad may have sent professional photographic portraits of themselves in uniform to be cherished by proud parents, wives and sweethearts thousands of miles away.

Remember, the style of the uniform might point to a career at a colonial outpost, or in a Boer War campaign. Scrutinise every item you find for vital clues.

Just as questions are raised when 'British' ephemera and family treasures are found in our ancestors' possessions abroad, similar queries may arise when foreign examples appear in their keepsakes here at home. For example, part of the *Natal Mercury* newspaper reporting the extreme weather conditions in the region during May 1940, found neatly preserved in the journal of a man who spent much of his life in Cumbria, requires our detective skills to find out why it was so important:

- Did the man have relatives who were living in Natal who had sent him the newspaper to show the extreme conditions they were experiencing at this time? Who were these relatives, and can we find out more about this side of the family?
- Why did they choose to live in Natal? Had previous generations emigrated many years earlier, or was this the correspondence from a short-term visit and simply memorabilia sent to relatives back home?
- As the newspaper is dated 1940 and the world was in the grip of the Second World War, could this have been sent home from a relative with military connections?

Paper ephemera are invaluable. Whether you have discovered a tattered, torn and delicate newspaper clipping or a pristine travel document that looks like it has never been looked at since the day it was created, both can provide facts and snippets of information which can prove crucial to your family story. Never dismiss items found in your forebear's belongings simply because they are no longer attractive to the eye, there is a reason why they were considered important enough to keep, it is your job to find out why.

8

INDIA

'There are no foreign lands. It is the traveller only who is foreign.'
Robert Louis Stevenson

As one of the most important outposts of Queen Victoria's British Empire, India – and Britain – have gained from sharing knowledge, customs and traditions, influencing each other's way of life for generations to come. But the integration of the differing societies was not easy and, at times, became fraught with difficulties and conflict.

MUTINY IN THE MAKING

In the first half of the nineteenth century, the East India Company ruled India on Britain's behalf. European influence over the nation was intended to benefit the country and its economy; instead resentment grew as citizens regarded the British occupation as disruptive, feeling that Hindu society was being affected by Western ideas.

The flashpoint came in May 1857, when the Indian Army rebelled against the British authorities and a period of violence and bloodshed ensued as European men, women and children were killed before retaliation attacks were taken by the avenging British armies. The uprising rapidly spread across the country, taking just over a year to quell the unrest. Finally, on 8 July 1858, with the last few enclaves of rebels defeated, a peace treaty was signed.

After a century of control by the East India Company, and the resulting conflict to dominate the country in what became known as the 'Indian Mutiny' or the 'Great Rebellion', British Crown rule was established in India. The British 'Raj' was a Hindi term meaning 'to rule' and described Britain's governing of approximately three-fifths of the subcontinent. While the remainder was under the control of local princes, Britain still exerted a fair amount of pressure on them to acquire dominance over all of India.

A Divided Society

After the mutiny, trust between the two nations broke down completely and a barrier was put up that resulted in segregation between the British and Indians.

Queen Victoria (who was made Empress of India in 1876) vowed that her government would work hard to better the lives of her Indian subjects. Sadly, their methods were not always subtle and included suppressing cultural practices in favour of educating the nationals in British modes of thought. In particular, the new government tried to stamp out practices that they did not agree with, such as the Hindu custom of 'Sati', which involved burning a widow on her husband's funeral pyre, or burying her alive in his grave. The women had no social standing in Indian society and although this 'final act of marriage' was supposed to be voluntary, it was not always the case.

You only have to read E.M. Forster's novel *A Passage to India* to understand the great divide between the two cultures. The differing ideals and opinions lasted until the end of the Raj in 1947, when the British provinces were partitioned into two separate dominion states, those of India and Pakistan. But there are always exceptions to the rule, and living in such close proximity, romances were established that crossed the boundaries. Relationships between 'white' and Indian nationalities went on to produce 'Anglo-Indians' who suffered a similar fate of segregation because of their mixed-race which, to many at this time, was considered impure.

Before the Mutiny interracial marriages were fairly acceptable and had little effect on a person's social standing, but after the Mutiny, the outlook began to change. As a direct result of the conflict, the British created a feeling of racial superiority and distanced themselves from their Indian counterparts.

As Britain prepared to build the foundations of modern India the gap between the ruled and the rulers grew considerably. British officials were located in every district in order to maintain law and order and establish a peaceful existence for all. With the help of intermediaries there was a need to try to get closer to the people while remaining cautious – memories of the rebellion were still very fresh in everyone's minds.

In order to reinforce their regime, the Crown encouraged Europeans to live and work in India. By the 1860s, waves of Englishmen arrived to build railways and cotton mills, while others established coffee and tea plantations, improving India's infrastructure and trading possibilities for the future.

Travel Transformation

A major turning point came in 1869 when the Suez Canal opened connecting the Mediterranean with the Red Sea. Instead of the four-month voyage via Cape Town, businessmen and merchants from Britain could get to India in less than three weeks, completely revolutionising travel to the eastern empire. The wealthy, and those unconcerned with the price of the fare, would reserve north-facing cabins on both legs of the journey to avoid the strong rays and heat from the equatorial sun, coining the phrase 'Port Out, Starboard Home' (POSH). During the day they took the sea air by walking the decks and playing shipboard games, while in the evenings they ate and drank from lavish menus and were entertained with concerts and recitals.

The Suez Canal ensured that travel to the region was both quicker and easier for British women; the resulting influx of spinsters creating a choice of wives for the British men already settled in the country. Now more than ever, it was frowned upon for an interracial marriage to take place. Despite this, there are numerous stories where mixed relationships evolved, some successfully, others not. Military men, civil servants and plantation owners continued to take Indian wives, fathering children known as 'Eurasian' offspring, due to their half-caste skin.

The women – and children from these relationships – were far from accepted in society, and even less so if a British man took a native wife back home with him. Life for them was often difficult, and their status was regularly unrecognised by their British contemporaries. Although there were some cases where these relationships were accepted, on the whole they were looked upon as taboo.

CLIMATE COUTURE

Dora de Blaquière was a knowledgeable writer on fashion and travel in the latter part of the nineteenth century. In June 1890 she wrote an article entitled 'The Purchase of Outfits for India and the Colonies', which not only gave hints and tips to the reader en route to far-flung destinations, but also paints a vivid picture for us as genealogists and social historians of what travel for ladies 'with means' was like at this time:

> During most of the year passengers through the Red Sea and also the Indian Ocean are obliged by the excessive heat to sleep on deck as the stifling air of the hot and confined cabins completely banishes sleep; the decks are more airy and certainly cooler, and beds are made up on them, one side being reserved for ladies and the other for gentlemen.

Rather quaintly, she notes that female passengers would require a 'print dressing gown of a dark colour' to put on over a night gown when sleeping on deck to preserve their dignity:

> The voyage to Hong Kong comprises the most numerous changes of climate... It lasts eight weeks and washing can be done at Suez, Singapore, and Columbo. When nearing Hong Kong you will need your warm clothing. For hot weather you will require six or eight cottons, prints or muslins, and a lace, or grenadine and silk, for evening, for onboard the P and O steamers going to Australia and the East there is a good deal of dressing for dinner, and a black lace dress is always suitable.

She also advises a white cotton umbrella, a shady hat, and a pair of 'galoshes' should the decks be wet.

For those travelling across the Pacific Ocean, she notes that the voyage usually lasts from sixteen days to three weeks, and points out that anyone travelling across the Pacific or Mediterranean after the month of April, would need to wash their dresses at various ports on the way, simply because of the heat. With regard to travelling to China, Dora explains that women should be aware of the changing climate across the seasons:

> In the winter the ladies wear much the same things as in England – a sealskin jacket, and a warm serge or cheviot are quite suitable. January, February, and March are very cold indeed; the latter part of March, April, and May are warm, and generally damp. June and July wet, and exceedingly hot, with breathless nights. August and September are drier, but hotter; and in September the nights begin to get cooler; October being the pleasantest month of all the year in China. For the summer months, the thinnest gowns and underclothes are needed; but like most places in the East, it is now thought well to sleep in flannel all year round.

One essential piece of advice that she gives which applied no matter where the final destination was expected to be, was not to forget:

> a small but convenient writing case, with one stiff side on which you can write on your knee, if necessary [...] Take only as much paper as you will certainly need, a few spare pens, and remember your own pen handle, sealing wax, and seal; a very safe travelling ink bottle, filled with ink, and, if possible, a small letter weighing machine.

I can imagine this going down well if I chose to add one into my holiday luggage today! She points out that: 'You will find a list of rates of postage to different countries of the world and the weights of letters at the end of any diary.' Interestingly, Dora describes the need to take a seal and sealing wax on the journey even in the 1890s when stamps would have been easily available:

> On the continent, when you wish to forward an unlocked parcel – such as a roll or rug – you must tie cord round it, and seal the cord at every knot. The Italian railways, for instance, refuse to take unlocked parcels, but will accept the seals willingly. It is sometimes wise, also, to seal your letters, as the seal retains much of its ancient prestige in foreign countries, and constitutes a defence to the gummed envelope which nothing else would do. So you should practice making seals until you can do one well.

Newspaper images are ideal for illustrating life on-board ship. This image from the *Illustrated London News* of September 1893 depicts the tradition of maintaining afternoon tea on-board ship.

In ensuring her readers took a writing case with them, she unwittingly enabled the surviving letters and diaries produced to become heirlooms of the future, avidly sought after by later generations of family historians. Dora de Blaquière died on 6 May 1901 at Sarnia County, Lambton, Ontario in Canada, aged 63. Her death certificate recorded her occupation as 'journalist'.

CASE STUDY: IN SICKNESS AND IN HEALTH

The further our ancestors travelled the more problems they encountered. Although the majority were eager, or resigned, to starting their new life abroad, not everyone reached journey's end.

Mal de Mer, Nausea, Seasickness – however you choose to phrase it – is an affliction that affects many sea travellers, no matter what their social status. Julius Caesar's military campaigns tell of vomiting recruits and sea-sick horses, Columbus was affected on his long voyages of discovery during the Middle Ages, and even Admiral Nelson – who first went to sea aged 12 – was said to be a chronic sufferer. Even our word 'nausea' has ancient maritime connections and derives from the early Greek term 'naus', meaning ship.

When French writer and traveller Maximilien Mission wrote his book *A New Voyage to Italy* in 1695, he noted that, 'the best remedy is, to keep always, night and day, a piece of earth under the nose'. By the nineteenth century, despite the numerous sea voyages taken throughout his career, Charles Darwin turned to his publisher friend John Chapman to send him a book about therapy for the malady; it advised applying ice bags to the small of the back to reduce the queasiness. A multitude of inventions hit the market from a vibrating anti-seasickness deck chair to an anti-motion sickness belt in order to try and alleviate the problem, but for most travellers, the discomfort had to simply be endured until their destination was in sight.

But as bad as the symptoms of seasickness are, illnesses suffered while onboard ship prior to the twentieth century could have fatal consequences. When voyages took weeks – and in some cases months – to reach their destination, deaths at sea were a much more common occurrence. Depending on the vessel and class of accommodation, conditions and sanitation varied, but even those travelling in first class cabins were susceptible to illness. The spread of disease – with little in the way of effective medicine and treatment to combat, or delay the symptoms – was extremely difficult to control. The duration of the early voyages meant that those who passed away could not be kept on board ship and instead required a burial at sea. We can read about these tragic experiences in history books, but to find an eyewitness account, which adds feeling and describes the events surrounding the death, gives us a whole new perspective on what our ancestors were up against. In his journal, solicitor George Russell Rogers vividly describes the death of his fellow passenger Mr Mumford:

> Thursday 18th June 1891 – during the afternoon the Doctor asked me to go into Mumford's cabin as he thought he wished to speak to me. I accordingly went to the poor fellow's berth and found him extremely weak and low, his breathing being still more distressing and difficult. It was evidently a great exertion to him to talk [...] The Doctor had asked him whether he had made a will. As he had not, he wanted to know whether I would mind making a short will for him and this I at once proceeded to do. I drew the document, read it to him, he thoroughly approved it so the Doctor examined it and Mumford then executed it in the presence of the Doctor and myself, the will then being handed to the Captain for safe custody.
>
> Friday 19th June 1891 – I went to (Mumford's) cabin where I found the Doctor who said that the poor fellow was rapidly sinking. His breathing was barely perceptible and he was in the last stages of exhaustion. The Doctor and I remained with him until 8.45pm when he died most peacefully and quietly without the slightest movement or sound. The Captain was summoned as he will have to make an entry in the log of the date and time of the death and of the latitude and longitude where it occurred. I then helped the Doctor to lay the poor fellow out, then his cabin door was locked and the key given to the Captain.
>
> Saturday 20th June 1891 – a burial at sea is, I think, of all funerals, the most solemn. To those who are on board ship when a death occurs and to experience for the first time the gloom cast upon the whole ship's company, it is very awe-inspiring. True, there are those who by habit have become accustomed to witness such things and it is strange to see how little they are affected by them. But with those to whom such an event is a new experience, it is different, though the dead may be unknown even by sight, it is impossible to feel anything but horror at the thought of leaving behind in the wide ocean, any member of the little community.
>
> Early this morning the sail maker went to poor Mumford's cabin and served up his remains in sailcloth enclosing an iron weight of about 56 pounds. The Union Jack was then thrown over the canvas coffin and remained there until the end of the service. At half-past ten punctually the ship's bell commenced to toll and the officers, middies and apprentices collected on the Quarter Deck just below the Poop where the Doctor and I joined them. The other passengers assembled on the Poop with their Prayer Books and everyone present wore mourning of some description. At 10.35, the Doctor commenced reading the service and at the same time the Steward, the Boatswain, the Carpenter and the Sail maker came slowly from the saloon on to the Quarter Deck carrying the

> body on their shoulders on a plank which was placed on supports opposite the Quarter Deck Port on the port side; the Union Jack still forming the Pall.
>
> The service proceeded to the words 'we therefore commit his body to the deep', when one end of the plank was raised there was a sudden pause and a splash, a gurgling of the water, the closing words of the service 'Blessed are the dead which die in the Lord' and all was over, the Ensign remaining half mast high.

This emotional scene, written by an eyewitness in his own hand, is extremely moving and poignant, and just goes to show the power that an original document or item of ephemera can have. Can you relate these experiences to those endured by your ancestor?

THE CLUE IS IN THE KEEPSAKE

Although numerous keepsakes are paper-based ephemera, this is not always the case. The single piece of luggage that your migrant forebear took with him may now be the fashionable trunk that resides in a bedroom or as a 'trendy' coffee table that is steeped in history. Similarly, the small leather suitcase that carried an individual's 'worldly goods' to the other side of the globe may now hold the family archive of photographs and letters for further generations to enjoy.

Investigate these pieces closely. Are there any labels that give clues as to their origins – a small manufacturer's tag might state the phrase 'made in Bradford', for example, or even give an address of the shop from which it was bought back in Blighty, even though the suitcase itself now resides thousands of miles away in India.

Items that you take for granted within the home may easily have had a 'double life' – what is now decorative, may at one time have been extremely practical.

MAKING A HOME FROM HOME

Despite its reputation for searing heat and the presence of deadly diseases, Calcutta became the administrative capital of Anglo-Indian society. The standard of living was high for those British who settled in the city at this time and, in many cases, much better than what they could have experienced back home. The wealthy took over palatial mansions and luxury bungalows to house their families and the servants they employed. European men were addressed as 'Sahib' – meaning 'sir' or 'master', while 'Memsahib' was the respectful form of address for the European females. Single men shared housing with like-minded merchants, bankers and businessmen, spending the majority of their days at work in their offices.

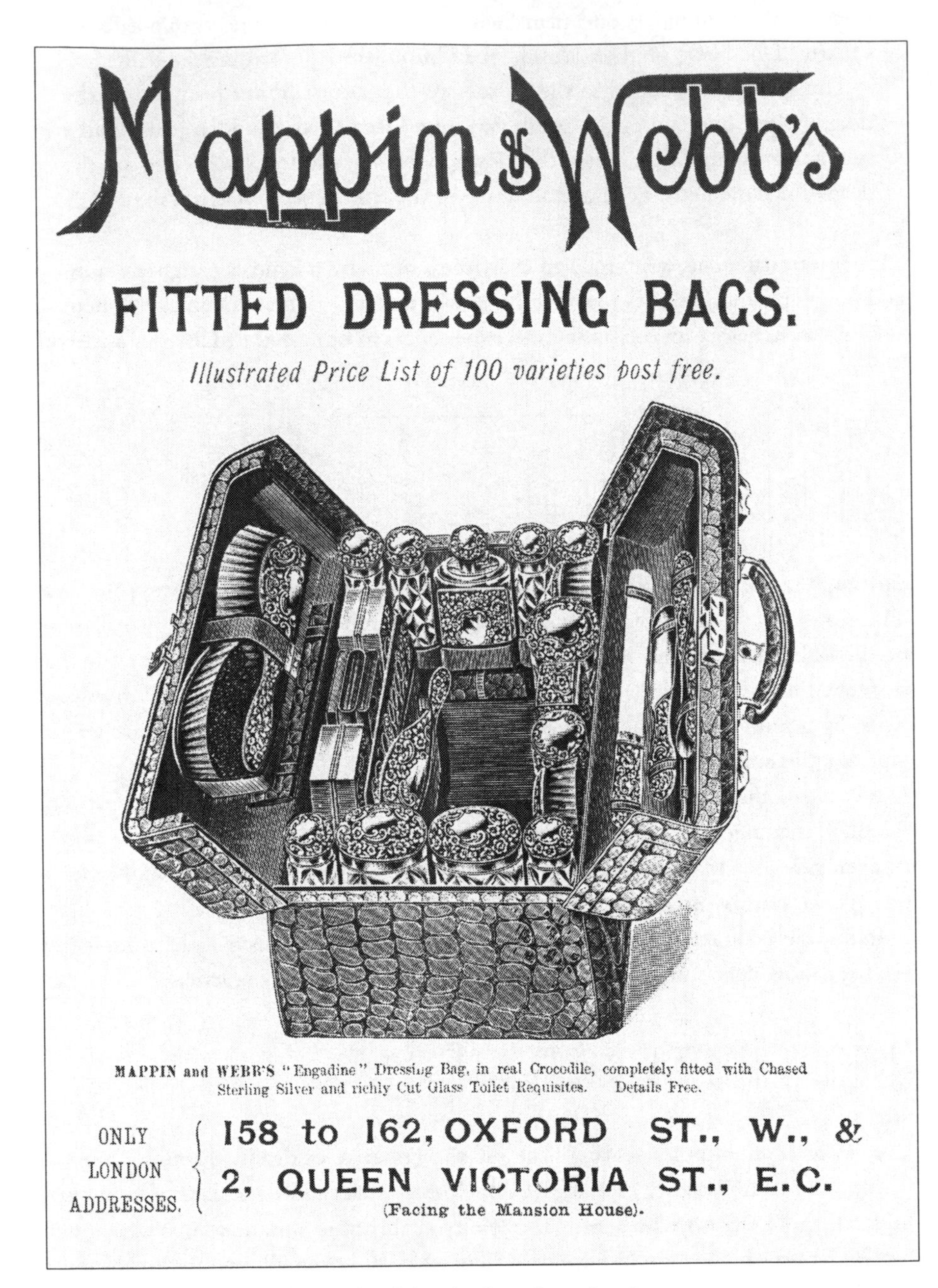

Advert depicting essential ladies' fitted dressing bags from the 1890s.

That said, the expat community always found plenty of time to socialise. During the evenings many congregated in Calcutta's Eden Gardens, taking a stroll, or listening to the regimental band. Their social calendars would be full of official gatherings and a week would not go by without a dance, or ball, being held – but even these were hierarchy based with the British having a strict precedence policy within their own class divisions.

Sport featured highly within the lives of the settlers bringing with them a little piece of British life to India. Small racecourses were established and Polo was enjoyed by those with a military background, enabling the men to show off their horsemanship and prowess. The women favoured tennis, and even the English hunt was replicated on Indian soil forfeiting the traditional beagles for a mismatched pack of dogs of varying breeds.

MERCHANTS AND THE MILITARY

Established in the latter part of the sixteenth century, when Queen Elizabeth I granted its official charter on 31 December 1599, the East India Company was given exclusive trading rights (for an initial period of fifteen years) with all the countries beyond the Cape of Good Hope. While its counterpart, the Dutch East India Company, had strong connections in the Spice Islands, the British East India Company concentrated its efforts on India's textiles, spices and opium.

The company needed a main base in India from where its ships could dock and offload its British wares before reloading with spices, sugar, silk and other commodities that could be transported back home. Surat on the west coast was chosen, and as British financiers saw vast returns for their investments, it wasn't long before foreign competitors wanted a slice of the company's success. The Indian Army was created to help provide protection by guarding its factories and warehouses. The term 'Sepoy' was used to describe an Indian soldier serving in the army of a European power.

When the company trading settlements split into three administrative divisions – known as 'presidencies' – in Bombay, Madras and Calcutta, it required three separate armies to help oversee their security. But in the year following the Indian Mutiny of 1857, the army command was transferred from the company to the Crown.

Although the East India Company finally ceased trading on 1 January 1874 – 274 years after its introduction – the Indian Army did not sever its links with Britain until India gained its independence on 14 August 1947. Clocking up two centuries of combined history, this union resulted in numerous British and Indian soldiers working side-by-side, and for the family historian, a wealth of military records lie waiting to be uncovered.

RESEARCHING THE RAJ

'Anglo-Indian' is a term often used to describe a person born of mixed British and Indian parentage. In many cases the female would be of Indian descent, but this was not always the case. Perhaps you have Anglo-Indian blood in your family tree, or are simply trying to investigate ancestors of British origin who lived in India? The best place to start your research is at the British Library's India Office Family History Search website at http://indiafamily.bl.uk/UI. Here you can expect to find over 300,000 births, baptisms, marriages, deaths and burials in the India Office Records of British and European people who settled, or worked, in India between 1600 and 1949. The collections include documents relating to the East India Company and other areas where the India Office had influence with details of civil servants, medical staff, railway workers, military personnel and numerous other official and non-official inhabitants, such as missionaries and merchants. Although not all records are accessible online, the information gathered may give you clues to follow your ancestor's trail.

Your next stop should be at the Families in British India Society at www.new.fibis.org, where a free database allows the searching of over 1 million names and provides an understanding of life in British India during different periods in its history.

Of real importance are the maritime records which detail the embarkations, disembarkations and notices of arrival of over 183,000 people who arrived in India by ship. This not only included foot passengers and crew but also those men who were recruited in Britain to join the East India Company's armies as well as those soldiers whose regiments were posted to India. There are images of the ships on which these long voyages were taken and the destinations to which they travelled. The site has links to a vast array of searchable photographs, personal papers, diaries, letters and documents helping to bring Anglo-Indian stories to life.

Don't forget, that this is also the ideal place to search for the thousands of European soldiers who served in the Bombay Army of the Honourable East India Company between 1795 and 1862. The online registers include not only the names of those men who enlisted, but also details of their careers in India (Bombay, now Mumbai) including their rank and unit, often a place of origin, the date they entered, the length of their service, and any promotions or transfers of pension arrangements. You may be lucky enough to discover the date they arrived in India and the name of the ship upon which troops were transported to their destination.

Remember, the India Office only holds information connected to British nationals overseas. If your British ancestor married an Indian national and you want to research the line further back, you will then need to follow the paper trail through the Indian archives to discover what records still exist. Indian ancestors who came to Britain can be researched through our civil registration documents and census records, but remember to check the spellings of surnames and those birth locations which may have been misspelt in translation.

Luggage labels can give clues to the countries and destinations visited.

MISSIONARY MOTIVATION

A life overseas appealed to so many of our ancestors for numerous reasons. From the late eighteenth century, a proportion of Christian believers felt that it was their calling to spread their religious beliefs around the globe. These men and women became known as 'Missionaries' who joined dedicated societies in order to travel to distant outposts and spread the Christian word.

If you think you know which society your ancestor belonged to, you can try to track down more information by visiting the website http://www.mundus.ac.uk – an online gateway to overseas missionary material held in over 400 collections within the UK. Searches can be made by personal names, organisation names, place-names and subjects, with clickable maps enabling you to pinpoint geographical locations. If your searches are successful you may need to make arrangements to visit the repositories in person to read the letters, newspapers, registers, magazines and other printed materials that are not available for viewing online.

Missionaries travelled far and wide throughout India, Africa and Asia. The International Mission Photography Archive (http://digitallibrary.usc.edu/cdm/landingpage/collection/p15799coll123) is a great place to view historical images from missionary collections around the world, while Yale Library (http://divdl.library.yale.edu/missionperiodicals/Results.aspx) has an extensive database of Missionary periodicals.

PASSAGES to INDIA, AUSTRALIA, &c., engaged free of commission. Outfits provided. Agency for officers and civilians of the E. I. Company's Service. By C. R. THOMPSON, LUCAS, and CO. London—Winchester House, Old Broad-street; Southampton—1, Queen's-terrace. Baggage and Parcels shipped and forwarded. Insurances effected.

EMIGRATION.—Passages to Australia, Tasmania, New Zealand, &c., may be secured through Messrs. S. W. SILVER and CO., Emigration Outfitters, 3 and 4, Bishopsgate-street (opposite the London Tavern), City. Letters of Credit granted, and reliable information from their numerous connections given, upon application as above, personally, or by post.

Emigration notices, such as this one advertised in the *Illustrated London News* of October 1857, provide fascinating details of shipping routes, vessels and destinations.

Essential Reading

The *India Man Magazine* provides a whole host of genealogical and historical information about the British in India and Southern Asia between 1600 and the twentieth century (www.indiaman.com).

DIGITALISED DIARIES

Autobiographies and memoirs written by an individual about their life and experiences are primary sources that can help to explain a certain situation or event to us in depth. The Duke University Libraries at http://library.duke.edu/digitalcollections/womenstraveldiaries/about/ provide a whole list of links to digitalised diaries written by British and American women who documented their travels around the globe. You can browse the pages written by Harriet Sanderson Stewart who, accompanied by her father, gave a detailed account of the ships, accommodation and countries that she visited; the description of life stationed in a garrison camp in North India by the wife of a British Army officer in 1865; the social engagements of a woman journeying through the West Indies, or the customs of the Lebanese as experienced by a viscountess in 1860. Vivid and full of life, these accounts were written in their own words using the vocabulary of the time. What is perhaps most exciting about this site is that each diary has been photographed so it is the author's own handwriting that you are reading – *not* a transcription – giving each story an even more authentic feel!

9

WEST INDIES

'For the execution of the voyage to the Indies,
I did not make use of intelligence,
mathematics or maps.'
Christopher Columbus

Formally known as the British West Indies due to its colonial history, this chain of islands stretches across the Caribbean Sea from Venezuela to Florida encompassing Barbados, Grenada, Jamaica, Montserrat, St Vincent and Trinidad to name but a few.

When the Europeans first encountered the West Indies in 1492, they were solely populated by their indigenous peoples, but the arrival of the newcomers brought great change, and not necessarily for the better. New diseases resulted in the deaths of many islanders who had no resistance to these unfamiliar maladies, and although they tried to protect their lands, the Spaniards and Portuguese took advantage and enslaved them to work on their plantations and in their South American gold mines.

By the nineteenth century, there had been decades of conflict as European countries attempted to claim the lands for themselves, culminating in disputes of ownership and territorial wars. Britain captured a series of islands from the French, Spaniards and Dutch, before offering sanctuary to those from non-British Islands during the Spanish American Independence Wars and the French Revolution. Consequently, the majority of ethnic groups in Anglo-Caribbean countries today have strong African, British and Asian Indian ancestry.

Migrants who located to the West Indies fell into three distinct categories. Firstly, there were voluntary migrants who, in most cases, had a choice in where they decided to settle. These included merchants, landowners, discharged sailors and soldiers, adventurers and travellers, and East Indian labourers. Secondly, were the involuntary migrants, who had little choice in where they settled and included transported criminals and African slaves. Finally, there were displaced migrants, which included refugees fleeing from war, those escaping religious persecution, and fugitive slaves attempting to avoid capture.

Remember, the original use of the term 'West Indian' can be a little confusing, as it was not only used to describe a person who was born, or had settled, in the West Indies, but also for a merchant or estate owner with land and financial interest on the islands, who lived in Britain.

THE SUGAR RUSH

In 1625, the first ship from England arrived at the island of Barbados with the intent of establishing a permanent settlement. Within twenty-five years, this island became the wealthiest colony in the British Empire, thanks to the growth and industry of its most precious commodity – sugar.

As a result, Barbados attracted immigrants from all levels of society, with vessels docking in Bridgetown on a daily basis. Convicts facing the death penalty were known to have been offered the chance to reform by being 'Barbadosed' – sent to the island instead of facing the noose. Indentured servants agreed to be bound to their masters hoping to one day acquire land for themselves, while at the other end of the scale, upper-class speculators arrived with the sole purpose of creating plantations that had the potential to multiply their existing wealth.

As the plantations grew and flourished there was an increasing need for further man-power to work them. Thousands of African slaves were shipped to Barbados and the neighbouring islands to meet this demand – a practice that would continue until the abolition of slavery in 1807. It would take another twenty-seven years before the slaves were actually granted their freedom, at which time many left the islands for good.

Slave Ancestors

Britain's colonial ties with the West Indies saw us inextricably linked with the slave trade – not only giving many of us ancestors who were slaves, but also the merchants and plantation owners who employed them.

Between 1640 and 1808 it is estimated that 60 million slaves were sent to the West Indies. Slave ships were used for their transportation. Closely packed inside every vessel, the human cargo had barely enough space to lie down, their comfort limited further as they were shackled to keep their movements restricted. The voyage must have been horrendous. Sickness was rife, disease spread rapidly and for many, death was inevitable. Once they arrived at their destination they were forced to complete various working tasks on the plantations, as domestics within the homes of their owners, or sold on to the highest bidders at auction for further labour intensive duties.

Trying to trace slave ancestors can be a difficult but not impossible task. You will need intensively to research the subject, gathering together snippets of information that will hopefully lead you closer to your goal. Before black slaves gained their freedom, individuals can be tricky to track down and identify, simply due to the fact that many did not have surnames and were instead recorded under the names of their owners.

Originally, any records created referring to individual slaves would have been kept within the personal papers of their owner, but on 26 March 1812, it was decided that a slave registry should be set up in Trinidad as a means of monitoring legally held slaves. Other West Indian colonies followed suit and the resulting documents now give us some of the most comprehensive records from the period 1812 to 1834. After 1834, former slaves began to appear on official documentation, enabling you to search for them through the normal channels.

Start by familiarising yourself with the websites and resources available on the Internet by using a search engine to narrow your research to the area most relevant to you. www.ancestry.co.uk has information on over 700,000 slaves, owners and family members on St Croix, as well as a searchable database of the slave registers of former British Colonial Dependencies during the period 1812–34; it is just a matter of seeking out details that help to build a background to your ancestor's story (http://search.ancestry.co.uk/search/db.aspx?dbid=1129). Although not available digitally, there is a small selection of records which relate to British slave owners and their slaves at The National Archives. Expect to find:

- The name of the owner and parish in which they lived.
- The name, age, gender and nationality of the slave.

As Britons we take our freedom for granted and it is hard to think of a person being 'owned' or as the 'property' of another human being, but that was the situation faced by slaves. They could only be released from this ownership by a court act, by deed, or through the will of their owner.

The complete abolition of slavery (in British law) eventually came in 1833, and plantation owners replaced their freed workers with indentured labourers who were often Asian – from India and China – who were now immigrants in the islands. The National Archives Colonial Office will hold any immigration records or indentures that exist regarding these labourers.

Following the Clues

Perhaps you are aware of family connections to the island and wish to see where the trail may take you. Start by contacting the Registration Department in Bridgetown, you can investigate the civil registration records of those ancestors who originated from Barbados. For births, these records date from 1890, for marriages from 1930 and for deaths from 1925. The address for postal queries is:

The Barbados Registration Department
Supreme Court of Barbados
Law Courts
Coleridge Street
Bridgetown, St Michael
Barbados

With any luck, your findings will help you to travel further back in time, so you will next have to consult the island's church records of baptisms, marriages and burials.

By 1640, English settlers had divided Barbados into eleven parishes with an Anglican church in each. Gradually, other religious denominations arrived and set up their own places of worship, including Catholics, Methodists and Moravians. Establishing the religious beliefs of a forebear can really help you to locate their records, but again bear in mind that the documentation that has survived varies from parish to parish.

Contact the Barbados Department of Archives who can verify which records have been microfilmed, transcribed or published, or why not search online at www.familysearch.org by visiting their 'help' section at https://familysearch.org/learn/wiki/en/Barbados, which provides details of where relevant information can be found.

THE BIGGER PICTURE

Britain does not hold records for its former colonies. Each island or territory in the West Indies has its own record office or archive; they are not centralised. The range of documents that have survived is purely reliant on the record-keeping of that particular country and upon the natural disasters that may have befallen it which have affected the storage and preservation of their holdings. Over the decades, earthquakes and floods account for the loss of a large percentage of ancestral documentation.

It should also be noted that prior to British rule, the West Indian mainland colonies and islands changed hands between various European powers, so many of their early records may still be housed in the archives of the countries of former ownership. For example, Trinidad was under Spanish rule until 1802, while St Vincent, Grenada and Dominica were governed by the French until 1763. Accordingly, not all records will be in English, so some translation from the original language may be required.

An excellent overview of the history and heritage of those with West Indian roots can be found on the The National Archives website.

Always try to establish as much basic information as you can to enable you to take your research to the next level. Ask yourself:

- Do you know your ancestor's religious denomination?
- What was their ethnic group? Were they of African, Asian or European descent?
- Do you know the island on which your ancestor was born? This is extremely important when trying to track down documents – remember, there is no central index as each territory/island has its own register offices and archives.

The Caribbean Surnames List is a central location where researchers post information about the West Indian families they are researching and their country of origin. It is the ideal place to question like-minded people who may have links to your family surname, share findings and extend your ancestral knowledge. Find out more at http://www.candoo.com/surnames/index.php?sid=34fb2498713bc8044f77091b1c40f92b. Similarly, Rootsweb has a Caribbean themed mailing list upon which to post your queries at www.rootsweb.ancestry.com/~caribgw/mailinglist.html.

CASE STUDY: MILITARY MEMORABILIA

Protecting the Eastern Caribbean between 1780 and 1905, and with dedicated West Indian regiments introduced from 1795, the British Army has a long history with the islands. Many of these soldiers, their families and their descendants made a life in the Caribbean and have helped provide today's inhabitants with their British military roots.

By tracking down ephemera that relates to your personal family story you will be amazed at the variety of documents and memorabilia you will find. Some will be 'one-offs', or of a limited quantity, while others will be in ready supply and easy to come by. Over the centuries different organisations, societies, trades, events and gatherings have all prompted printed records of their existence to be produced.

One example, relevant to those ancestors who were also ex-servicemen, is their 'official' journal entitled, *Our Empire – the British Empire Service League*, whose strap line promised to 'Unite Ex-Service Men's Organisations in Great Britain and Ireland and the Overseas Dominions'.

The British Empire Services League was founded in 1921 in Cape Town, South Africa by Field Marshal Earl Haig and Field Marshal Jan Smuts. By April 1925, when the first issue of the monthly journal was published, their patron was HRH, Edward the Prince of Wales.

The vision of 'Our Empire' was to link ex-servicemen throughout the world, telling them of the conditions that governed the lives of their contemporaries who had settled in other areas coloured in red on the map; opening their eyes to the wider opportunities in parts of the Empire they had only previously heard about and sharing the latest news from around the globe. This was summed up with the message:

THE R. M. S. P STEAMSHIP "ATRATO"

Image of the Royal Mail Steam Packet Ship the *Atrato* and its passenger list from a voyage taken in 1906.

LIST OF PASSENGERS

—PER—

R. M. S. "ATRATO"

Leaving NEW YORK, March 31, 1906.

OFFICERS OF THE STEAMER.

Commander = = H. J. BOBY, R.N.R.

Chief Officer ..	J. WATTS.
2nd Officer ..	M. TAYLOR.
3rd Officer ..	A. BAKER.
4th Officer ..	R. G. CLAYTON.
5th Officer ..	H. R. ELLIS.
Surgeon	L. SELLS.
Purser	H. V. STURGESS.
Asst. Purser ..	E. F. JEFFREY.

Chief Engineer ..	C. MURCHISON.
2nd Engineer ..	W. J. EVANS.
3rd Engineer ..	W. HOBSON.
4th Engineer ..	L. ROSS.
5th Engineer	H. D. McINTYRE.
6th Engineer (Senr.)	W. GIBBONS.
6th Engineer (Junr.)	T. YEATES.
Refrigerating Engineer	D. BERTRAM.

Chief Steward	C. FRANCK.
Stewardess	MARY ROGAN.
Assist.-Stewardess ..	A. REA.

> The children of the British Commonwealth of Nations enjoyed an immeasurable advantage over most of the other peoples of the Earth. They are many nations, but they speak one tongue [...] Canada, Australia, South Africa, New Zealand – each has its own 'dialect', its peculiar intonation; but the language is the same. This is the glorious channel – the tongue of Shakespeare, of Raleigh, Frobisher, Drake, and Cork – through which we hope to link the outposts of the Empire with every other part of it; the centre with the circumference.

If you come across copies of this publication you will find that the initial eighty-page editorial is crammed with information about British nationals who now resided in the Colonies. From articles covering the use of guns and rifles in North America to hunt moose, caribou, antelope and bear, to ranching in Rhodesia and wheat farming in Canada, topics are covered which give information about those who have already made their homes in these countries, while answering the questions of others whose move overseas is imminent.

The letters page shows just how far reaching this journal was with 'stories' sent from South Africa, Sydney and Winnipeg; there is even an interesting feature discussing the difficulties faced over wireless transmission communications and the possible solutions for broadcasting over widely scattered areas in the colonies ... a service the majority of us take for granted today.

Published between the wars, the inclusion of political cartoons reflected the issues of the day; it is interesting to note that many of the problems are still our main concerns nearly a century later. Industrial strife, reduced pensions, the cost of living, disablement and unemployment are all highlighted and topped with the caption, 'Heaven help me if I win another war.' If only the readers knew what lay ahead and how true the sentiments of the cartoon remain. It is fascinating how a simple piece of ephemera can help us to understand and empathise with our ancestors despite the difference in the areas in which we live.

BRITISH CARIBBEAN LINKS

Migration between Britain and the West Indies has been constant in both directions since the seventeenth century. Landowners, merchants and plantation owners from Britain may have settled for long periods in the West Indies but they often sent their children home to be schooled in Britain accompanied by their West Indian servants. Once discharged, those serving in the Army, and merchant seamen, sometimes decided to settle in Britain and although white West Indians found it easier to integrate into British society, it was not so easy for the black migrants.

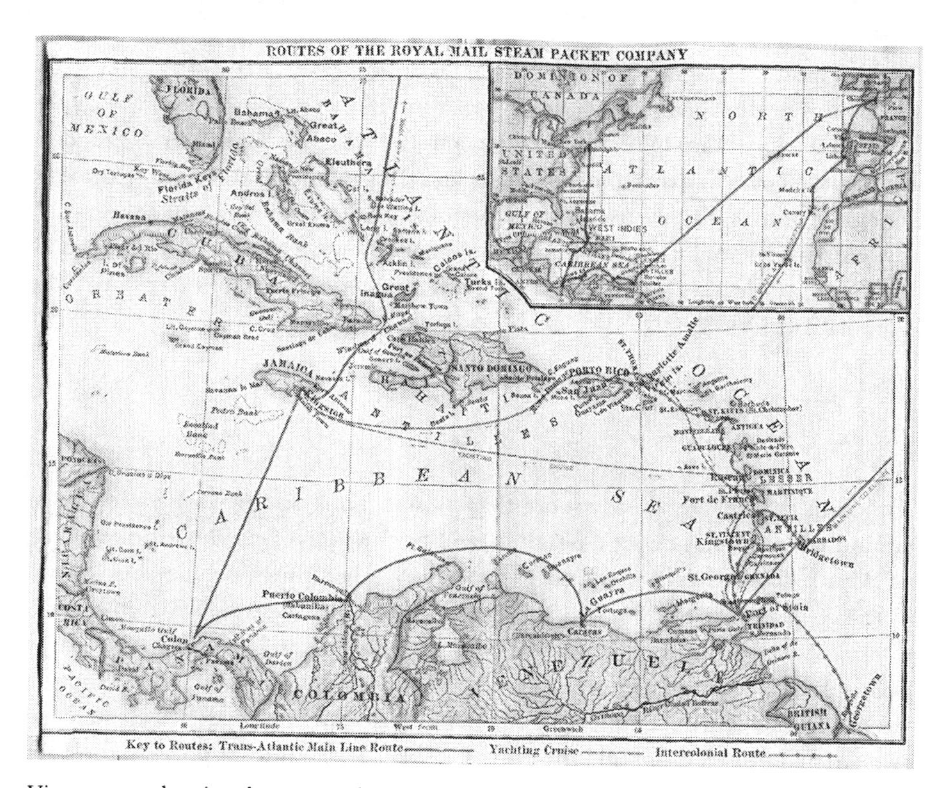

Vintage map showing the routes taken by the Royal Mail Steam Packet ships around the West Indies.

Remember, Britain was not the only destination of nineteenth-century West Indian immigrants. The abolition of slavery enabled many to start new lives in commonwealth countries, British colonies and other foreign destinations seeking employment in construction jobs such as building the American railways and the Panama Canal. There were a number of 'official establishments' that dealt with the movement of migrants around the British Colonies, including:

- The Colonial Office – established in 1854 but held the records of its predecessors since the sixteenth century.
- The Dominions Office established in 1925.
- The Commonwealth Relations Office formed in 1947 which combined with the Colonial Office in 1966 to create the Commonwealth Office.

For more information on these departments and acquiring access to the documents they hold, visit The National Archives online help guide at http://www.nationalarchives.gov.uk/records/research-guides/british-colonies-and-dominions.htm.

Despite over 300 years of steady migration of West Indians to Britain, very few passenger lists exist before 1890 – those that do are housed at The National Archives.

As West Indian immigrants were considered British subjects, the government registered very few ships and passengers arriving from this part of the Empire.

Until the First World War, passports were not required by ordinary citizens, only by government officials and merchants in an effort to ensure safe passage through foreign countries. This in itself makes pinpointing the movements of those without passports before this date slightly tricky. After 1917, passports were introduced by the Foreign Office with details of applications and those issued to be found at The National Archives.

THE *EMPIRE WINDRUSH*

Although there were already more than 75,000 black and Asian people settled around the ports and major cities of Britain by the mid-1940s, the greatest influx of West Indian settlers arrived on 22 June 1948, when the passenger ship known as the *Empire Windrush* docked at Tilbury. The British Nationality Act of 1948 gave all Commonwealth citizens free entry into Britain and provided the starting point of mass migration from the West Indies to what was viewed as the 'mother country'. Initially, a government newspaper advertisement prompted 490 men and two women from Jamaica and the other Caribbean islands to respond to the offer of employment and cheap tickets to Britain. At this time, jobs in the West Indies were in short supply, while in Britain, industry was booming and the factories and coalmines required workers to help increase trade and to assist with post-war reconstruction.

Within hours of the migrants arriving – officially welcomed from representatives of the Ministry of Labour, the Colonial service and local authorities – those who were not staying with friends and relatives already settled here, were shown to temporary accommodation in the converted former air raid shelters in Clapham Common before signing up for work permits and papers at the Labour Exchange. Eighty-two of the men had volunteered to join the Armed Forces so were housed in a hostel in Wimpole Street before they received their training and postings.

The experience was undoubtedly exciting for the young migrants, with the opportunity for a new start and a means of building a future in Britain, but it could not have been easy. At this time, Britain had a variety of racial prejudices which, in turn, impacted on the newcomers when they tried to find their own accommodation. The colour of their skin resulted in them not being welcomed by some landlords and neighbours, and they were barred from certain establishments like bars, clubs, restaurants and even specific jobs because of their ethnic origins.

Despite these hurdles, many settled and integrated into what was becoming a multicultural Britain. West Indian communities sprang up, especially around the London area, with the inhabitants contributing to community life. One of the migrants – Sam

Examples of foreign currency collected whilst travelling around Columbia and Panama in the early 1900s and then pasted into a travel journal.

King – even became Southwark's first black mayor, prompted by his services to the community, along with his work on Brixton's *West Indian Gazette* and in helping to establish the Notting Hill Carnival.

The *Empire Windrush* was not the only vessel to bring migrants over from the West Indies and the SS *Orbita*, the SS *Reina del Pacifico* and the SS *Georgic* soon followed, although it was the *SS Auriga* – which left Kingston in Jamaica on 2 August 1955 – that had an unprecedented number of passengers. Some 1,100 people were on board and like those that had arrived before them, the mix of skilled and unskilled workers hoping to improve their training, came to fill jobs and enjoy the adventure.

If you believe that your ancestor came to Britain by the *Empire Windrush*, or one of the many other vessels that followed in its wake, start your search using the inbound ships passenger lists, found at www.nationalarchives.gov.uk, which lists migrants that arrived in UK ports between 1870 and 1960. You can also download a sample of the *Windrush* documentation at The National Archives website. As well as the passenger's port of embarkation, you can find details of the individual's proposed address, occupation and intended future residence. Similarly, if you know the Caribbean island where your ancestor was based prior to their move to Britain, you may be able to unearth departure lists that have survived in the archives or customs departments in their country of origin.

The first issue of the *British Ex-Serviceman's League* journal. Was your ancestor an ex-serviceman of the British Empire?

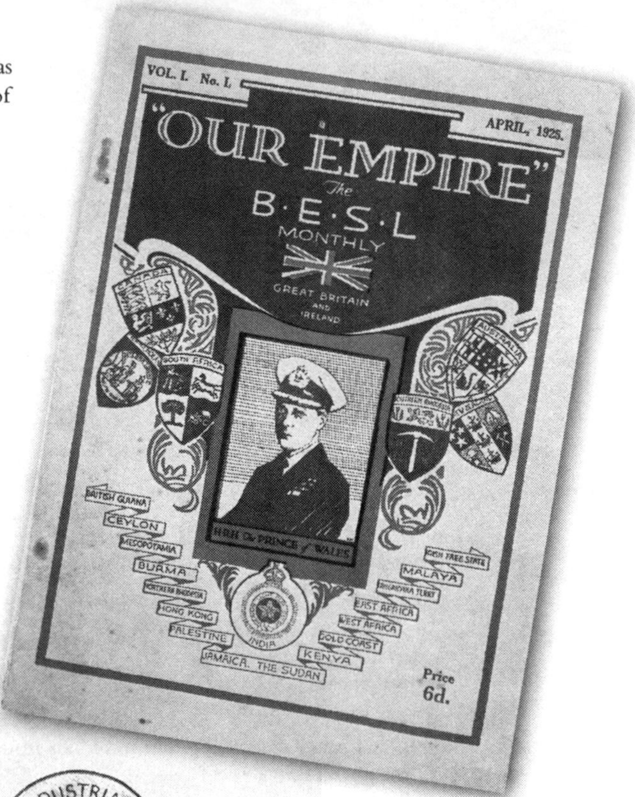

VOL. I. No. I.
APRIL, 1925.
"OUR EMPIRE"
The B·E·S·L MONTHLY
GREAT BRITAIN AND IRELAND
H.R.H. The PRINCE of WALES
BRITISH GUIANA
CEYLON
MESOPOTAMIA
BURMA
HONG KONG
PALESTINE
JAMAICA. THE SUDAN
INDIA
KENYA
GOLD COAST
WEST AFRICA
EAST AFRICA
MALAYA
IRISH FREE STATE
CANADA
SOUTH AFRICA
AUSTRALIA
Price 6d.

"Heaven Help Me If I Win Another War"

Reproduced by courtesy of *London Opinion*

Cartoon from the *Our Empire* journal depicting the current issues in the world at the time. Unemployment, reduced pensions and industrial strife – our ancestors were facing similar dilemmas to our own today!

Those who stayed here would have applied for UK citizenship and the naturalisation records for the period 1948 to 1987 can also be found at The National Archives.

Transcripts of personal migration stories along with photographs, newspaper articles and case studies can be found at The National Archives website. They help to give us a real feel of why these individuals chose to leave their country of origin, their experiences during the journey, the emotional aspect of being separated from friends and family back home and the difficulties faced when integrating into their new communities and jobs in Britain.

EPHEMERA – TOP TIPS!

If your ancestor travelled to Britain on one of the above mentioned vessels, track down any newspaper reports of their arrival in the country. Press coverage would have been top priority to portray our good relations with our Caribbean cousins, so small details could well be included that you wouldn't find anywhere else.

The discovery of a collection of foreign currency provides us with clues as to the destinations visited by our ancestors. Do your research to work out when the notes were issued (the imagery, themes and the denominations will help pinpoint the era) and you should be able to whittle down a timeframe as to when your ancestor was travelling. Equally, if you know the locations they visited, why not consider acquiring period currency from those countries to illustrate their journeys – a fantastic visual aid to genealogical memoirs if you are lacking in relevant photographic images.

10

GERMANY/HUNGARY

'Civilisation has ever accompanied emigration and conquest – the conflict of opinion, of religion, or of race.'
Alfred Russel Wallace

When George I came to the throne in 1714, his Hanoverian connections prompted a rush of German-speaking people to migrate to Britain. Musicians, bankers and artists were just some of those that arrived to make their mark in our financial institutions, galleries and theatres. But the migrants were not restricted to the wealthier classes. People from all sectors of society found a home here, bringing with them their trades and skills to establish businesses – not only in London but in many towns and cities.

Cabinet makers, shopkeepers, pork butchers, bakers, tailors and those in the sugar refining industry were just some of those that arrived from the early eighteenth century onwards. During the nineteenth century, while in the peak of the Industrial Revolution, the need for skilled labour made Britain an attractive proposition and Germans with trades to offer were virtually guaranteed to find work.

It is perhaps hard to believe that until 1871, the German Empire did not exist. Before this date German-speaking parts of Europe were divided into separate states, the smaller ones gradually incorporated into the larger ones. Prussia was one of the larger regions and through war and conflict, managed to conquer those less powerful, resulting in their inhabitants fleeing to Britain in search of safety. Political refugee Karl Marx was just one of those migrants who was exiled in London when the German states attempted to set up the Democratic German Confederation in his homeland in 1848.

As well as providing a safe haven, Britain also practised the same faith as many German Protestants, making it a little easier for the religious refugees to mix in with the locals. As in all immigrant communities, their own place of worship was soon established. German Protestant churches appeared in Britain from the seventeenth century, while the German Catholic Church was set up in the capital during the nineteenth century. Their registers – which can prove very informative – often include the place of origin of the individual, helping you to trace their story even further back. The Anglo-German Family History Society http://www.agfhs.org.uk has indexed many surviving records and by becoming a member you can request their help in trying to find your migrant ancestor's entries.

ARCHIVAL ANALYSIS

When researching your German ancestry you should first establish the town ('Stadtarchiv') or city archive ('Kreisarchiv') nearest and most relevant to where your forebear was based. Although very few are indexed, individual states created headcounts to record the inhabitants within a particular village, town, or city, which may prove helpful as national census records were never made. However, from 1876, inhabitant listings known as 'Einwohnermelde' were introduced, which give detailed accounts of each resident.

The division of the country can make tracing your early German family history a little challenging, but once you start looking, it is surprising what unique records were kept by each administration. For example, the Catholic priest of the former kingdom of Württemberg created a register of everyone living within his parish – no matter what their religion. This register, or 'Familienregister', was organised by family and included the names, and important dates of birth, marriage and death of those within it. War has naturally meant that some documents have not survived the conflicts but those parish registers that remain will either still be kept at the parish church, or have been handed over to be housed at the local archives. As Germany was not unified until 1871, the start of civil registration differed from area to area and can vary with each district as to how much information each record contained. By the mid-1870s, most certificates offered similar information to their British equivalents.

Once you have established where you think a particular birth, marriage or death may have taken place, you will need to contact the local civil registration office – or 'Standesamt' – to see when their records began and to acquire a certificate. Bear in mind that there are no national indexes for BMD events in Germany. Visit the website http://www.amason.net/hessen/archives.htm for a comprehensive list of archives and databases that can aid you in your quest to uncover more about your German ancestry. From church, state and civil records to military organisations and maps, you are guaranteed to find something of interest!

GERMAN EMIGRATION

In many German states, being able to emigrate was not necessarily a straightforward procedure. Permission had to be granted and to enable an individual to be considered they had to prove that their parents were provided for – or that they had passed away – that any debts they may have were settled, or would be settled before they left the country, and that they had performed their military service. There were obviously those that managed to dodge this procedure, but for anyone who applied via the official channels, their records would be filed under emigration – or 'Auswanderung' – at the local archives.

Despite these strict regulations, very few records of passengers leaving Germany exist and those that do – mainly from Hamburg between 1850 and 1934 – can be viewed online at www.ancestry.com. Be aware that there is a gap in the records between 1915 and 1919 due to the First World War. The database includes images of the original passenger lists and shows that although one third of the people originated from Germany, nearly two-thirds actually came from Eastern Europe, especially those travelling between 1880 and 1914. These passenger lists also provide details of 750,000 Russian Jewish immigrants who sailed to the United States, and make interesting reading for those with Jewish ancestry (see Chapter 11).

This archive has only been partially indexed at present, so you may have to refer to the online hand-written indexes, which enable you to work out whether your ancestor was a 'direct passenger' (travelling to their destination on the same ship that they left Hamburg on) or whether they were an 'indirect passenger' (changing ships en route). With over 5 million records of individuals included in this database, it is an extremely important resource to mine. The records are in German, so expect to have to translate the wording.

Over the years, the amount of detail requested on the passenger lists varied, but you can gather much personal information from this one piece of documentation. The most basic data included the name, age, birth date and birthplace of the passenger, but you may be lucky enough to discover a person's original nationality, marital status, religion, occupation and even whether they had carried out military service. The shipping line on which they were travelling, the port and date of departure as well as their port of arrival and intended final destination might also be listed.

If you do have trouble locating your ancestor, consider searching using spelling variants of their name. Try to think how many ways in which a particular surname could have been spelt if it had been misheard when completing the forms. Extend the time frame in which you believe your ancestor emigrated to include a wider search period and remember to check both the direct and indirect indexes in case your ancestor changed ship en route. Sadly, it may simply be a case of your ancestor emigrating from another port, rather than Hamburg, where the passenger list information for their intended voyage was not recorded.

Norddeutscher Lloyd
Bremen.

A beautifully illustrated German shipping line brochure and menu list from 1899, preserved as a keepsake from one of the passengers of this particular trip. Have you come across similar items in your ancestor's possessions?

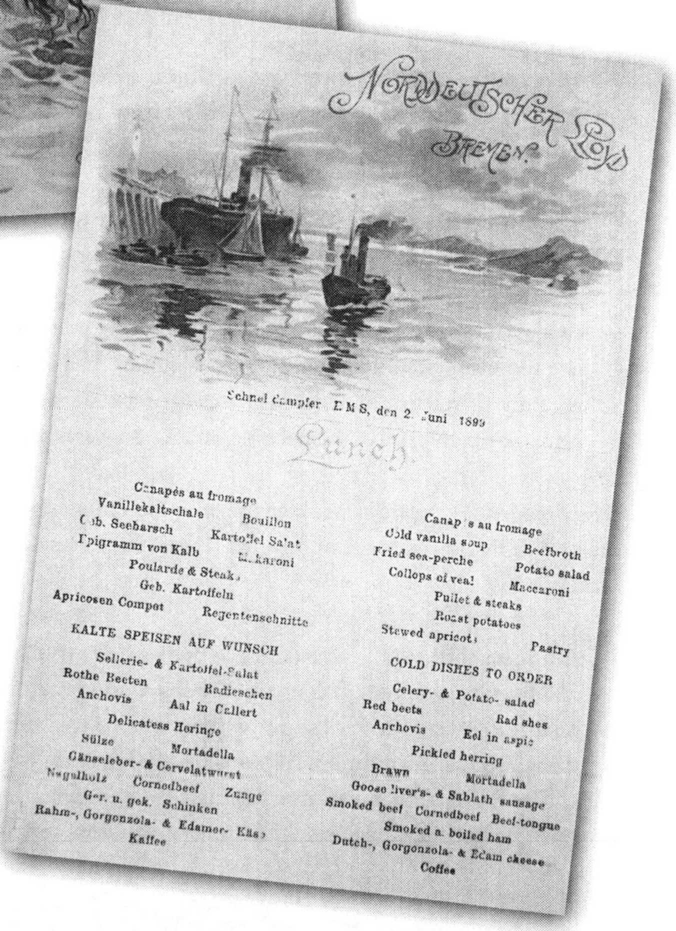

Norddeutscher Lloyd
Bremen.

Schnelldampfer EMS, den 2. Juni 1899

Lunch

Canapés au fromage
Vanillekaltschale
Bouillon
Geb. Seebarsch
Kartoffel Salat
Epigramm von Kalb
Makaroni
Poularde & Steaks
Geb. Kartoffeln
Apricosen Compot
Regentenschnitte

KALTE SPEISEN AUF WUNSCH

Sellerie- & Kartoffel-Salat
Rothe Beeten
Radieschen
Anchovis
Aal in Gallert
Delicatess Heringe
Sülze
Mortadella
Gänseleber- & Cervelatwurst
Nagelholz
Cornedbeef
Zunge
Ger. u. gek. Schinken
Rahm-, Gorgonzola- & Edamer- Käse
Kaffee

Canapés au fromage
Cold vanilla soup
Beefbroth
Fried sea-perche
Potato salad
Collops of veal
Maccaroni
Pullet & steaks
Roast potatoes
Stewed apricots
Pastry

COLD DISHES TO ORDER

Celery- & Potato- salad
Red beets
Radishes
Anchovis
Eel in aspic
Pickled herring
Brawn
Mortadella
Goose liver's- & Sablath sausage
Smoked beef
Cornedbeef
Beef-tongue
Smoked a. boiled ham
Dutch-, Gorgonzola- & Edam cheese
Coffee

CASE STUDY: A MEMORABLE EXPERIENCE

For those of us born after 1950, most of our literary encounters with British and German history during the first half of the twentieth century is dominated by war. But for those actually living in this period, that was not always the case, and between the two conflicts, Germany was a popular destination on European tours. In September 1929, St Annes resident Charles Doeg recorded his own travel experiences, which were later published in his local newspaper:

> It is not often one has the opportunity of visiting the continent from Liverpool in the luxurious manner recently afforded by the enterprise of the Canadian Pacific Railway Company, in placing at the disposal of the travelling public one of their magnificent liners, the 'Montrose', which recently left Liverpool for three days voyage to the handsome and busy city of Hamburg; to return again to Southampton after three full days ashore.

Charles's enthusiasm for travelling by ship is evident as he points out various shipping lines upon arrival in Hamburg – the largest port in Germany, referred to as 'the gateway to the world':

> As we approach our destination, we come across the famous Vulcan shipbuilding yards, and the fine fleet of the Hamburg American ships with their rather picturesque funnels; and four busy little tugs take possession of our monster ship, two at the stem and two at the stern and draw us along carefully and slowly to our mooring place. We had just caught sight of the North German Lloyd 'Europa' recently the victim of a serious fire. She is a sister ship to the famous 'Bremen', now the greyhound of the Atlantic, and is being refilled following the fire.

His detailed descriptions of their travel arrangements between Hamburg and Berlin gives us a first-hand account of what it was like to travel across country in Germany at this time:

> A non-stop express covered the 170 or 180 miles to the huge city in three hours and fourteen minutes. It is one of the finest and fastest runs in Germany, along a remarkably smooth track, and the train arrived to the minute. From the train, if desired, one can communicate outside by wireless.
>
> The famous firm of 'Cooks' – the traveller's friend – had, in Hamburg, not only provided a return travel ticket, arranged for a supplementary ticket (costing

> four marks each way for this special train from Hamburg to Berlin), and also phoned to the hotel in Berlin for rooms, which were ready at our disposal on arrival. This service was most helpful and just the kind of hotel we should have selected; the bedroom costing but seven marks per day, hot and cold running water in each well furnished room. The hotel is the 'Hotel Prinz Wilhelm' in Dorotheen Strasse. We were struck by the openness and spaciousness of many of the streets, the beautiful parks and shady boulevards. The New House of Parliament is a magnificent structure [...] and from a musical point of view, one felt envious of Berlin's three State Opera Houses.

Reading his journals, Charles's love of transportation is obvious, and he even gives us his opinion on the developing traffic light system adopted in Germany:

> The automatic street signalling is in general use, and one could not help noticing that not only motor drivers, but also pedestrians find this system most helpful, for they all look up at the signals before crossing the streets. On taxis and on other cars the mechanical signals showing which way you are turning are compulsory; we should do well to institute similar regulations in this country.

GERMAN INTERNMENT

As we have already discovered, large numbers of German migrants chose the United Kingdom as their home long before the early twentieth century, but when the First World War broke out in 1914, they faced suspicion and even more upheaval as people questioned their purpose for being in the country. Camps were set up in Knockaloe and Douglas on the Isle of Man and any German men between the ages of 18 and 50 were interned. History repeated itself by 1939, when German Jews – who fled to Britain to escape the Nazis – were naturally faced with the same feelings of mistrust and doubt as the world once again became ravaged by war.

The International Committee of the Red Cross (www.icrc.org) will provide a search of their internment records free of charge if requested by the individual concerned, or their next of kin; in other cases a nominal fee will be charged. Once the internee's name has been found, the entry could shed light on their original birthplace. This is an extremely useful resource, as most of Britain's internment records were destroyed in enemy bombing during the Second World War.

Digitisation is well underway for these First World War archives and it is hoped to be completed by early 2014. It is therefore necessary to fill in an online request form if you are enquiring about any civilian internee or prisoner of war who was involved in twentieth-century conflicts. During the 1939–45 conflict, information can again be found on the Red Cross website, or at The National Archives, which also records those internees who – to establish whether they were to be set free or interned – were taken before a tribunal. This documentation can provide an intriguing insight into your immigrant ancestor's war years.

The ICRC has literally thousands of records, photographs, films and audio archives. Established in 1863, its mission is to provide humanitarian help for people affected by conflict. Based in Geneva, Switzerland, this independent, neutral organisation takes its lead from the rulings put in place after the Geneva Conventions of 1949. Another important service offered is to trace the victims and their families of Nazi persecution. The wealth of information that their archives provide is phenomenal and charts the fate of over 17.5 million people. Of these, the documentation relates to victims of the Holocaust, those detained in Nazi concentration or work camps between 1933 and 1945, displaced persons under the care of international relief organisations after the Second World War, and children separated from their parents as a result of war.

The International Tracing Service (ITS), operating from Bad Arolsen in Germany (and via the website http://www.its-arolsen.org/en/homepage/index.html), makes the important statement that:

> in the coming years it will no longer be possible to obtain direct testimonies from survivors of Nazi persecution. Therefore the unique documents preserved in Bad Arolsen will play a crucial role in testifying of this dark chapter of human history [...] and will carry on with its traditional work providing information to survivors and their families for as long as it continues to receive requests.

BORDER CONTROL – HUNGARY

When following your forebear's trail abroad remember that over time national boundaries in foreign countries have changed; an area that was once in Russia could now be in Romania, or even Poland, while a city that was formerly in Germany, might now belong to the Russian Federation.

Over the last century, Hungarian borders, place names and internal boundaries have changed considerably so the key to success when researching German/Hungarian ancestors is organisation. By obtaining maps of the area you want to research – or even full country maps – from different periods, you can begin to establish where your ancestor was located. For example, some former Hungarian cities have now become amalgamated into the countries of the surrounding nations.

Try to establish when your ancestors arrived in Britain from Hungary by searching for them on the census. For example, if they appeared on the 1901 record but not on the 1891 enumeration, you can target your research to this particular decade.

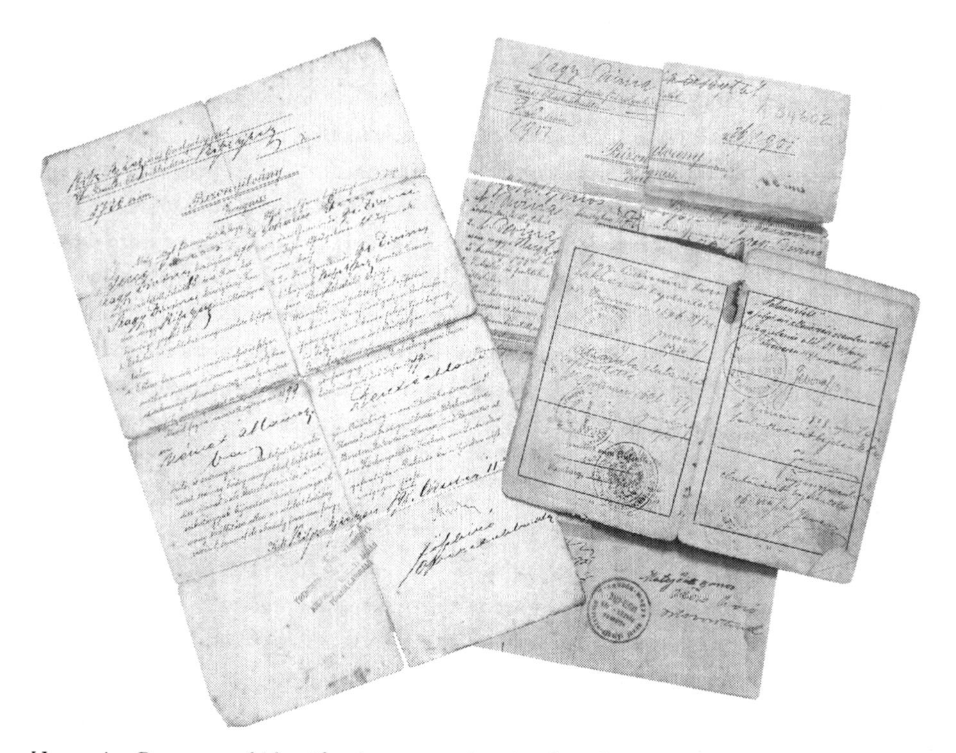

Hungarian Passport and identification papers showing the official stamp, which proves this passenger travelled via the German port of Hamburg. Look closely at your ephemera and memorabilia to see what clues you might have missed.

The National Archives at Kew provides lists of naturalisation from the period 1844 to 1934, so checking here may uncover future research possibilities if you manage to locate your forebear within these documents.

Once you've traced your ancestor through the British records, you can proceed back to their country of birth and try to establish a link in the Hungarian records. It is worth remembering that in their own country, Hungarians write the family surname first, so although a person may have been known as Janos Geres in Britain, you will now have to search under the name of Geres Janos. A useful addition to their twentieth-century records is the inclusion of a mother's Christian and maiden names, helping to distinguish between those with similar names. This information is a vital piece of evidence in establishing an additional generation in your tree as traditionally women dropped both their Christian and maiden names upon marriage and instead added the suffix 'ne' to their husband's first name.

If you wish to search census records the best place to start your enquiry is at The National Archives in Budapest. Here, they will be able to confirm what documents still exist for each area and in what year the censuses were taken. The data contained in each varies greatly. An alternative resource is to establish what tax records are available from your ancestor's place of birth. These were created by the Church and used for calculating the tithes payable by the residents in certain dioceses. They can provide a treasure trove of information about a family and date back much further than the census.

The majority of Hungary's Church records dating to 1895 are held on microfilm in the Hungarian National Archives. Baptisms, marriages and deaths between 1850 and 1895 are recorded in pre-printed books with sections that allowed the priest to write in specific details such as names and dates. Prior to this, the documents were mostly hand drawn and written. While there was a lot of intermarriage between Christian denominations, it is important to note that it wasn't until the 1780s that Emperor Joseph II allowed Protestant churches to keep Parish records. Before this date all registers were Catholic, with Protestant events denoted with simple phrases such as 'LUTH', meaning Lutheran.

HUNGARIAN JEWS

Although I have tried to focus on Jewish research in Chapter 11, a note should be made in this chapter regarding those Hungarians of Jewish extraction. You may find this area of your research a little 'hit and miss' with regards to what you will uncover and how far back you can trace your family line. Joseph II declared that all Jews living in Hungary should adopt surnames in German so this may initially impede the tracking down of your individual's origins. Although many Jewish records were destroyed during the war, all is not lost …

A national census recorded all the Jews living in Hungary in 1848, which can be viewed at The National Archives in Budapest, and makes essential viewing if your forebears resided in the country around this period. Follow this up by contacting the Hungarian and Jewish Museum and Archive, which holds the census records taken that refer to the Jews in the country between 1827 and 1853. For further information visit www.fsz.bme.hu/hungary/budapest/bpmuz/bpmuz19.htm.

Similarly, a fabulous online research guide to Jewish Hungarian ancestry has been produced by the Centre for Jewish History and can be downloaded online at http://researchguides.cjh.org/Hungary.pdf.

Sadly, Civil Registration did not begin in Hungary until October 1895. These documents were sealed for 100 years, so the amount of information available to the family historian is naturally limited and can be difficult to obtain.

CASE STUDY: GLEANING THE FACTS

Language is always a barrier, but in this modern age of technology there is no need to be put off if the memorabilia or ephemera you discover are not written in English.

LESSONS IN LANGUAGE

Not only is the order of the person's name important but also the language in which the original records were written. Prior to 1844, Latin was the language used in Hungary. Later, Hungarian was widely used, along with German. This also applied to the written word with Catholic records written in Latin and Protestant documents written in Hungarian or German. When trying to research your ancestral name remember that the German language also influenced the writing and spelling of a person's name.

Before passports became compulsory thousands of people travelled without one, therefore, to discover one of these documents relating to your ancestor is a massive bonus – no matter what language it was written in.

Engage the services of a professional translator, ask the advice of someone who speaks the language, or use the free translator tools on the Internet to convert the text into something readable. Even if you can only pick out certain words or phrases, with a little diligence, it is possible to begin to decipher the document. The website http://translate.google.co.uk enables you to simply type in the words, sentence or paragraph that you wish to translate, click the buttons to request a conversion from Hungarian to English, and wait for your new information to be revealed. Be prepared for some words or phrases to be 'lost in translation' but you should at least be able to fathom out the meanings and get the gist of what has been written.

In my example, the passport and papers of Janos Geres are in very poor condition yet peppered with facts that will help advance any further investigations. The papers have been folded and unfolded so many times that they have worn badly along the creases and parted company, but these four quarters *are* legible. If you find a document in a similar state, don't be tempted to cellotape the pieces together – the tape will gradually discolour and look even more unsightly. Instead, lay the quarters onto a scanner and scan the complete piece, then you can use this copy to work from and keep the original in a safe place.

As for the badly worn passport with its tattered cloth covers, the damage is only cosmetic and the paperwork is still intact and the lettering still readable. The condition of both of these items tells a tale in itself. The documents were likely to have been presented for inspection on numerous occasions throughout their long journey to prove the identification of the owner and to officially show the countries he had travelled from and was travelling to ... so although they may look a little worse for wear they record an important passage of time.

By translating documents you can increase your chances of finding further information about the individual to which they belong, and in turn, look out for all the records where their details may have been included. The word 'Hamburg' on the hand stamp which marks the passport can easily be identified and leads us to understand that this would be the port of departure from which the individual left Germany. Investigate further by checking the records at www.ancestry.com and then use this information to cross-reference the details with the various passenger lists. On this occasion, more research revealed Geres' arrival in America and his completion of a Petition for Naturalisation in 1904.

Similarly, the date of birth given on the passport can be used to confirm that you are tracing the correct person across all documentation, so each seemingly small piece of information gleaned can provide clues to trace an individual's travel plans or proposed route, making any item of ephemera found, a real gem for genealogists.

11

JEWISH MIGRANTS

'Emigration, forced or chosen, across national frontiers or from village to metropolis, is the quintessential experience of our time.'
John Berger

An Edict of Expulsion was proclaimed by King Edward I in 1290 banishing the entire Jewish population from our shores; it would be another 400 years, under the ruling of Oliver Cromwell, before their re-admission was allowed.

Jump forward to the end of the nineteenth century and large numbers of Jewish families flocked to Europe to settle in countries such as Holland, Germany, Poland and the UK to avoid the difficult conditions they were experiencing in Eastern Europe and Russia. In Britain they quickly established communities incorporating their own worship in synagogues alongside that of Reform, United and Independent churches.

CASE STUDY: IN NEED OF EMPLOYMENT

The *Oxford Dictionary* definition of ephemera is: 'things that exist or are used or enjoyed for only a short time.' These 'things' are usually paper based – letters, diaries, theatre programmes, tickets and newspapers – which have avoided being thrown away and have survived to tell a tale of a different era.

For family historians, ephemera is doubly beneficial, as not only do we revel in owning an item that once belonged to our ancestors, but we also appreciate that ephemera – not necessarily in the possession of our forebears – still has the potential to inform us about their lives. Newspapers, journals and printed publications are a good example of this.

First, a carefully preserved copy of *The Graphic* newspaper might have once been purchased and enjoyed by your great-great-grandfather – a fabulous keepsake just on those merits alone, but on further inspection the articles, adverts, images and opinion pieces within can help to shed light on the world your forebear was living in. An article published in the late 1890s helps us to understand the diverse skills and trades of the Russian Jews who were eager to find work as soon as they arrived in Britain. Scour original printed publications to enhance your knowledge of specific periods of our history:

> Forty of them, including about a dozen women and children, had just arrived by a Hamburg vessel, all apparently in excellent health, notwithstanding the hardships through which they had passed. Among them were a carpenter, two tin workers, two millers, two tailors, three cigar makers, a brush maker, a tanner, two employees at a grain warehouse and two traders. Most of these immigrants were provided with addresses to which they were directed under proper guidance.

The writer points out that due to their eagerness to work, find homes for their families or to continue their journey on to America, these immigrants would not 'become chargeable to any parish' and would sustain themselves. Despite this, it was also believed that their skills were wasted:

> Ignorance of the vernacular [...] also of the special methods of English trades, and a general feeling of strangeness and timidity in their novel circumstances, keep them from occupations in which they have had training and experience, and induce them to join the army of workers already engaged in cheap shoe and clothing trades. Toiling for barely enough to keep body and soul together, the struggle at first is terribly severe. The labourer has scarcely passed out of the unskilled stage, when he is able to earn, when in full work, as a tailor from 7/– to 8/–, and as a boot maker from 6/– to 7/– a day, women's earnings amounting on the average to half that sum.
>
> The complaint one hears on all sides is not, as one would expect, that the hours are too long, or that the work is too heavy and monotonous, but that there is not enough of it.

These comments provide a brief glimpse into the great labour problem that was not only experienced by our own nationals, but also by the immigrants who came here. Surprisingly, over 100 years on, not a lot has changed.

GET YOUR FACTS STRAIGHT

The term 'Ashkenazi' derives from the word 'Ashkenaz', which is Hebrew for Germany. These Jews were of Central or Eastern European descent and approximately 120,000 arrived in Britain between 1880 and 1914 from Russia and Poland.

The term 'Sephardim' derives from the word 'Sepharad', meaning Spain, and refers to those families of Spanish or Portuguese origin. Today, many Sephardim Jews are from North Africa or the Middle East.

WIDENING THE NET

Initially, when starting your Jewish genealogical quest, you will need to employ the same research techniques as if you were trying to locate anyone else who lived in Britain. Gather together any old documents, ask family members for their recollections, jot down name variations, and try to establish your ancestor's approximate date of arrival.

Once you have confirmed that your Jewish forebear settled in Britain, you can begin to build a picture of their lives by researching the community they lived in. By referring to maps and topographical guides in the local archives, and trade directories at www.ancestry.co.uk or historicaldirectories.org, you should be able to determine what kind of area they were living in, what the housing was like, and whether the living conditions were good or bad.

Where possible, use the census to see if other families with Jewish sounding surnames lived nearby and look closely at what they listed as their occupations – were they working in a whole variety of jobs, or did they bring their skills with them from their homeland? Different nationalities are often known for excelling at particular vocations. For example, Jewish people are often connected with tailoring or jewellery trades.

Refer again to specialist trade, commercial and historical directories, such as White's, Pigot's and Kelly's, to see if your ancestors had their own family business, giving you another avenue to follow as you try to verify where a business was based and if the building they worked in still exists.

Local newspapers are ideal for enlightening us as to how immigrant communities were perceived. Study them over a number of decades to see how thoughts and feelings changed towards the newcomers and how they integrated with the locals. When you've found references to your Jewish ancestors on the census and other civil registration documents you can flesh out this information by searching synagogue records.

You may be lucky enough to uncover a marriage contract which provides the date and place of birth of those who were born abroad, giving you the potential to take the family line back even further.

Don't forget to seek out newspaper references to family events. The *Jewish Chronicle* (which can be researched online at www.thejc.com) reported births, betrothals, marriages and deaths. Similarly, a wealth of information can be uncovered if you happen to find an obituary referring to your Jewish forebear. The details revealed can help you to make links between other family members, information you may not have been able to discover anywhere else.

By verifying a place of birth – either from census returns, marriage contracts or naturalisation papers – you can begin to work backwards. Remember that the records of the Latter-day Saints are not confined to purely Christian entries, so try your luck on the website to see what facts you can confirm. https://familysearch.org.

Top tip – when researching Eastern European names, the spellings can change considerably from document to document. Where possible widen your search using the Soundex facility to include all forms of the name by how they 'sound' regardless of how they are spelt.

Why not consider joining a Jewish related group or society? Their knowledge of specific records, and help with language barriers when deciphering old Hebrew documents and memorial inscriptions, will definitely be an advantage.

The Jewish Genealogical Society of Great Britain or 'JGSGB' (www.jgsgb.org.uk) promotes and encourages the study of Jewish genealogy – if you have the time and are able to travel, think about enrolling on a beginner's workshop, or attending one of their talks. In early 2010 they released the 1851 Anglo-Jewry Database – a collection of approximately 29,000 records covering the lives of more than 90 per cent of the Jewish population living in the British Isles in the mid-nineteenth century. Searchable by both members and non-members, this resource is one of the most important databases relating to this area of research. Their knowledge and online aids to understanding Synagogue marriage authorisations can be a great help to the novice family historian, while their library of Jewish genealogical books is unrivalled by any other in Europe.

Remember to ensure that official records were made; many Jews were registered in the Church of England parish registers, so don't limit yourself purely to Jewish based records when trying to find your forebears.

Perhaps your ancestors settled in the capital, then why not visit London's Museum of Jewish Life based in Finchley. Their archive includes many personal records and documents with photographs of Jewish social history in the London area and oral collections of past residents. An appointment is required to be booked in advance so consider combining your visit by enrolling on one of their Family History Workshops, which are held periodically throughout the year. Find out more at http://www.jewishmuseum.org.uk.

THE RUSSO-JEWISH IMMIGRANT.

Seek out vintage articles about the lives of immigrants, such as this one depicting the problems faced by Russian Jews living in London in the late nineteenth century.

The International Jewish Cemetery Project (www.iajgsjewishcemeteryproject.org) aims to catalogue every Jewish cemetery or burial site listed by town or city, country, and geographic region around the world – an extremely helpful database to use as you follow your ancestor's trail.

Once your research takes you back overseas, your first port of call should be to join one of the many genealogy societies that exist around the world. They will be able to explain where different records and registers are housed, and may even be able to put you in touch with like-minded genealogists researching the same family line. An initial search for a suitable society can be done online and once you've made contact you can follow the leads wherever they may take you. It may be worth hiring a private researcher in the country of origin who can concentrate on your case, would be well versed in deciphering Jewish documents, and provide essential help in translating any paperwork into English.

JEWISH REFUGEES

In 1938 the views of the Nazi Party brought about the increased persecution of the Jewish community in Germany and in order to escape their anti-Semitic laws many chose Britain as a place of refuge. As a result, over 13,000 people (10,000 of them children) had arrived here by 1939, prompting the government to fear that this sudden and continued 'invasion' would create a huge unemployment problem, and so they began to look for ways to repatriate the newcomers. Temporary shelters were erected in existing Jewish communities, but because many had come from enemy territory, they were initially treated with caution – and sometimes hostility – and placed in internment camps, often alongside the enemy, until their background stories were investigated.

The National Archives has an excellent online help guide to enable you to track down any existing records relating to interns during both the First and Second World Wars (www.nationalarchives.gov.uk/catalogue/RdLeaflet.asp?sLeafletID=224&j=1).

The Holocaust

Those unable to escape from Nazi persecution faced a terrible fate during what became known as the Holocaust. By researching this emotive subject on the Internet you will discover there is a wealth of databases and websites that can fully help you to find out more about those involved in this period of our history.

Start your research at the JewishGen website (www.jewishgen.org) – an affiliate of the Museum of Jewish Heritage and a living memorial to the Holocaust. One of its most comprehensive collections is its Holocaust Database, which comprises of 2.4 million entries with information gathered from over 190 sources. These sources include:

- Jews who resided in Krosno, Poland before 1941.
- Danish deportees.
- Auschwitz Work Cards.
- An American military government compiled list of Jews showing the survivors and victims of concentration camps.
- Polish Medical Questionnaires – of over 2,000 Jewish medical personnel.
- Jewish refugees from the Soviet Union.

The component databases with some of the largest number of individuals recorded includes:

- The Bedzin census of Poland from 1939 containing the information of over 20,000 Jews who were remunerated in this city at the start of the Second World War.
- The World Jewish Congress Collection with data on more than 72,000 Holocaust survivors.
- Claims Conference Data on Hungarian and Romanian Jews.
- Schindler's list, totalling 1,980 inmates in Oskar Schindler's factories in Poland and Czechoslovakia.

These are just a fraction of the collections held on the site and it is not until you view their extensive lists at www.jewishgen.org/databases/Holocaust that you realise the research possibilities you are able to carry out online.

To enable you to use the site to its fullest there is a 'frequently asked questions' area, a 'first timers guide', and FREE online classes that are designed to educate while providing specialist help from experts, allowing you to connect with like-minded researchers and discover more about resources available to you in this specialist area of genealogy.

Finally, there is the opportunity to donate to the ongoing work involved in creating this genealogical archive – which includes the translation into English of memorial books written after the Holocaust – as well as providing ways in which you can honour a family member on a special occasion and remember those no longer with us.

If you find Polish Jews within your ancestry, follow the links to the www.jewishgen.org/Communities page of the website. Here you will find a database of Jewish communities, their historical names and jurisdictions, providing the perfect place to pinpoint your ancestor on the map. The JewishGen Gazetteer also enables you to search Jewish localities in fifty-four countries stretching across Europe, the Middle East, Central Asia and North Africa. This powerful tool helps you to map a place name displaying information to within a 10-mile radius of the location.

The 'family trees' section is particularly helpful and contains the details of over 4 million people with Jewish ancestry worldwide. Consider using online translation aids to decipher Hebrew, Russian, Yiddish and other languages – http://translatorbar.com allows free translation to and from any language and enables you to download a 'translator toolbar' to your computer for future use.

12

POLAND

'Not all those who wander are lost.'
J.R.R. Tolkien

Poland has a diverse and complicated history. Before the First World War, it was actually split between Russia – which controlled the larger share – Germany (formerly Prussia), and Austria. During the Second World War, Hitler and Stalin divided the lands between them and it did not become the country we know as Poland with its present-day boundaries until 1946. These changes in boundaries can cause some difficulties for the family historian as records were produced in the language of the governing country. Despite this, these records are likely to have remained within the same area and have been deposited in the local archives.

Prior to Poland's EU membership in 2004 and its resulting effects on migration by its citizens, the greatest influx of Polish immigrants to Britain was during the early- to mid-twentieth century. Many fled their homeland under traumatic conditions when Europe was in the grip of war. Prior to this, religious persecution was the main contributing factor to their movements.

Each governing country had different religions. Russian Poland had large numbers of Jewish communities and pockets of Russian and Greek Orthodox worshippers. In the former Prussian Poland, many were Lutherans, while in Austria the majority followed the Roman Catholic religion. As borders and governing countries changed, there was strong opposition between the differing religions resulting in many emigrating to escape the trouble which ensued. This was not just a nineteenth-century problem where the Jewish took flight from the Russian 'pogroms', but continued well into the twentieth century with the German invasion and the Holocaust. Those that fought for freedom and joined the Free Polish Forces also felt the need to flee the country and sought sanctuary in Britain. During the 1950s, '60s and '70s, many escaped from behind the Iron Curtain, not returning until after its collapse in 1989.

ENQUIRE AND INVESTIGATE

Those who settled here during this time may have left evidence of their past in the form of personal family papers, letters, naturalisation papers, passports and travel documents which should give you a clue as to their original hometown or village. Interviewing your living relatives for information about your Polish ancestor is likely to shed light on the reasons behind their emigration. Be aware that the details may be very hard for some people to recount, so always use sensitivity and understanding with your questioning and don't push certain subjects until the individual is ready to talk further.

At the forefront of those directly affected by the conflicts of the Second World War, 160,000 Polish servicemen who had fought alongside our own British soldiers in Europe, and were mainly anti-Communists, were in no hurry to return to their homeland, which was now ruled by the Soviet Union. To demobilise these Polish servicemen, the Polish Resettlement Corps (PRC) was formed in 1946, which allowed them to enlist for the term of their demobilisation. Once discharged, they could go on to make new lives in Britain, joined by their wives and families from Poland. The addition of these dependent relatives took the number of Polish immigrants at this time to over 200,000. Records of the PRC are held in the Army Records Centre of The National Archives at Kew. Any documents that were written in Polish usually have English translations.

For those with ancestors who arrived in Britain much earlier than these dates, civil registration records could hold the key to revealing family information. Birth certificates should reveal a mother's maiden name and address, allowing you to cross-reference the results with details found on earlier censuses. Marriage certificates not only show the female maiden name but also the names and occupation of the couple's fathers; these clues may seem small but when combined with other household information you can begin to work out when your ancestor arrived in Britain. By focusing on a timeline of events you can then concentrate on seeking out naturalisation papers and passenger lists to follow the trail back to Poland.

LANGUAGE BARRIERS

When tracing your Polish ancestry it is important to first try and establish your family's place of origin. Even if you are lucky enough to discover a possible location on a document or British census record there are still hurdles to overcome. Remember that some spellings may have been lost in translation, and even that earlier Polish names may have been different from their modern equivalents.

Cabinet cards and photographs were hugely important to travelling ancestors and emigrants, helping to keep the memories of their loved ones back home alive.

Poland has had such a volatile history that many of its records have been written in different languages, depending on who was governing the country at the time, which can undoubtedly cause the researcher a headache. Early Roman Catholic registers were written in Latin, Lutheran registers were usually written in German, while Orthodox records were created in Ukrainian, Polish, Old Church Slavonic or Russian, so unless you're a bit of a linguist, you're going to need a translator to help with your latest mission. Depending upon the amount of correspondence you need to write, and the documents you need to decipher, this will not come cheap, but can be viewed as a worthy investment if you learn more about your family's heritage.

REVEL IN THE RESEARCH

The description on www.polishroots.org hints at Poland's diverse associations, while concisely summing up its aims:

> PolishRoots covers all areas that were historically part of the Polish Commonwealth, from the 16th through the 18th centuries, throughout the

> years of partitions by Prussia, Russia, and Austria, through its rebirth in 1918, subsequent domination during World War II and post-war occupation, to its present freedom struggle for independence through the latter 20th century.
>
> We also promote Polonia, areas of Polish presence throughout the world regardless of ethnicity, religion, or political views. We cover everything Polish whether you have ancestry there for 500+ years, or you shop at a Polish deli down the street.

So there it is in a nutshell! Visit the site and from immigration to ethnicity, culture to customs, you can immerse yourself in the Polish way of life and understand more about the country's history. A whole section has been dedicated to genealogical research giving links to specific archives, libraries, organisations and societies that can help you pinpoint the best place to start your search. Along with this extensive list are numerous links to Polish themed collections and archives around the world – ideal if your ancestor emigrated to a Polish community in a different country.

A helpful section includes 'Tips on Translating' and gives examples of Polish expressions and words which have then been translated into their Latin and English equivalents, as well as the meaning and 'usage' of the particular phrase. This can be extremely beneficial when trying to transcribe documents, letters and journals written in the native tongue.

DID YOU KNOW?

With regards to civil registration, early Poland followed the procedures of their governing countries, so start by checking www.familysearch.org for those records which have been microfilmed. When the Poland we know today was formed in 1946, a standard civil registration process was put in place allowing you to apply for birth, marriage or death certificates of your ancestors from the local archive in the region where the event took place.

13

SPAIN

'Travel makes one modest, you see what
a tiny place you occupy in the world.'
Gustave Flaubert

Again and again we begin to see that war and conflict often dictates the direction in which a family's nationality can take them, especially when our ancestors flee their birth countries in order to find a safe place to settle. These links are often discovered quite by accident.

THE SPANISH CIVIL WAR

When the Basque city of Guernica was bombed by a legion working on behalf of General Francisco Franco, little did anyone realise that the repercussions of these actions would be felt in Britain for many years to come.

The destruction of property and civilians in the ancient Basque capital was part of Franco's campaign against the existence of the Spanish Republic in the north of the peninsula during what was to become the 1936–39 Spanish Civil War. Many that survived the attack sought sanctuary abroad. Although the British government was adamant about following its policy for non-intervention in the conflict, the 'Basque Children's Committee' – an offshoot of the National Joint Committee for Spanish Relief – was set up enabling 3,800 Basque children to be evacuated to England and Wales for the duration of the war. It guaranteed a fund of 10 shillings per child per week to ensure their care and education.

In May 1937, the ageing steamship SS *Habana*, escorted by a British convoy of two naval warships – the *Royal Oak* and the *Forester* – arrived at the port of Southampton. On board were 3,840 Spanish children, 80 teachers, 15 Catholic priests and 120 voluntary helpers. Their journey had been a tough one from the moment that the children had been taken to the Spanish quayside by a train. Here, they had boarded the vessels and emotionally left their homeland behind, undergoing a gruelling sea voyage, encountering a storm in the Bay of Biscay, which resulted in terrible seasickness, long before they sighted the British coast.

Initially, these children were sent to a camp in Eastleigh, Hampshire before being found new homes across England and Wales. Bristol, Bradford, Cambridge, Oxford, Keighley, Caerleon, Hull, Leeds, London, Maidenhead, Manchester, Witney, Swansea and Worthing were all to play host, and although many of these children returned home after the conflict ended, some 250 remained in Britain rebuilding their lives and having families of their own.

Have you discovered Basque ancestry in your family tree?

In November 2002, 'The Basque Children of '37 Association' was set up to reunite these once displaced children of war, helping to preserve and document their stories. Plaques were placed in locations around Britain where the children had found temporary or, on some occasions, permanent homes, marking their 'traumatic adventure' in history. To find out more about this Spanish evacuation visit the website at www.basquechildren.org where you will find tips on how to research these children, as well as articles, photographs and details of the whole operation.

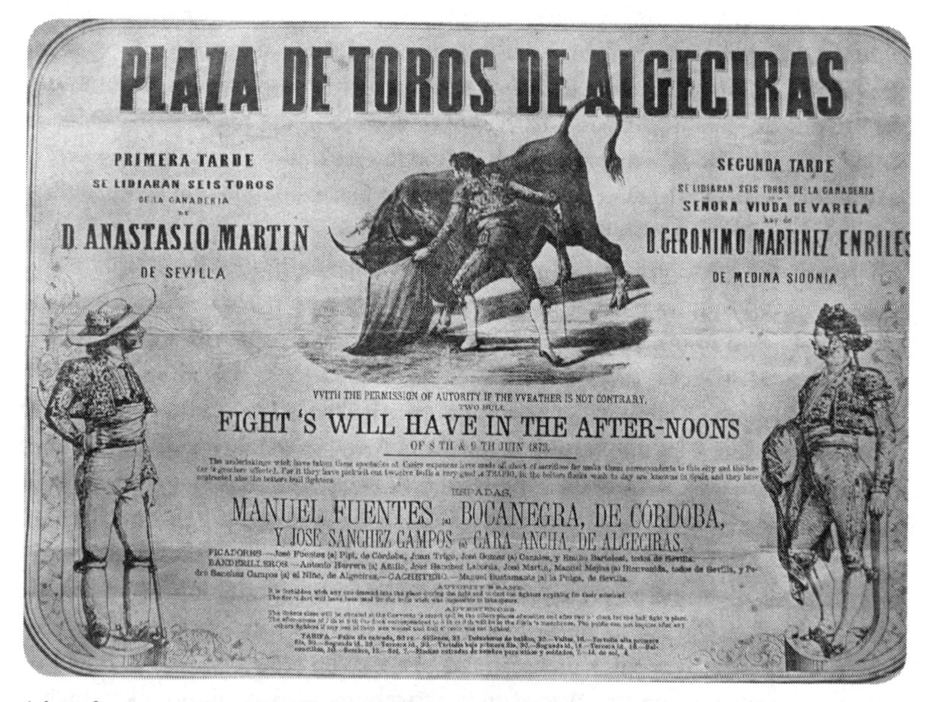

Advert from a 1902 Spanish bullfight. Adverts and pamphlets from specific events and entertainments tucked inside our ancestor's belongings can show us how they spent their free time.

A Welsh Connection

The lack of official intervention to quell the raging civil unrest resulted in individuals from other countries feeling strongly enough to travel to Spain to fight fascism by joining the cause to restore freedom and democracy. Comprising of 40,000 volunteers from across Europe, the International Brigade was established. Of the 174 men who enlisted from Wales, 118 were from the mining valleys of the South; 33 of whom were to lose their lives. Their jobs as colliery workers made them sympathetic to the plight of the Spanish. Often the Welsh volunteers were men who were unemployed due to their trade union activities and beliefs, or ex-servicemen. Find out more about their experiences at www.agor.org.uk/cwm.

The Welsh contingency only accounted for some of the many volunteers who left Britain to provide assistance. If you believe your ancestor played their part, why not visit The National Archives website to browse the digitalised records of The International Brigade Association and Friends of Republican Spain (KV5/112)? This annotated list details those who fought in the Spanish Civil War and includes a Roll of Honour of those who lost their lives. The collection is broken down into those nationalities who were involved, making it easier to pinpoint your ancestor if they were not a British national.

An excellent website can be found at the Warwick Digital Library (http://www2.warwick.ac.uk/services/library/mrc/explorefurther/digital/scw), where material from the Modern Records Centre of the University of Warwick has been added. It makes essential reading if you want to understand more about the effects of the Spanish Civil War on Britain, the attitudes of the British and French governments, the response to organised labour, the care of refugees, and the International Brigade. A wide selection of ephemera from this period has been digitalised allowing you to read and download images of documents, opinion pieces and relevant propaganda – perfect for adding examples to your own family stories.

The Archives Hub, http://archiveshub.ac.uk/features/spanishcivilwar.shtml represents over 220 institutions across the country and is a great place to discover unique and little-known resources that can help support your ongoing research. For those wanting to investigate further, use this site to find links to organisations, books and specific collections. Additionally, there is information on where to find examples of ephemera produced by the Spanish Republican Army in the 1930s, photographs of civil-war volunteers, memorials and ceremonies held to commemorate those who fought, as well as directions on how to track down video footage or the recollections of those who were involved, or affected, by the conflict. From Swansea University (which holds recorded interviews of war veterans from the South Wales mining communities) to the Bateman collection at Bristol (with its selection of printed ephemera), there is material in these archives just waiting to be discovered.

Don't forget the Imperial War Museum's website, www.iwm.org.uk, which is home to one of the most important collections of posters in the UK – many examples can be found at the online resource for visual arts – www.vads.ac.uk – by entering 'Spanish Civil War' in their search facility.

Building an Archive

Due in part to the Spanish Civil War taking place within living memory, historical items of memorabilia can regularly be found on auction sites such as eBay. Think about honouring your forebear by collecting newspaper clippings recording the unfolding events of the conflict, war correspondent pictorials and freedom fighter badges – just some of the items listed for sale which are ideal to illustrate this turbulent period of your family history.

Look out for identity cards and identifiable photographs of Republican soldiers and militia; flags, propaganda material and postcards with a military theme can all help us to get an insight into the tensions and atmosphere encountered at this time.

Seek out specialist dealers on the Internet for more unusual pieces but do your research beforehand so that you have a good knowledge about what you are buying. Remember:

- Where possible examine items before you purchase them to ensure they are in the best condition that you can afford.
- Establish that the item you are buying is an original and not a reproduction. It can be difficult to tell the difference so if you are not sure seek the help of an expert.
- As with any paper ephemera, display out of direct sunlight, or store in acid and lignin free folders to prolong its life and condition. Consider the purchase of the best storage for all your memorabilia as an investment.

SPANISH LINKS – IT'S ALL IN THE NAME

Whittling down exact places of origin for a foreign immigrant ancestor can sometimes be difficult if all you have to go on is the name of the country. This can be even harder without the help of census, BMD records and parish registers to provide clues.

Locating the passenger list of the voyage taken by your forebears is obviously your best bet, but failing that try to study your ancestor's name.

Ask yourself – is it possible that their name has been anglicised? Write down spelling variants and say the name aloud to see how it could have been interpreted. Using your results, carry out Internet searches to see if you can establish a geographical location for the surname. Similarly, does the name itself describe the location? Or, is it a description of a particular occupation? It is surprising what leads you can find if you take your train of thought in a new direction. From this you may not be able to get the name of an exact town or village, but you can certainly close the net on possible areas and even dismiss unlikely candidates.

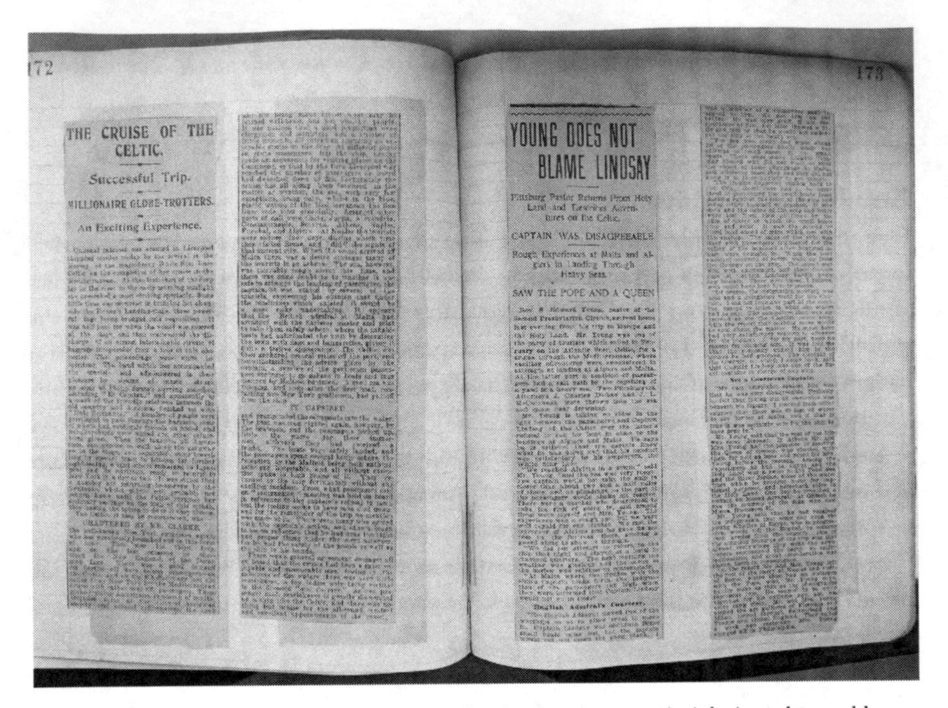
THE CRUISE OF THE CELTIC.

Successful Trip.

MILLIONAIRE GLOBE-TROTTERS.

An Exciting Experience.

YOUNG DOES NOT BLAME LINDSAY

CAPTAIN WAS DISAGREEABLE

SAW THE POPE AND A QUEEN

Newspaper cuttings lovingly pasted into scrapbooks can give us an insight into the world our forebears lived in.

ANCIENT ASSOCIATIONS

An injection of foreign ancestry can appear with the branches of your family tree at any point in history. Step back in time to the Medieval period when the son of King Edward III – John of Gaunt – was preparing to marry Princess Constance of Castille. The princess came to England accompanied by Dona Sanche de Ayala – a Castilian young woman of aristocratic birth – who remained in Britain when she married the English knight, Sir Walter Blount. The couple's descendants gave generations of Britons ancient Spanish roots. This is an example of just one of the occasions when our ancient British and Hispanic ancestry has become entwined.

Helpful Hints:

- Over the centuries, Spaniards have travelled to British shores for trade, or to escape wars and disputes within their own country; some settled here permanently, while others moved back to their homeland at a later date. If you have found links to forebears emigrating from Spain before 1790, a number of passenger lists still exist that can be accessed at the General Archives in Seville.

- Since the early 1700s, anyone of Spanish descent was referred to in their written records by two surnames; a similar example in Britain would be known as a 'double barrelled' name. In Spain, the first of the two surnames would denote the surname of the individual's father, while the second would denote that of the mother. This is an extremely important consideration when trying to trace a specific line and can help you to determine the difference between the maternal and paternal sides of a family.
- Civil registration did not begin in Spain until 1 January 1872. Obtaining details of these events can be frustrating as there are no indexes to these records so you really do need to have as much information about a person as possible before you make your enquiry. If you are lucky enough to track down a birth record you will be rewarded with not only the details of the individual, but also the names and birthplaces of the parents and all four grandparents. The initial search may prove difficult, but the outcome has the potential to rapidly confirm the surnames of several generations.
- By the mid-1800s, parish priests were required to submit duplicate baptism, marriage and burial records to the city authorities. Later, when left wing radicals showed their opposition to religion by burning Spain's churches, much archival material was lost forever so these duplicates provide another avenue of research for you to try.
- Church records were kept by law in Spain from 1570 onwards and those that have survived contain similar information to their British equivalents. Bonus details came in the 1700s when the spouses of the deceased were named, while towards the end of the eighteenth century, grandparents were named on baptismal records. These registers may still remain at the parish church, or now reside at the local archives.

14

ITALY

'To travel is to live.'
Hans Christian Andersen

ITALIAN INFLUENCE

By the 1851 census, approximately 4,000 Italians were living in England. The majority of these came from the mountain and lake regions of Italy, bringing their artistic talents to Britain in an attempt to earn extra money before returning home in time for their harvests. Their traditional craftsmanship earned them a reputation as skilled workers known for creating intricate pieces of furniture and precision instruments such as clocks and barometers.

Within thirty years, Britain saw an influx of Italians who followed their predecessors, eager to escape rural poverty in their own country. Happy to take on a variety of employment roles from shopkeepers to figurine makers, many chose to settle here for the long haul. Men brought their wives and children, while those who were single married local women and started their own families, establishing small communities – collectively known as 'Little Italy' – not only in London, but in towns and cities across the UK. The number of immigrants who settled north of the border has resulted in an estimated 80,000 Scots of Italian descent living in Scotland today; many of these can trace their roots to the Tuscany and Lazio regions.

Although their choice of occupations was diverse – encompassing ships' chandlers and coal miners, plasterers and organ grinders – the Italians also brought with them their passion for food, especially ice cream. Their skills and culinary knowledge rated them as some of the best ice cream makers in the world, and they shared the results of their secret family recipes with their customers to create a regular income.

Initially, Italian vendors would travel the streets with brightly coloured carts – pulled by pony or pushed by hand – and sell their ice cream from their own pitch or round.

Gradually, they would rent or purchase premises to build successful businesses, often choosing to employ friends and relatives who had travelled from the same villages back home in Italy. This provision of employment to other family members is always worth bearing in mind when trying to establish further links during your research.

Italian immigration to Britain decreased considerably during the First World War, and when the Italians initially chose to support the Germans during the Second World War, enforced emigration restrictions and the internment of Italian males during the conflict meant that numbers did not really increase again until the 1950s.

EXPLORE ALL POSSIBILITIES

It is well known that Italians are extremely family orientated, and for the genealogist this can cause some problems when trying to fathom out ancestral relationships. The same Christian names were regularly duplicated down the generations, making it difficult to differentiate between those with the same name.

In Italian records this was overcome by adding a reference to the individual's father's name, indicated with the word 'di'. For example, Antonio Lorenzo would be listed as Antonio Lorenzo di Luigi – making it a little easier to work out that Antonio was the son of Luigi, allowing us to confirm those ancestral links. On some occasions the name reference was to the individual's mother, while the replacing of the word 'di' with the term 'fu' indicated that at the time the record was created the parent of the individual was deceased.

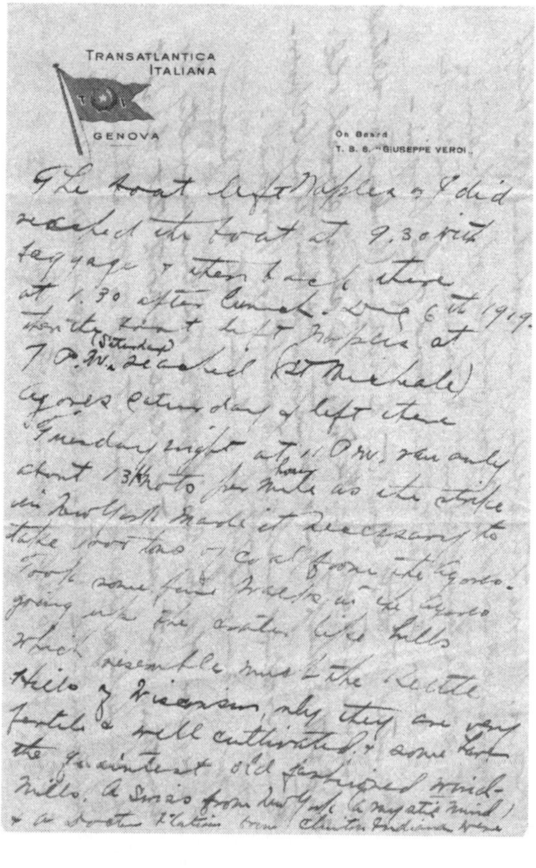

TRANSATLANTICA ITALIANA
GENOVA

On Board T. S. S. "GIUSEPPE VERDI"

The boat left Naples & I did
reached the boat at 9.30 with
baggage & stayed back there
at 1.30 after lunch. [illegible] 6th 1919.
[illegible] boat left Naples at
7 P.M. (Saturday) reached (St Michaels)
Azores Easter day & left there
Tuesday night at 11 P.M. ran only
about 13 knots per hour as the strike
in New York made it necessary to
take [illegible] tons of coal from the Azores.
Took some fine walks in the Azores
going up the [illegible] like hills
which resemble much the Kettle
Hills of Wisconsin, only they are very
fertile & well cultivated, & some [illegible]
the quaintest old fashioned wind-
mills. A Swiss from New York (a mystic mind)
& a doctor [illegible] from Clinton Indiana [illegible]

This letter was sent from Transatlantica Italiana Genova on-board the TSS *Giuseppe Verdi*. Letters and diaries make essential reading, as we can discover our ancestor's thoughts, feelings and observations.

It was often common practice for the surname to be listed before the Christian name. This custom not only took place on the majority of Italian civil records but also on gravestone inscriptions and was continued by some immigrants on their earlier records when they settled in Britain.

As you can see there are many opportunities to be confused when tracing Italians by name, but there are also some bonuses. For example, women kept their maiden names throughout their lives making it much easier to trace the female line.

Remember, surnames can also be extremely helpful when trying to establish the place of birth of your ancestor. Often local in origin, try focusing on the distribution of the name across Italy and you may be able to pinpoint an area from which the family initially came. Try the Italian surname distribution search engine to find out more – http://italia.indettaglio.it/ita/cognomi/cognomi.html.

For those who decided to make Britain their home, it was a regular occurrence to anglicise their surnames, so although most Italian surnames end with a vowel, spellings may have changed slightly as the decades have passed. This is most noticeable on census returns so do not be too quick to dismiss an individual just because the spelling is not as you had expected. Check back and compare any changes that may appear on other official documents for consistency.

Hotel memorabilia and ephemera from an Italian trip.

A 1902 journal noting a traveller's visit to Sorrento in Italy. The vivid details of his trip are unlikely to be found anywhere else, making it a primary resource for genealogists and historians.

Civil Registration

Italy's civil records – known as 'Stato Civile' – are held in the Archivio di Stato of each city or provincial town. With twenty regions divided into provinces – many named after one of the cities in their region – this duplication of place names can initially seem a little puzzling when you begin your search. The bonus is that once you locate your records, they are generally far more informative than the UK equivalents. On the majority of birth records the parents' father's names are recorded – giving you an extra generation – while in marriage records, *both* parents of the bride and groom are included, and also noted on death records.

Church Records

Just like in the UK, ecclesiastical registers are held by the parish in which the church is located. Be aware that early records may be in Latin rather than Italian. Additional birth information includes the names of the godparents, while for marriage records – as in civil registration – the names of both parents of the bride and groom were noted. In burial registers you may be lucky and even find the cause of death included. Some areas created records known as 'Status Animarum' meaning 'State of the Soul', which were compiled by the clergy for tax purposes and are similar to census returns with regard to their detailed information as they provide a register of the people living in a specific parish and the events related to them.

Military Records

Since 1865, it has been compulsory for every Italian male – when reaching the age of 18 – to register for military service. These registers are a vital source of information for anyone tracing their male Italian ancestors. After a period of seventy-five years, these 'Registro di Leva' are transferred to the state archives where they are available for viewing. (This website provides a useful list of addresses for Italy's State Archives when wishing to correspond by letter – http://www.gentedimareitaliangenealogy.info/files/Italianstatearchives.html.) Usually indexed, these registers include a place of origin, the names of an individual's parents, their occupations and physical descriptions and even notes about their ability to read and write. A record was then made to confirm whether the conscript was finally accepted for military service. If they were, you would need to refer to the 'Registro dei fogli matricolari', a register that would provide information on his service, where he was posted, whether he was promoted and the date and details of his discharge. These records are invaluable.

Tracing Italians in British Records

Along with a number of Protestant and Jewish Italian immigrants, the majority practiced the Roman Catholic faith. For anyone tracing Anglo-Italian ancestry the best place to request advice on how to find out more about the religious denominations and the survival of the relevant records is to contact the Anglo-Italian Family History Society, www.anglo-italianfhs.org.uk. Their website also provides details of the current project to index the Italian Civil Records – over 2 million have already been indexed but more help is needed and volunteers are required – perhaps this would be a fascinating way of learning more about your own Italian connections!

The Archivi Sistema Archivistico Nazionale is the official National Archives of Italy (http://www.archivi.beniculturali.it). Here, you can discover what collections and information is held by each State Records Centre in order to get the most out of your research. Use this site as a portal to locating specific documents, publications, images and alternative resources.

CASE STUDY: THE TOURIST TRAIL

Perhaps you're trying to track down a globe-trotting forebear who you believed may have travelled to Italy for business or pleasure? Towards the end of the nineteenth century, frequent travellers enlisted the services of agents to help them during their stay in certain locations abroad. These agents gave advice on where to eat, what to avoid, provided communication where necessary with the locals, and helped guide their clients around the sights, landmarks and places of interest. Just like today, they had printed cards that they handed out to increase their business and to provide potential customers, or those they had already managed to engage, with their contact details and credentials.

The discovery of one of these cards, or promotional material from hotels and tourist attractions within your ancestor's possessions, may give you new leads to follow and help you to confirm the period in which they visited this country.

This tourist trail can begin with a letter sent home from onboard an Italian vessel; this may be to a loved one or perhaps a business colleague. The correspondence may even have been written in the Italian language, suggesting that the traveller was a regular visitor to this country. Hotel pamphlets and trade cards might require more investigation to see if the accommodation still exists, but remember that businesses within the tourist trade are often family concerns which are passed down and still in operation in some form or other today. I found an example of this within the journal of American traveller Abraham Pease, who visited, recorded and photographed aspects of his stay at the Hotel Jaccarino near Sorrento at the turn of the nineteenth century. This hotel still exists today.

With this in mind, have you ever considered 'walking in your forebear's footsteps' by travelling to the destinations that they once visited? This would be the perfect way to bring this phase of your family history quest to a fitting conclusion. A planned trip to see the sights they had seen, to document the similarities and changes, and to compare their recorded thoughts and feelings with your own is guaranteed to provide you with lasting memories that not only reach far into the past, but also provide the basis for further research for future generations!

FAMOUS IMMIGRANTS

IN SEARCH OF FAME AND FORTUNE

While some immigrants floundered in their adopted countries, never fully settling into their new lives, others flourished. There have been thousands of success stories, but some have been more famous than others.

United Kingdom

Ignatius Sancho: born on a slave ship in 1729, he became the first black person to vote in a British election and, after a successful career as an actor, writer and composer, became the first African to be given an obituary in a British newspaper.

Sigmund Freud: the Austrian 'father' of psychoanalysis, who fled the Nazis and made London his home, remaining there for the rest of his life.

Karl Marx: the German philosopher and 'father' of socialism was expelled from Paris in the 1840s and, like Freud, chose London as his home, his final resting place being an ornate tomb in Highgate Cemetery.

United States of America

Others chose the 'New World' in which to 'reinvent' themselves and share their talents with others:

Irving Berlin: the Russian-born songwriter, born in 1888, moved with his parents to New York when he was just 4 years old. Their decision to make a new start in America gave Berlin opportunities he might never have realised back in Russia, and by his early 20s he had published his first song. From these simple beginnings, he went on to write 800 more, many of which became the best-known show songs of all time. He had a long and successful career and left a legacy of stage productions such as 'There's No Business Like Show Business' and classics like 'White Christmas' and 'God Bless America', which are still played to this day. Berlin passed away in New York City on 22 September 1989, aged 101.

Albert Einstein: the German physicist moved to Switzerland in search of better educational facilities. Graduating from the Federal Institute of Technology, he accepted a position as a clerk in a Swiss patent office in 1902 to enable him to work with new inventions. Within three years he had published five papers, one in particular being his 'Special Theory of Relativity'. When he released his updated 'General Theory of Relativity' in 1916, his talents were becoming recognised worldwide, culminating in him receiving the Nobel Prize for Physics in 1922. The effects of the First World War had caused Einstein to become a pacifist, so in 1933, while visiting America and with war once again on the horizon, and upon learning that the Nazi Party had come to power, he decided to renounce his German citizenship and remain in the United States. There, while realising that the Germans were working on creating an atomic bomb, he advised President Roosevelt of the potential effects it would have in Nazi hands. Although he understood that the US had to develop the bomb first, Einstein spent the rest of his life working for peace, passing away on American soil in 1955.

Joseph Pulitzer: the Hungarian-Jewish publisher quit Europe for America in 1864 to fight in the American Civil War. He remained in America after the conflict and found work on a German-language newspaper in St Louis. Within a few short years, he had become publisher, and eventually the owner, of the *St Louis Post-Dispatch*. Through his newspaper, he managed to expose wrongdoers, tax dodgers and corruption. He soon gained the favour of the public when he bought *The New York World* and became the publisher of the best-selling newspaper in the country – partly due to raising public donations to build a pedestal for the Statue of Liberty so that it could be shipped from France. Pulitzer's standards of editorial excellence led to a legacy, which lived on after his death in 1911. The Pulitzer Prize is an annual series of awards for journalism and is highly coveted within the field.

Cary Grant from the UK, Sophia Loren from Italy and Arnold Schwarzenegger from Austria all found fame in American showbiz.

Australia

Famous Ten Pound Poms have included: the Bee Gees (pop group), the parents of Hugh Jackman, Kylie Minogue, Prime Minister Tony Abbott and former Prime Minister Julia Gillard.

CONCLUSION

As we have discovered, sea travel and emigration have touched the lives of literally hundreds of thousands of our ancestors. The countries that I have chosen to focus upon are by no means an exhaustive list as there are countless incidents and episodes in world history that have had a domino effect on our forebears' decisions and choices. My aim was to target those destinations and events which created the greatest impact on migrants from the United Kingdom and foreign nationals who chose Britain as their new home.

I hope the advice and guidance will provide a starting point for you to further your own research. Look for evidence in public records relating to your own ancestor's movements and team your findings with any clues you may find in personal memorabilia or ephemera that has been passed down within the family to enable you to follow their trail overseas.

We should never dismiss the importance of sea travel within our investigations as one single voyage had the power to change the direction our genealogical roots have taken. This area of research can lead you to uncover stories about your forebear's lives that you never knew existed. Events in history – which you had previously only read about – come to life when you realise that *your* ancestor was actually there, may have been involved, or was directly affected by the consequences of it.

Be open-minded and realistic about what you hope to find. Organise your facts, scrutinise your findings and delve into obscure and unusual resources to piece together the family jigsaw. Most of all, remember the saying, 'the journey of a thousand miles begins with one step' – get your detective hat on and enjoy your own voyage into the unknown!

ESSENTIAL RESOURCES

The National Archives – www.nationalarchives.gov.uk
Ancestry.co.uk – www.ancestry.co.uk
Findmypast – www.findmypast.co.uk
The Genealogist – www.thegenealogist.co.uk
The British Newspaper Archive – www.britishnewspaperarchive.co.uk
The Ephemera Society – www.ephemera-society.org.uk
Ephemera and Collectable Book Fairs – www.etcfairs.com

The National Archives of Australia – www.naa.gov.au
The National Archives of America – www.archives.gov
The French National Archives – www.archives-nationales.culture.gouv.fr
The Library and Archives of Canada – www.collectionscanada.gc.ca/index-e.html
The National Archives of South Africa – www.national.archives.gov.za
The National Archives of India – http://nationalarchives.nic.in
The Polish State Archives – www.archiwa.gov.pl/en/state-archives.html
The German National Archive – www.bundesarchiv.de/index.html.de
The National Archives of Hungary – http://mlp.archivportal.hu
The National Historical Archive of Spain – http://www.spainisculture.com/en/archivo-biblioteca/madrid/archivo_historico_nacional.html
The Italian Archives – www.archivi.beniculturali.it

FURTHER READING

Migration Records by Robert Kershaw (paperback). Published February 2009 by The National Archives. ISBN 9781905615407. A fantastic guide explaining centuries of movement to, within and beyond Britain's shores.

The discovery of a voyage taken on one of the world's most famous passenger ships can take your research off in a new direction as you aim to acquire as much information as possible on the vessel and its history. William Miller is an acknowledged world expert in this field and has written over seventy books on the subject of passenger ships – a number of these are available from The History Press, www.thehistorypress.co.uk, and are well worth seeking out if you wish to find out more about life on the ocean wave.

Consider purchasing the republished *Map of Mail Steamship Routes* from The National Archives bookshop. Originally produced in 1937, it was commissioned by the General Post Office to depict steamship routes that carried the UK's mail during the 1930s and illustrates the voyages taken by shipping vessels such as the SS *Great Eastern* and RMS *Queen Mary*. Essential if your ancestor travelled aboard a Royal Mail Steam Packet ship!

INDEX

Lightning Source UK Ltd.
Milton Keynes UK
UKOW04f1045110614

233215UK00002B/5/P